COTTON'S LIBRARY

Also by Matt Kuhns

*Brilliant Deduction: The Story of
Real-Life Great Detectives*

COTTON'S LIBRARY

The Many Perils of Preserving History

MATT KUHNS

Lyon Hall Press
Lakewood, Ohio

Copyright © 2014 by Matthew John Kuhns

All rights reserved. No part of this book may be used or reproduced in any manner whatsoever without written permission from the publisher except in the case of brief quotations embodied in critical articles or reviews.

Published in the United States by Lyon Hall Press, Lakewood, Ohio

Every reasonable effort has been made to respect the owners of material reproduced in this book, but if any rights have been overlooked, the author and publisher welcome notification of the error.

Library of Congress Control Number: 2014913646

ISBN-13: 978-0-9882505-4-3

Printed on acid-free paper

All illustrations and photos are the work of the author except as noted.

Designed and typeset by Modern Alchemy LLC

Dedicated to
the British taxpayer

CONTENTS

Introduction   x

FOUNDATION

1. Dissolution and Recovery   2

The Diary of Edward VI   15

2. The Collector   18

3. Uses and Users   31

The Lindisfarne Gospels   42

4. The Insider's View   45

Anglo-Saxon Mappa Mundi   56

5. Sorting Things Out   60

Codex Purpureus fragment   72

6. Enemy of the State   75

INTERREGNUM

7. War and Peace   92

The Liber Vitae   102

7. Declassification   105

The Pearl Poems   117

9. The Three Rivals   120

The Julius Work Calendar   137

10. The Terrible Calamity   140

11. Sifting the Ash   153

RESTORATION

12. Dr. Sloane's Museum   168

    Anglo-Saxon Pennies   181

13. The Turning Point   185

    Magna Carta   195

14. Sir Frederic Madden   198

15. Peace and War   215

    Beowulf   228

16. The British Library   233

Acknowledgements   248

Discovering More   249

Index   262

"The Library of Sir Robert Cotton (1571-1631) is arguably the most important collection of manuscripts ever assembled in Britain by a private individual."
– C.J. Wright, former head of manuscripts, The British Library

"A large proportion of all the great documents that had survived from a thousand years of British history. [Cotton's library is] perhaps the most valuable single bequest ever made to the nation…" – Justin Pollard, historian and author of *Alfred The Great: The Man Who Made England*

"Indeed it is a remarkable circumstance, that no collection, perhaps, was ever exposed to so many dangers and vicissitudes as the Cottonian Library…"
– *The Morning Chronicle* (London), Sept. 5, 1823

Introduction

IN 1684 SIR JOHN COTTON faced a dilemma. After decades of fruitless searching, he had, at last, found the illuminated Book of Genesis lost from his late grandfather's library more than 50 years before. The prospect of finally returning this jewel to the family's renowned collection must have seemed a minor miracle, well worth all the effort, but for one small problem. The holder demanded £40 for its return.

Significant as £40 was in the 17th century, Sir John could afford it. But should he submit to the indignity of purchasing back what was indisputably his family's own property, and indeed still bore the Cotton arms on its binding? Having acquired the book through some unknown chain of intermediaries, a Lady Stafford now insisted that it had never been the Cottons' book at all but merely loaned to Sir John's father at one point, who then had it rebound. The claim was patently false, and Sir John knew it, but proving such in court would be an expensive gamble. He was prepared to negotiate, instead. He had offered Stafford as much as £30 already. But she refused even this small concession to his self-respect. He could pay the full ransom, try his luck with a lawsuit, or do without.

Eventually Sir John did recover his book, now recalled as the Cotton Genesis, closing one chapter in a story combining a valuable historic document with aristocracy, generosity, injustice, mischance and more than a touch of absurdity. In that sense the full story of the Cotton Genesis, famed for illuminated miniatures, is itself something of a history in miniature of the whole Cotton library. Like many items in that library the Genesis had passed through a rich history of its own before the library's founder, Sir Robert Cotton, ever set eyes upon it. "One of the earliest Christian books in existence," per Cotton biographer Hope Mirrlees, this Greek manuscript of the Genesis story was already 1,000 years old when visiting bishops presented it to King Henry VIII. Its illustrations may have provided the inspiration for mosaics in St. Mark's Cathedral in Venice. In England, Henry's daughter and eventual heir Elizabeth rediscovered the book in royal archives, bestowing it on Sir John Fortescue, who had tutored her in Greek. Fortescue, in Mirrlees's words, then "mindful of posterity, added it to the riches of the Cottonian treasure-house."

The best-known portrait of Sir Robert depicts just one book to represent all the wealth of that treasure-house. The choice of the Genesis is some indication of its great importance to him. Despite this, he loaned it out readily, with the same generosity he applied to any and every item in his private library. In 1617, Cotton sent the Genesis back across the Channel to the French scholar Nicolas Claude Fabri de Peiresc, patiently waiting five years for its return without a word of due dates or fines. Cotton was just as liberal with his own country's men of letters, not least Thomas Howard, 14th Earl of Arundel and patron of Cotton's later career. The Cotton Genesis was one of a number of valuable items loaned to Arundel and then lost, in many cases permanently, in the troubled years between Cotton's death in 1631 and Arundel's in 1646.

Sir Robert's son and grandson made loyal efforts to preserve what remained of the library through the years of England's Civil War and subsequent upheaval, and to restore some of the losses afterward. No doubt they related a particular interest in the lost Genesis to their unofficial librarian, the antiquary William Dugdale; his preserved letters record his efforts to relay that interest to correspondents throughout Europe for nearly 30 years. In 1656 a fellow librarian, who had served the Countess of Arundel, responded to an inquiry from Dugdale that he had not seen the Genesis among the cart loads of antiquities "convaighed away out of England" by the late countess. Another letter indicates that Dugdale nonetheless pestered the man for information about the book at least once more.

Such persistence finally paid off, though locating the Genesis with Lady Stafford was only the beginning of another campaign. After attempting to negotiate on the Cottons' behalf, a Gilbert Crouch wrote to Dugdale that Sir John's offer of £30 remained unacceptable to Stafford. She would have £40, "and will not take one farthinge less... Therefore (if Sr John have soe greate a minde to the booke) in my poore Judgm^t he were better give this other tenn pounds, than runn the chardge and hazard of a suite."

In the end, the aging baronet simply capitulated to Lady Stafford's terms, and bought back his family's manuscript. Even then, the adventures of what the Cottons cataloged as "Otho B VI" were by no means complete. (Most Cotton manuscripts are assigned to one of 14 groups, named for Roman emperors or their contemporaries for reasons examined later.) Over the following 300 years, the Genesis shared with its sibling volumes remarkably varied fortunes. Sir John's will bequeathed the library to the nation, in hope, perhaps, of preserving the library from a

Sir Robert Cotton with the Cotton Genesis
After an engraving by George Vertue

quarrel among heirs. The collection fell victim to quarreling nonetheless, with its de facto keeper at one point locked out of his own library—not for the first time in the collection's history. A parsimonious and neglectful British government then nearly accomplished what previous centuries of war and other perils had not, and in 1731 the library was preserved from incineration by a scandalously thin margin. For many individual volumes that margin was too thin, and the Cotton Genesis was reduced to smoldering fragments scarcely 40 years after Sir John had swallowed his pride to recover it.

Neglect and fire still did not write finish to the history of the Cotton Genesis or to that of the Cotton library. Eventually arriving, in both cases somewhat the worse for wear, at the British Museum, they became founding pieces of a new national collection. Occasional accidents continued for many years; astonishingly, the Genesis fragments went through an entire second cycle of loss, rediscovery and repurchase. But with time, the British Museum repaired both its own mistakes and many made by those who preceded it. Since the mid-19th century, Cotton's collection has enjoyed the attention long overdue to a national treasure. Generations of conservators have gradually restored much that was written off as a loss, including even pieces of the Genesis. Curators have abetted and encouraged public appreciation for the library's contents through exhibitions and publication, including a growing online replica. The permanent Treasures of the British Library exhibit in its St. Pancras home includes a lengthy list of Cotton collection highlights, among them the Lindisfarne Gospels, the unique manuscript of *Beowulf* and one of four surviving copies of Magna Carta.

If the Cotton library is enjoying a second golden age, however, much of its modern brilliance is still a reflection of its first golden age in Sir Robert Cotton's time. Bringing together great prizes of antiquity, Cotton made them—and himself—central to the intellectual life of his era. Though he rarely played a leading part personally, Cotton and his library were closely connected to nearly all who did in early 17th-century England's scholarship, arts and government. Cotton advised the day's foremost politicians, and even the crown; he contributed to and edited the works of a modest revolution in historical scholarship; he gathered up the endangered records of his country's past and present with one hand, and supplied them to nearly every memorable individual and enterprise within reach of early Stuart London with the other.

That very closeness of Cotton and his library, to the most powerful persons of a fractious era, eventually imperiled both. The collection's subsequent, remarkable survival is worth studying for many reasons. The individual documents preserved by (and in some cases in spite of) Sir Robert's successors include many of the foundation stones of British history and Anglophone literature as we know them today. Those documents' survival *as* a largely whole collection provides an invaluable context for better appreciating them. Last, but by no means least, the details of that survival through four centuries of tragic, bizarre and not-infrequently comic hazards constitute the makings of a remarkable tale.

Cotton's Library is my attempt to tell that tale. In doing so, I owe much to a vast and growing bibliography of scholarly works about the library, as well as a surprising number of books for more popular audiences. This latter category is the origin of my own interest. In reading about the history of one or another of the collection's more prominent works some time ago, I gradually realized that parts of the story were curiously familiar. Indeed I had read of the same events multiple times, over a number of years, as without even realizing it I had acquired four or more books that owed and acknowledged a significant debt of their own to items preserved by Sir Robert Cotton. The curiosity thus aroused led into one of the most remarkable rabbit holes in the realm of bibliography; one could spend a lifetime exploring its innumerable trails and at least a few people have done so. My own attempt to map its larger structure would not be possible without their work, duly acknowledged herein.

Nonetheless, until now, no one in its four-century history

has prepared a single, complete narrative of the Cotton library. Such a want is almost a theme through the library's story. Generations of researchers have bemoaned the shortcomings of a series of imperfect catalogs, and though Cotton and his library are the subject of a handful of books, more than one scholar has expressed astonishment at the continued absence of a comprehensive scholarly biography. These challenges I, too, shall leave for abler researchers; I make no claim to have assembled a complete encyclopedia of the library (much as I would, very likely, readily devour such a volume at this point). But I believe that the *story* of the library, of its adventures and of the larger patterns among them, is more than ready to be told. The pieces are there, and have only wanted someone to come put them together.

Which situation also has its thematic resonance in the library's history, and offers the perfect place to begin.

A brief further note about the text, first: as nearly all of the sources for Cotton and his library are British in origin, a majority of the quotes herein employ British spelling. It could therefore be preferable to apply the Queen's English throughout, and add "ue" to every instance of the word catalog, e.g., quoted or otherwise. Unfortunately for the purposes of uniformity, all of my own habits and reference materials alike employ American spellings, and quotes from the library's first hundred years or so frequently include archaic and improvisational English (which I have retained per convention), ensuring something of a carnivalesque text no matter what my approach. My apologies to any readers disconcerted by the result; two people separated by a common language, and all.

PART ONE
FOUNDATION

CHAPTER 1
Dissolution and Recovery

I F THE CENTURIES-SPANNING STORY of the Cotton library has any one, genuine beginning, it is the Dissolution of the English monasteries. Thirty-five years before Robert Cotton's birth, King Henry VIII set into motion a transformation of English society with great consequences for the future collector and his collection. In both cases, the results were largely unintended accidents. But then, much the same description might be applied to the entire endeavor.

The Dissolution, from the perspective of more than 450 years' subsequent evaluation and reevaluation, appears curiously to foreshadow Sir John Seeley's remark about Britain's later acquisition of empire in a fit of absentmindedness. A close scrutiny of *The Dissolution of the Monasteries* by Joyce Young suggests that it made substantive contributions to neither religious reformation, nor crown revenues, and for that matter never even "in so many words, dissolved" England's religious houses directly. By itself it merely completed a decline of monastic communities that modern scholars can trace as far back as the 1300s.

At the Dissolution's outset, that decline may only have been dimly evident. Very quickly, though, cautious initial encroachments revealed a tree ready to fall with the slightest push. Material gain was central to Henry's supplying that push, even if the results for his exchequer proved impermanent. In addition to their prime land holdings, English monasteries of the late 1530s held considerable treasure as a legacy of past prosperity. Instructions to commissioners inventorying dissolved houses' property emphasized land, plate, and precious ornaments. More mundane commodities were by no means ignored; the eventual haul of lead bells and roof tiles was so great as to inspire rumors, not entirely fanciful, that obtaining monasteries' lead for armaments was Henry's true object. Commission lists also record nearly everything else that might be picked up or pried up, including "corn, cattle, bedding, napery, vessels, kitchen stuff, buttery, pantry and other implements and utensils of household... tables, forms, standards, brewing vessels..." Curiously, from a modern perspective, the one consistent omission is books.

When the Middle Ages' monasteries are recalled today, likely as not it is for their legacy of manuscripts. Beautiful decorative illumination, volumes of Latin text preserving classical learning through the medieval darkness, all carefully produced by robed brothers toiling in the scriptorium; these are the real treasures. For Henry VIII's commissioners, by contrast, all this was little more than scrap. The only documents demanded by their formal instructions—hardly lacking in detail—were property records and deeds. In theory, other papers or parchments might have been encompassed by general injunctions to secure all of a house's "movables." In practice, whole shelves of manuscripts ended up as waste paper, often literally.

The preface to John Bale's *The Laboryouse Journey* records the results that he witnessed, firsthand: "A great nombre of them whych purchased those superstycyous mansyons, reserued of those lybrarye bokes, some to serue theyr iakes, some to scoure theyr candlestyckes, and some to robbe their bootes. Some they solde to the grosers and sope sellers, & some they sent ouersee to the bokebynders, not in small nombre, but at tymes whole shyppes full…" The "jakes," it's worth emphasizing, was Tudor slang for the toilet.

Bale was one of a small group, including John Leland and Laurence Nowell, who led the way in trying to save England's history. They worked to preserve as much as possible from incidental annihilation, as well as from the intentional purge that followed it. Under Henry's son Edward—whose conception had motivated so much of the Henrician reform program in the first place—what had been driven more by convenience than conviction changed in tenor dramatically. The government of Edward VI pursued Reformation with genuinely religious fervor, and books were no longer overlooked bystanders. The Act against Superstitious Books and Images of 1550 demanded forbidden volumes be surrendered to crown officials, and "openly burnt or otherways defaced and destroyed." Primarily secular collections were no guarantee of safety, either, and England's university libraries suffered enormously during Edward's brief reign.

That more of the English language's heritage was not lost owes as much to the last Tudor king's early death from illness, at age 15, as it does to preservationists' quiet disobedience. Under more accommodating governments, however, England's bibliophiles could act more boldly. Catholic Mary Tudor is often remembered for burning people, but she suspended her half-brother's aggressive policy of burning books, and their half-sister Elizabeth made no effort to revive it. To the contrary, under Queen Elizabeth, the salvage of England's libraries became an object of the court, both formally and informally.

Court astrologer John Dee personally assembled an enormous collection of books, eventually numbering perhaps 3,000 volumes. Elizabeth's close advisor William Cecil, and her chosen

Archbishop of Canterbury Matthew Parker, shared with Dee an interest in piecing back together the nation's history as well as a sense of urgency in doing so. Dee and Parker both wrote to Cecil of their concern for the vast number of books and manuscripts still in peril, as a result of the upheavals decades before; Cecil supplied patronage to historians, in addition to collecting, himself. In a 1568 letter that C.E. Wright credits to "the guidance of Cecil and Parker," Elizabeth proclaimed a royal interest in recovering dispersed monastic libraries.

By the 1570s, then, the bewildering variety of Tudor policy had given birth to both a crisis in English historiography and a subsequent enthusiastic campaign to address it. When the future collector and antiquary Robert Cotton entered the world three years after Queen Elizabeth's proclamation calling for preservation of ancient records, he was indeed, in the words of Justin Pollard, "born at exactly the right time."

Robert Cotton was born, on January 22, 1571, into favorable circumstances in more ways than one. The Cottons were not at the pinnacle of English society—Hope Mirrlees suggests ancestry including a moneylender, a Barbary merchant and even a pirate—but they had done very well out of the land bargains resulting from the Dissolution. Cotton's family also enjoyed a measure of older, inherited wealth through Mary de Wesenham, along with a claim to descent from the Scottish hero Robert the Bruce. The Cottons possessed an estate at Conington, in Huntingdonshire, approximately 70 miles due north of London. Conington was not necessarily the seat of a great lord, less still the nearby Denton home where Cotton was born; descriptions of the surrounding fen country at that time include terms such as "odd," "melancholy," "unhealthy" and, above all, "wet." But even a family seat in the fens offered benefits to the future path of Robert Cotton, beyond just the cash rents of his eventual inheritance. The country had once been rich with great religious houses, such as Sawtry Abbey. Some of Sawtry's land had since enriched the Cottons, but remnants of the manuscripts loosed from the abbeys made Huntingdonshire a promising home for a collector, as well.

For Robert Cotton, it was in the long run a second home, all the same. From childhood onward, his true home was London. His family's prosperity financed an enviable education including Jesus College at Cambridge, and later study at Middle Temple, one of London's Inns of Court. Cotton's most important years as a student, however, were those spent at London's Westminster School. There he fell under the sway of William Camden and of documentary history.

Camden was both heir to the early antiquaries like Bale, Leland and Nowell, and the first major English proponent of a new evidence-based secular history emerging across the Channel. In Camden's day, English history was still as much mythology as documented fact, even among such scholarly treatments as existed. Formal history curricula at the universities were largely concerned with classical antiquity; the prevailing narrative of England's own past was peopled by figures like Brutus the Trojan, King Arthur, and other misty heroes. Even after Camden, generations passed before popular myths gave way entirely to more skeptical inquiry, and in his own later writings Cotton mostly preferred working around the old legends to challenging them head-on.

The larger project of studying, as well as salvaging, England's historical record nonetheless found an important champion in Camden, and Camden found his greatest acolyte in young Robert Cotton. By his late teens, Cotton was well on his way to a lifetime passion for history and its records. Three items in his eventual library bear the date "1588" in Cotton's handwriting, including a 10th-century manuscript and a 15th-century copy of the *Polychronicon*, a world history by Ranulf Higden. Around the same time, Cotton began assembling notes for a parish-by-parish history of Huntingdonshire, likely inspired by a vogue for county history projects among the previous generation of antiquaries. (His results were similar to theirs; Leland's project aborted after he lost his reason, while Cotton apparently never progressed beyond a list of the local parishes' names.) Given the tall ambitions of his adolescence, it's certainly plausible that Cotton was even partner with his old teacher in forming London's first Society of Antiquaries as early as the 1586 release of Camden's *Britannia*, for which the society may have been a kind of promotional book group that took on a life of its own.

By his late twenties, Cotton was not only an active participant in the Society of Antiquaries, but also setting out in Camden's company for a season of archeological field work. As an active search for artifacts of the nation's distant past, their 1599 expedition to northernmost England was little short of revolutionary. It was probably the greatest adventure of Cotton's life up to that point, as well. Mirrlees remarks that "I can think of no journey we could take to-day which would be its equivalent in danger and daring. The Border ballads were not only still being sung, but being lived, and if the Queen's writ ran north of the Humber, it certainly did not run smoothly, for it was not until 1603 that peace was brought to the Borders."

For Camden and Cotton the lure of discovery outweighed any local dangers. The land adjoining Hadrian's Wall offered a wealth of monuments and other artifacts compared with the south, where most Roman traces had been either concealed by development, or else quarried for it. The experience may not have been entirely agreeable, as Cotton never again ventured so far from home. But the products of his and Camden's six-month tour were quite enough to contribute to both men's projects for long after, anyway.

The interest of his mentor Camden and other contemporaries in rediscovering Britain's history, in something of a companion effort to the era's voyages of exploration and colonization overseas, certainly motivated Cotton's creation of a great private library. It was not his only motivation. As with nearly any question about the man and his library, the answer is complex. His library's treasures eventually served political, ecclesiastical, social, legal and financial ends at one time or another, from which much may be inferred. Cotton himself, however, has left behind little account of his own thoughts on the matter.

The picture that emerges from the studies of Cotton's life is at once both remarkably full, and oddly incomplete. Incomplete in the sense that, for all of the detailed records about his activity that survive, a fully rounded sense of Cotton as a person seems elusive. He left an extensive paper trail as a librarian, propertyholder, academic and courtier. But the gaps include much of his correspondence and other personal papers, as well a collection of printed books that might have constituted a more personal library. Portraits and busts permit looking Cotton in the eyes, in a sense, yet they leave one guessing what was behind them. The effect is somewhat like the enigma that shadows his close contemporary, Shakespeare, and multiple students of Robert Cotton's history have expressed sentiments similar to those of Sidney Lee, that "It is impossible to describe very definitely Cotton's personal character."

What remains is nonetheless full in the sense that Cotton's activities seem so many, and diverse, that one might puzzle at where he possibly found enough time until reminded that he never needed a "real job" in his life. As a young man, he struggled with at least a relative want of cash, borrowing from moneylenders including one of his uncles. The death of Cotton's father in 1592 did not lead to immediate financial ease, either; as eldest son

DISSOLUTION AND RECOVERY 9

he was the primary beneficiary, but his father had dealt generously with a second family begun after Robert's mother died. Sorting out administration of the portion he did receive kept Cotton frequently occupied in Huntingdonshire for a number of years. His eventual arrangements, however, appear to have been effective. Though beset by many troubles through his subsequent life, money was rarely among them.

Marriage to Elizabeth Brocas the year after his father died also helped to shore up Cotton's financial position. Mirrlees notes that, "In accordance with the prudent customs of his family Cotton had married an heiress." The subsequent history of their marriage suggests that quite possibly this quality outweighed personal compatibility, too. Judging from his extensive circle of friends, Cotton had a considerable capacity to charm, and per all accounts he employed this *pour chercher la femme* both before marrying and after. He later spent several years and possibly more than a decade living with the widowed Lady Hunsdon, perhaps as her lover but certainly in the context of an overt separation from his wife. Eventually, the Cottons patched things up. Nonetheless a reputation as something of a rake attached to Sir Robert through the end of his life.

If by some measures Robert Cotton was a wealthy playboy, in his defense he was, again, hardly an idle playboy. He devoted the greatest portion of his ample time and energies to a combination of scholarly research and public service. The nexus of both pursuits, for many years, was the Society of Antiquaries of which he had likely been a founding member.

The term "antiquary" has become somewhat anachronistic, ironically enough given that the one common thread to the antiquaries' loose-knit community was interest in the past. Graham Parry, studying these proto-historians in *The Trophies of Time*, writes "How might one define an antiquary? ... the spread of scholarship they engaged in was so broad and variegated that it defies definition." This was very much true of the core group including Camden and other of Robert Cotton's fellow travelers. Like Cotton, they reacted to the context of their time more than to a single organized program. Someone simply had to take an interest in the nation's documentary past if it was to survive. In addition to ex-monastic manuscripts in danger of becoming lavatory paper, England's government records were nearly as endangered, simply by their expansion beyond rudimentary archives' capacity. Preserving all of this fit very naturally with the antiquaries' one unifying interest, in the origins of things.

It also fit the spirit of the times, up to a point. Relative stability and prosperity under the Tudors had stoked an appetite for taking pride in the nation's accomplishments, at the same time that still-contested separation from Catholic Europe spurred a search for antecedents of a native English Christianity independent from Rome. Traditional stories like Joseph of Arimathea in Glastonbury, or Lucius, the dubious first Christian king in Britain, fell somewhat short of the new standard Camden was trying to introduce to English history. As a group the antiquaries devoted less effort to questioning those old legends than to piling up other, more scholarly rigorous evidence beside them, but the result of their exploration fed later historians somewhat like the alchemists' experiments served the advance of scientific chemistry.

In Cotton's time, antiquarians remained in the early days of even their rudimentary efforts. Their whole project was faintly suspect. Even as the need was readily apparent to the antiquaries and their patrons, what would become a respected interest for gentlemen a century later was at its outset disdained by many as rooting around in a dusty dark age past, while a true renaissance of classical greatness beckoned. Perhaps, though, the antiquaries' support of one another was all the stronger for it.

The Society of Antiquaries that met in London for approximately the last 20 years of Elizabeth's reign seems a distinctly cozy association. Its members were predominantly lawyers, clerks, and heralds from the close world of the London court; many were graduates of the universities, but neither the academic world nor the clergy had a significant presence in the Society. Meetings were largely devoted to topics of interest only to the members—what was the origin of this title, or that legal tradition—explored in relatively casual discussion. Rules required everyone speak, though even the briefest statements were judged adequate and "debates" generally finished without any formal conclusion.

Within this relaxed atmosphere Cotton, who was generally a supporting player in more public forums, achieved considerable prominence for himself. In *Medieval History in the Tudor Age*, May McKisack affirms other authors' impression of Cotton as a respected, well-prepared contributor: "...Cotton used an impressive range of documents to illuminate the history of trial by battle. These included the Red Book of the Exchequer, the Parliamentary and Plea Rolls, and the Close and Patent Rolls, as well as in a number of French, Spanish, and papal records." Cotton's peers took notice. Gradually, inside the Society of Antiquaries' supportive environment, the emergence of Cotton's library as a resource to be reckoned with had begun.

By the closing years of Elizabeth's reign the growing profile of Cotton's collection, combined with the Society's concentration of a general interest in better preserving the nation's records, inspired what may be the Society of Antiquaries' most important, if indirect, legacy. Together with James Ley and John Doddridge, Cotton petitioned the queen to build upon the foundation of their group a national center for antiquarian research, "The Academye for the Studye of Antiquity and History Founded by Queen Elizabeth."

Their proposal, probably submitted in 1602, was both ambitious and detailed. The petitioners outlined ideas for both rules and officers, including a president, two librarians and a number of permanent fellows, all to pledge both the Oath of Supremacy to Elizabeth and guardianship of the library. The academy would have combined Cotton's and other antiquaries' collections with the accumulated books and manuscripts of England's sovereigns, to create a great national library. This and the academy's other projects would be responsible to an oversight group including the Lord Chief Justice, the Archbishop of Canterbury and other eminences. Suggestions for siting the academy included "some convenient room in the Savoy, which may well be spared" as well as "the dissolved priory of St John of Jerusalem," the latter particularly appropriate given the petition's multiple origins in the Dissolution.

Cotton and his cosignatories accompanied the proposal with a compelling list of arguments. The queen's own call for better care of the nation's "ancient monuments" would at last be achieved, with historical records both preserved and made reliably accessible for study. The academy would supply a valuable focus for the native historical study "which the Universities, being busy in arts take little care or regard." In demonstration of this value, the petitioners pointed to King Edward I's claim to Scotland and Elizabeth's father's assertion of an independent English church, both of which had employed arguments from historical precedent. Cotton, for that matter, might have brought up his own service to Elizabeth herself; though his career as a courtier was but recently commenced he had already advised the crown in seeking diplomatic precedence over Spain. He and the other antiquaries certainly implied that an academy might advance such work, as well, and might even become an advanced training center for high office with the addition of foreign language and geography departments.

For good measure, the petitioners also made a point of noting rival governments taking up similar plans. In broad outline, their proposal was neither new nor unique, even in their own country. The Tudors had already received such proposals at least as far back as Henry VIII's reign. Leland petitioned Thomas Cromwell, one of Henry's prime agents in carrying out the Dissolution, about a formal program to arrest the wreckage of the nation's libraries. In 1556, John Dee sought Queen Mary's support "for the recovery and preservation of ancient writers and monuments" in a national archive. Elizabeth had heard multiple exhortations to follow up her 1568 letter with more substantive measures. Dee may have raised the matter again during the years when he had the ear of the queen; Archbishop Parker certainly did so. As did Sir Humphrey Gilbert, whose own plan for a "Queen Elizabeth's Academy" even included deposit rights to new-published works.

Cotton and his friends may have considered this history and, with youthful enthusiasm, believed that the moment had arrived. Their older associates may have had comparatively low expectations. This might explain the absence of other names from their petition, not least that of Camden who seemingly might have lent a measure of gravitas to an effort he can hardly have opposed. Nonetheless, the academy just might have come closer to fruition than skeptics imagined. Another member of the antiquaries' Society, Richard Carew, wrote a few years later that "in the late queene's tyme it was lyklie to have received… extraordinarye favour from sundry great personages" and that only Elizabeth's death in 1603 prevented the scheme's realization. The possibility is almost as tantalizing to imagine now as it must have been to the ambitious 30-year-old Cotton: a great national research library and living monument to the Elizabethan "Golden Age," which would today be entering its fifth century. Alas, for both Cotton and counterfactuals, such was not to be. Historians have considered various reasons for the plan's failure; McKisack questions whether the petition ever reached Elizabeth herself, while an older tradition suggests that some form of grant had even issued, only to be voided by the change in government. Resistance by the universities also comes in for some suspicion, despite the proposal's claim that the academy would not be a competitor.

The history and habits of Elizabeth suggest that the petitioners may simply have been struggling against the Virgin Queen's most dependable instinct: prefer stalling for time to decisive actions whenever possible, especially when the latter would cost money. For most of a half-century Elizabeth routinely made a virtue of delay, and on balance England prospered. By her final years, however, even the famously frugal Elizabeth was struggling to balance her accounts. Funding a glittering new academy would have been a marvelous idea to praise—then defer until later. "Later" ran out for the last of the Tudor dynasty in March of 1603.

By itself, this need not have meant any obvious consequence for the antiquaries' proposed academy, besides a change of name. Given Cotton's initial flourishing under the new reign, James's accession might well have seemed an encouraging development. Nonetheless the petitioners' hopes were disappointed again. Whatever the reason, or reasons, "The Academye for the Studye of Antiquity and History" met the same government reluctance as every such proposal to come before it, and all those that followed for more than a century. In the meantime, if England's antiquaries were to have a center for their work and the preservation of the nation's documentary heritage, it seemed one of them would have to provide it himself.

EX LIBRIS
THE DIARY OF EDWARD VI
Nero C X ff. 10–83

If any item in the entire Cotton library seems calculated to attract both scholarly and popular interest, it must be Nero C X. On one hand, it is an English king's personal record of his life and reign amid pivotal years for the Reformation. On the other, it is *the secret diary of one of the royals*, and a doomed young prince, at that; tabloids in both Britain and theoretically republican America would bid fortunes for its like, today.

This manuscript is something of an odd text, for all that, and in some ways confounds conventional ideas of a diary. In that sense its entries' nature complements and highlights the larger oddities of the reign of Edward VI. The long-sought male heir of Henry VIII, Edward succeeded his father at age nine, then fell ill and died six years later just as he was growing into a more confident and independent role. His diary is thus as much schoolboy's journal as chronicle of a king. Most scholars presume the diary was originally an assignment for one of his tutors. Edward began the manuscript in 1550, but the first section is a summary of his life up to his 1547 accession, plus events of his first three years as king. After completing the account more or less up to the present, however, he may have decided to extend the exercise for his own purposes.

Edward continued making diary entries thereafter until late 1552.

Few entries include much in the way of an inner life. In the early section, Edward frequently refers to himself in the third person, and even after he takes up contemporary events the text is as much a summary of court events as it is a personal diary. Despite which, it possesses extraordinary interest for the simple fact of what it records; even at its most clipped and detached it is a king's firsthand account of the events of his own reign. In a 1966 study of the work, Wilbur Kitchener Jordan observed that "in English history, and very possibly in European history, there is no historical source quite of the nature of the Chronicle of Edward VI. It... not infrequently constitutes our only source of information for events of considerable significance."

Perhaps the most fascinating parts of the diary concern arguments with Princess Mary, Edward's much older half-sister, about her steadfast loyalty to Catholicism. Edward's reign pressed England further and more firmly toward Protestantism than any other, and the rejection of this program by a close relation who was also next in line for the throne was inescapably state business. Yet it was also obviously a deeply personal conflict, as is plain even in Edward's stilted prose. In 1551, Edward recorded how

> The lady Mary, my sister, came to me to Westminster, where after greetings she was called with my council into a chamber where it was declared how

long I had suffered her mass, in hope of her reconciliation, and how now, there being no hope as I saw by her letters, unless I saw some speedy amendment I could not bear it. She answered that her soul was God's and her faith she would not change, nor hide her opinion with dissembled doings. It was said I did not constrain her faith but willed her only as a subject to obey. And that her example might lead to too much inconvenience.

The presence of Edward's diary in the Cotton library offers its own poignant juxtapositions. Though a Protestant himself, Sir Robert Cotton generally viewed Catholicism as an object for skeptical exchange and analysis; a relic, but a relic to preserve and study. By contrast, Edward sought to erase the Roman church from England entirely. His Act against Superstitious Books and Images of 1550 condemned the illuminated manuscripts and saints' lives that Cotton eagerly archived in his library decades later, and had Edward enjoyed the longevity of his father or his half-sister Elizabeth, the Cotton library might have been very different indeed. In that sense, for the collection that Nero C X now shares with numerous "superstitious books and images," the most important part of Edward's diary is nowhere in the text, at all, but rather in the many entries that were never made.

CHAPTER 2

The Collector

SOME YEARS AFTER JOHN DEE joined his late queen, his legendary library found itself broken up for sale. It was a sad irony given Dee's alarm on behalf of collections scattered by the Dissolution of the Monasteries, and his petition for a national sanctuary for their fragments. But the decline in Dee's fortunes from their Elizabethan peak had left behind a deeply indebted estate. With no national library to extend them shelter, his thousands of volumes were fair game for both creditors and fellow collectors. Sir Robert Cotton, knighted by King James in 1603, hoped for a nobler fate for his own library despite having gotten no further than Dee with petitioning for a national repository. But first, he needed a library worth preserving. In building such a library he felt no hesitation picking over the collections of fellow bibliophiles, ironies or no.

Much of the Cotton library was assembled through such scavenging. Authors frequently quote John Aubrey on how "manuscripts flew about like butterflies" in England, at the turn of the 17th century, and important work remained for those motivated to recapture them. But 60 years had passed since the Dissolution's initial crisis and opportunities. By the time Cotton began collecting he had missed out on the first wave of salvage buying. As a second-generation collector, his own great opportunities were often dependent on deaths among the previous generation.

In this, Cotton does indeed seem to have come along at "exactly the right time." Beginning around the time of Dee's death at least six more major collectors followed the late mystic in as many years, just as Cotton was enjoying heightened connections and resources thanks to court patronage. In 1609, Cotton managed to secure a few items from Lord Lumley's collection, although in competing against Prince Henry a number of choice items understandably escaped. The prince's own early death just three years later presented a second chance, however. That same year saw off William Dethick, followed two years later by Cotton's great patron the Earl of Northampton, both collectors of note.

Estate sales were by no means Cotton's only source. The fate of his acquisitions from Northampton points toward another, which may have been the most important of all. Colin G.C. Tite, among the leading scholars of the Cotton library, notes that a prayer book handwritten by Northampton himself is today part of the preserved collection of his nephew Thomas Howard; as Earl of Arundel, he was the major patron of Cotton's later career. Tite suggests that Cotton, "ever an eye to the main chance," likely passed it along knowing from experience that generosity had done more for his library than greed. Though the Cotton collection benefitted often from timely death, its development into not only a great but an active, living library, depended most of all on good friends.

Over the years, in collecting for his library, Cotton acquired books by nearly every means fair or foul. A rumor alleged that before his death Dr. Dee had buried manuscripts of his work in a field—and that Cotton subsequently bought part of Dee's estate in order to dig for them. Though almost certainly apocryphal, the tale recorded by Aubrey in *Brief Lives* is fully consistent with Cotton's passion for the chase. His library served many purposes, even in his own lifetime, but one of the most important reasons for its existence is undoubtedly its owner's simple joy in assembling it.

The records of Cotton's library transactions, assembled in turn by the patient work of modern scholars, are familiar to anyone who has been or known an eager collector. Cotton had his "want lists." He engaged various "spotters" to extend his quest through his own country and abroad; Sjoerd Levelt has documented how a number of Dutch manuscripts came to the Cotton library via the commercial consul for the Netherlands, Emanuel van Meteren. Cotton arranged trades with other collectors. He certainly paid out of pocket for manuscripts, if needed, and his rent books confirm that he had the means to buy in bulk in an era when notable manuscripts might still turn up as packing material in a shop from time to time. Cotton also pursued manuscripts that collectors had already recognized and become correspondingly more demanding in selling. Occasionally Sir Robert was outmaneuvered on a key deal, sometimes even by a good friend.

Much more often, though, Cotton was receiving books from friends rather than losing out to them. For *Sir Robert Cotton, 1586–1631*, Kevin Sharpe reviewed surviving records and found surprisingly little evidence of purchased material in the library, concluding that "with the evidence we have, it is hard to avoid the conclusion that Cotton, like Matthew Parker, acquired the bulk of his library by gift rather than by purchase." Plenty of anecdotal evidence supports the possibility. His scholarly correspondent de Peiresc sent copies of the latest works off the presses of France. His friend John Weever wrote of discovering manuscripts in a chandler's shop once, and promptly turning them over to "the onely repairer of ruined antiquitie whom I knew."

The ill-fated Greek Genesis was a gift to Cotton, as were both copies of Magna Carta that his library eventually boasted. Donors had no shortage of reasons to enrich Cotton's library; Weever's confidence in the library as a safe store was shared by many, while Mirrlees has suggested that at least a few items may have represented "peace offerings from guilty borrowers." Whether from guilt or gratitude, Cotton's generous lending and assistance with research certainly inspired many friends to offer gifts. Few of them would have struggled to think of something he would like.

As attested by the opening pages of too many period books to record, friends to Cotton and his library were everywhere among early Stuart literati. Camden dedicated an edition of *Britannia* to Cotton, who supplied much of its source material. The jurist John Selden dedicated multiple works to him, praising Sir Robert's "inestimable library" as well in *The Historie of Tithes*. Francis Bacon's *Historie of the Raigne of King Henry the Seventh* credits Cotton's assistance. Edmund Bolton, a poet as well as a historian,

Two versions of Sir Robert Cotton's coat of arms
The design at left was used most frequently.
From *C.J.H. Davenport's* English Heraldic Book-stamps *(London, 1909).*

observed to Cotton that "The world sees that no worthie monument of witt and learning comes forth but with honourable acknowledgement of help from you…" Hope Mirrlees notes more prosaically that "there are very few Jacobean books on history or antiquities which do not contain some expression of gratitude to Cotton or to his library."

The tremendous value of Sir Robert Cotton's collection to contemporaries, and their resultant gratitude, are perhaps best appreciated within the context of the larger history of England's libraries. Prior to the Dissolution, the great collections of books and manuscripts were almost exclusively those of monasteries. Though these had numerous shortcomings as public libraries, they did provide known places to turn, and even engaged in some limited lending. But the visitations of Henry VIII's commissioners brought all of that to a swift end.

The libraries of Oxford and Cambridge survived, as institutions. But even after they began rebuilding from the depredations under Henry's son, they too remained very limited resources. Both universities restricted in-person access to their collections, and borrowing material was an actual physical impossibility within a "chained library." J.N.L. Myres explains in *The English Library Before 1700* that such a library's books were "chained to the presses of sufficient length to enable them to lie open on the desks but not to be removed to any other part of the room." Myres adds that the printing press, by dramatically reducing the labor required for book production, effectively made such systems obsolete by the mid-16th century… yet as J.C.T. Oates points out in the same anthology, Cambridge delayed a general unchaining of books until after 1627, while Oxford "kept its chains until late in the eighteenth century…"

Cotton, by contrast, not only lent books but often neglected to make any bother about recovering them. His was a private library, and if a complete stranger knocked on the door Cotton could have and may well have sent him packing. But on the whole the Cotton library was a champion of accessibility, not least because of its location. Sir Robert and his books moved around a few times before settling in Cotton House, as close as any place has come to being *the* physical location for the Cotton library. But just being in London made the library far more accessible to the capital's scholarly and political community than either of the universities could be, in an age of slow overland travel. Once the library settled in Cotton House, around 1622, it could scarcely have been more centrally located anywhere in the city. In the middle of the Palace of Westminster grounds, amid various official record offices and close by the Houses of Parliament, Cotton was able to establish a national library almost literally by the back door.

Well before the Cotton library moved to Westminster, Cotton himself was becoming nearly an honorary resident. He entered Parliament for the first time in 1601, and at the Earl of Northampton's direction performed some modest service for Elizabeth's government. Under King James, both Northampton and Cotton then began to ascend the ladder of favor and influence even higher, from the new king's first day.

Henry Howard, Earl of Northampton, was connected in one way or another to most of the important people, groups and government projects of his era. In the 1590s, he briefly aligned himself with the dynamic Earl of Essex, before prudently moving to Robert Cecil's camp in time to avoid Essex's downfall; he and Cecil then collaborated on the tricky project of planning for a succession that was officially treasonable to discuss. Their gamble paid off when James moved swiftly to occupy the throne of England. While Northampton's relationship with the new king was often strained, he wielded considerable influence at court for the rest of his life. James wryly captured both of these aspects in dubbing Northampton, Cecil, and Howard's nephew the Earl of Suffolk his "Trinity of Knaves."

For Northampton's own close advisor, relations with the new sovereign were in many ways warmer still. The Scottish James was an awkward outsider suddenly thrust into the very center of England's turbulent court, and Robert Cotton offered a small measure of kinship, figuratively and even literally. Cotton was a descendant of Scotland's revered king Robert the Bruce, and if it was a distant connection, Cotton's new enthusiasm for this shared heritage apparently pleased James, who took to calling him "cousin" in addition to including him among the many knighthoods awarded in 1603. (Cotton himself took to signing his name "Robert Cotton Bruceus," thereafter.) Beyond this, James was himself a credible amateur scholar. As the man who eventually gave both patronage and his name to the Anglophone world's most enduring translation of the Bible, and once avowed that "Were I not a king, I would be a university man," he likely recognized a deeper kinship with "cousin" Robert.

Despite shared interests, King James's friendship with Cotton did not extend to the Society of Antiquaries or its projects. The proposed academy and national library remained a dream. If another clue to its rejection were needed, in addition to cost and inertia, one might readily be found in the Society's general decline under James. By 1607, London's first Society of Antiquaries ceased formal meetings, and an attempted revival several years later proved abortive. In both instances royal disapproval played a significant role.

Details of the Society's history are sometimes uncertain, but most sources support the conclusion of Sir Henry Spelman, who wrote some years after its demise that "his Majesty took a little Mislike of our Society." Amateur antiquaries discussing etymology and topography must appear, at this distance, a harmless club of eccentrics, hardly material for a "treasonous cabal." But by the early 1600s, the Society had in fact strayed some way into contemporary politics. Several members of Parliament had joined, including vocal critics of royal prerogative. More to the point, perhaps, in English politics of their era the distant past was generally inseparable from contemporary arguments.

One of the few things Parliament and crown could reliably agree on even as other differences sharpened was the importance of *precedent*. For James, an organized society of MPs and lawyers scrutinizing questions of precedent likely seemed distinctly unnecessary, particularly once direct questions into law and Parliament joined the relatively nonpolitical agenda of earlier days. The Society's closed proceedings probably did little to help; whatever their reasoning, they certainly courted suspicion in advising members that "Yt is desyred that you bringe none other with you, nor geue anie notive unto anie, but to such as haue the like somouns."

Some evidence points to a last minute attempt to foreswear subjects of political controversy and assuage royal mislike, but it apparently came too late. Though a Society of Antiquaries did return to London eventually, it was not for nearly a century. In the meantime, Cotton may have been disappointed by its disbanding but he had plentiful compensations, not least the king's exemption of Sir Robert's own research into matters of precedent. James and his "knaves" were quite content to support an individual antiquarian or two, as long as he labored under their supervision. Throughout the Stuart dynasty's early years in England, Cotton was kept busy marshaling arguments for one royal project after another. He eagerly produced evidence for James's personal claim to the crown, as well as the sovereign's general claim to preeminence over Parliament. He aided Bacon on James's desired union of England and Scotland (without success), and Northampton on peace negotiations with Spain (with better results, including a minor triumph in defending English trading activity in the Americas). In all these projects and more besides, Cotton was constantly drawing on documents from not only his personal library, but government archives; significantly, he did not always concern himself with maintaining a distinction between them.

The Cotton library of today most often enjoys attention for the *Beowulf* manuscript, the Lindisfarne Gospels, Magna Carta and other "crown jewels." For much of Cotton's lifetime, though, many of these items were either absent from his library or else unrecognized as noteworthy. Both his copies of King John's great charter were late acquisitions, while *Beowulf*'s ascent to literary fame only began in the 19th century. In the era of its founding the Cotton library's reputation owed considerably more to documents that seem relatively mundane, at least from the perspective of the uninitiated.

The extensive state papers collection among the Cotton manuscripts nonetheless offers its own claims to interest. For students of English history or heraldry, 200 volumes of records from Henry VIII through James I offer an invaluable resource. Tite declares that the collection as a whole traces "the transactions and preoccupations, major and minor, of English government at the time," transactions in some instances recorded nowhere else. For more general audiences, though, Sir Robert Cotton's state papers archive may hold greater interest for how he came by it.

Thomas Wilson, appointed the first keeper of the state paper office by James I, saw Cotton's private archive as little short of grand larceny. Wilson repeatedly criticized the ongoing drift of government papers into Cotton's library. More than once, he actively sought to contest it. When Robert Cecil died Wilson sought to secure the late secretary of state's papers before Cotton could get hold of them. In this, and a similar struggle for the papers of his colleague Arthur Agarde, Wilson met with no more than partial success; in general, his efforts must be regarded as a signal failure. Yet for what it may be worth, Wilson had a point.

Cotton certainly did help himself to the records of England's government, not only those that might be deemed privately held and therefore fair game, but those on deposit in official archives, as well. Kevin Sharpe notes that Cotton's library was as indispensable to heraldry as the College of Arms, "if only because Sir Robert had much of the material... which should more properly have been deposited there." Few such proprieties ever restrained Cotton. Through the Society of Antiquaries, of course, he knew many of the heralds and record keepers personally. He could bolster acquaintance with formal credentials, after he began regular work as a court researcher under James. In this pursuit, in particular, it seems Cotton developed a habit of taking his work home. Tite sums up the controversy over Cotton's state paper collection memorably, observing that "There is an impression that every time he visited the various archives of government he came away with his pockets crammed with booty."

At the same time, Tite is one of multiple authors who have rallied to Cotton's defense. Cotton's contemporaries recognized and shared much of their reasoning. Even among the official record keepers, Cotton's accumulation of state papers mostly met with acquiescence and even active support because, in most instances, Sir Robert seemed a better custodian of them than the state itself.

A typical tourist's itinerary for London can reveal a good deal about their reasons. Into the 19th century, government scattered its records among makeshift stores anywhere that offered room. Careful visitors to Westminster Abbey will note that its Chapter House was once a state archive. The Tower of London's exhibits note that Tower Records Office only closed in 1858, and that complaints of "the poor state" of records recurred throughout most of its history. Chancery records were divided between archives at the Tower, the Abbey, the Rolls House in Chancery Lane, and individual court offices. The records of important minsters were, as noted, often treated as personal papers.

By Elizabeth's time people recognized the chaos and began efforts to introduce a system into it. But formal progress remained elusive long afterward. In the meantime, as with a national library Sir Robert Cotton was ready to supply the want of an ordered, central archive for England's state papers, and friends among the clerks and archivists and political class were ready to support him. Sir Thomas Parry, ambassador to France in James's early years, donated papers to Cotton. Very likely other courtiers followed suit, as Cotton proved himself a capable and open-handed librarian. Thomas Wilson could warn against permitting one of Cotton's cronies to replace Arthur Agarde at the office of the exchequer after Agarde passed away, but as usual his attempts were sabotaged by his own side.

Like Wilson, Agarde was a reformer who devoted himself to ordering and protecting his office's papers; unlike Wilson, Agarde saw no conflict between this and Cotton's private collecting. After Agarde's death, Wilson petitioned the king himself to secure the late archivist's own valuable files, but Agarde had made perfectly clear his desire that many choice items go to none other than his close friend, and fellow Society of Antiquaries alumnus, Sir Robert.

Tite's image of a gentleman plunderer, stuffing manuscripts into his pockets with permission or without, is still difficult to efface. More than one chronicler records how Cotton once borrowed an ancient manuscript of Bede from St. John's College, Oxford, seemingly with every intention of keeping it. Cotton entered the volume into the catalog of his own library, and there part of it remains. Sir Robert surrendered back the volume after desperate pleas for its return and, finally, even promises of "recompense" by Archbishop Laud, who brokered the loan; even then, Cotton took the liberty of tearing out an entire section to hold back for himself. A similar story involving a large compendium borrowed from the City of London does not aid Cotton's reputation, nor does his employing as librarian one Richard James, who once boasted of having "gott away many of those manuscriptes from ye good olde man [Oxford scholar T. Allen] and conveyed them away to London to Sir Robert Cotton's studie..." Reading of a friend once warning Cotton, in advance of a meeting with Sir Thomas Bodley, that he should hide away any valuable tomes that might be easily concealed owing to Bodley's reputation for helping himself to such items, one must wonder which man should have been more on his guard.

Yet Bodley did not shun Cotton, and very few others did, either. Throughout his life Cotton enjoyed the friendship and frequent praise of exactly the sort of scholars and collectors most likely to have items on one of his want lists. While making some allowance for his charm and political connections, Cotton was never a true royal "favorite," either. Wilson notwithstanding, instances of outright thievery must realistically have been few and forgivable, at least in context of the countless transactions Cotton made over his career as bibliophile. Taking was constantly twinned with giving, including to Bodley; Sir Robert was one of the first donors to Bodley's planned library at Oxford, by his own choice rather than any unwitting loss.

Sir Robert Cotton was, in the end, simply a contradiction that cannot be entirely resolved. He unquestionably pursued books, manuscripts and other "ancient monuments" with passion, and regularly with aggressiveness that at least brushed the bounds of theft. At the same time, he was so generous with his own collection as to confound any idea of a rapacious hoarder. Reviewing Cotton's policies as librarian, one is left with the strange but inescapable impression that getting *back* a book of one's own from Sir Robert was frequently more difficult than obtaining the loan of even the most valuable of his.

An episode reported by Mirrlees reinforces that impression while offering a perfect vignette of Cotton's habits in all their amusing, infuriating, yet oddly consistent splendor. In 1620, nearly 50 years old, Sir Robert Cotton found himself being scolded by his uncle John for loaning out a manuscript borrowed from their mutual acquaintance Sir George Buc. Cotton had promised Buc to "keep it always in [my] own possession and where it should be ready at all times, if it were called for," a promise Buc had insisted on before parting with it for very good reason. He was correspondingly so anxious for the manuscript's return as to enlist familial guilt for the same reason: he himself had only been borrowing the book from another friend before charming, earnest, endearing old Cotton had somehow talked it away from him.

CHAPTER 3

Uses and Users

MANY OF THE VOLUMES in the Cotton library are compendiums. Inside, one may find formerly loose codices, and even odd scraps, bound together by Sir Robert or successors according to often-obscure systems. One of the folios in the volume labeled Julius C III is a hastily scribbled, barely legible note to Cotton himself. Edward Edwards identified it as a message dispatched from the privy council chamber by Robert Cecil, and in *Lives of the Founders of the British Museum* quoted the gist of its entreaty: "If you be not here with those precedents for which there is present use, we are all undone, for his Majesty doth so chide, that I dare not come into his sight."

To modern Anglophone societies, animated by an ideology of constant progress and growth, the obsession with precedent that characterized Cotton's age can appear backward and even baffling. Despite the massive changes of the Renaissance and Reformation, so obvious from the perspective of four centuries later, English political arguments were shaped by a determined insistence that change in the workings of society was not only unwanted, but unthinkable. Improvement on ancient tradition was impossible; at most, reform could merely restore what had fallen into error. In practice, this attitude allowed considerable scope for argument and innovation, owing to very vague concepts of how ideal traditions of the past functioned. Even in practice, however, a viable policy demanded some sort of historical precedent no matter how loose.

Ministers might, then, quite sincerely fear being "all undone" by want of appropriate precedents. In all fairness to them, it's worth considering that contemporary legal and political arguments may differ from those of the Stuarts more in style than in substance. As recently as Britain's 2013 parliamentary debate about military intervention in Syria, reporters found themselves reaching back to the 18th century for context, and pointing to royal prerogative in explaining the prime minister's options for declaring war. In America, proper interpretation of the Constitution provokes furious argument, year in and year out. The politics of precedent may operate under other names, but has not vanished entirely.

England has never had a formal written constitution, at all. The office of its prime minster is defined more by custom than law, and may even be said not to exist. Those traditions that resemble a prime minister's role are nonetheless relatively settled, today, compared with the decades before England's Civil War. Then, precedent was used to advance transformative policy, but it also defined government's structure even under the status quo. The most basic rules defining a government position were matters of antiquarian interest: what office was responsible for what, who was senior to whom, how an appointee was chosen. If this or that point had not come up in recent memory, the only hope of dependable resolution lay in old parchments—and a man familiar with them.

Every time Cotton ransacked the archives on a council commission, it enhanced his mastery of indispensable precedent. Such missions grew the physical resources of his library—through self-authorized permanent loans—and his general familiarity with the nation's records, whatever their location. The combination kept Sir Robert much in demand throughout James's first decade as king of England.

For his patron Northampton, Cotton was effectively an on-call research secretary, or even chief of staff. Northampton entrusted some matters to Cotton almost entirely; a tract against dueling written for the earl is one of the small number of finished works on Sir Robert's personal bibliography. Cotton also informed and advised Northampton on many more weighty issues. From the prosecution of the Gunpowder Plotters, to debates over the coinage, in Kevin Sharpe's words "Henry Howard turned to Cotton as his right-hand man."

King James relied, in turn, on both men, turning to them with some of his government's most recalcitrant problems. The poor state of England's navy and the poor leadership behind it were perfect subjects for the time-honored practice of delegating work to a committee; as one of its leaders, Northampton delegated much of the labor of investigating the navy to Cotton. Though his experience as an antiquary was likely of limited help, Cotton threw himself into the work, spending 12 months interviewing witnesses and recording details of corruption and mismanagement. The earl shared his dedication, preparing with Sir Robert's help a detailed plan of reform. Northampton even lobbied for a second commission in 1613, after James responded to the first with the equally time-honored tradition of study, praise, and inaction. The second effort nonetheless fared little better than the first.

By that point, experience may have tempered Cotton's enthusiasm with realism, and even a touch of cynicism. Sharpe dates to 1613 a rare expression of his subject's candid thoughts, describing the court as "a swarm of busie heads which measure the great Mysteries of state by the rule of their self conceited wisdomes." Still, Cotton carried on. Though by no means disinterested in personal advancement, he seems to have genuinely believed in politics as an opportunity, and even obligation, to serve.

His efforts were not all in vain, either. Crown revenues were another intractable problem entrusted to Cotton and his patron, and here they achieved at least short-term success. Cotton once again conducted extensive research, this time mainly among the documentary sources that were his forte, and prepared a kind of white paper on "Means for raising the king's estate." His suggestions ranged widely, from detailed income-generating precedents that might be revived, to warnings against monopolies and debasing the coinage, to general strategies for either collaboration with Parliament or unilateral action based on royal prerogative. Cotton also recognized that any real cure for the royal finances would require greater discipline in the king's personal expenditures; that his report did not shy from saying so demonstrates the author's confidence in his standing with James.

That standing received another boost shortly after Cotton's work on revenues. In June 1611, James's government raised Cotton to the newly reintroduced rank of baronet. Being the product of an undisguised cash outlay may have diluted the honor somewhat. But a paid-for revival of baronets was at least Cotton's own idea, a detail that should have provided some satisfaction even if credit has never been completely resolved. Just as failure is an orphan, the profitable sale of baronetcies eventually drew at least three other claimants to its parentage, including Robert Cecil and Northampton. Whoever played what part in the scheme's execution, however, Cotton himself certainly found the essential precedents for an order of "Baronnetz" just below barons; at least one such document is still in his library today. Amid the initially brisk sales that followed, royal praise was likely more than adequate to spread around anyway. It was not quite adequate to provide Sir Robert with a freebie. But if nothing else, in buying the 36th of the new issue on June 29, Cotton proved that he would take his own medicine.

Among Cotton's legacies, his library has long outlasted the Cotton baronetcy, as well as overshadowing it and most of his other achievements, generally. Somewhat curiously, his formal production as a scholar is no exception. Cotton was educated, obviously both interested and rich in material, and hardly lacking in ambition. Yet he published little, and relatively modest essays like his tract on dueling make up the greatest part of that, as well as of the anthology published after his death as *Cottoni Posthuma*. His most extensive, finished work of history was probably "The life and raign of Henry the Third," and even it was a modest essay primarily intended as a parable for his own era.

Many factors could explain the brevity of Cotton's bibliography. In an essay for *Sir Robert Cotton As Collector*, Nigel Ramsey suggests that Sir Robert simply "lacked the depth of knowledge to write a full-length work on any aspect of English medieval or Tudor history." Absent any firm evidence proving otherwise, some sort of deficiency along these lines is plausible, but Cotton had no shortage of other excuses. He was busy, of course, assembling a library, curating his collection, and serving tirelessly on government commissions. Though his involvement in Parliament and in managing his estates may have been limited, they too must have placed some demand on his time.

Cotton was also constantly supporting others' projects. In some cases, his aid was so substantial that it may be fair to regard them as his projects, in fact, as much as their official authors'. His involvement with more than one of Camden's works, as well as with John Speed's 1611 *Historie of Great Britaine*, verged on coauthorship. Sir Robert not only provided much of their raw source material, but also prepared extensive notes, edited early drafts and may well have written some sections entirely. *Britannia* may have begun as primarily Camden's work, but it become more and more a collaboration with Cotton with each revision. In piecing together pre-Roman history though Iron Age coins, Camden must have relied almost entirely on his friend, whose impressive coin collection was in some ways just as significant as his library (and indeed an integral part of it). Francis Bacon suggested that one of Camden's later projects, the *History of Elizabeth*, ought to be regarded as Cotton's work outright.

Countless other, more modest collaborations added up to claim another large share of Sir Robert's time. Edwards recounts that, "In later days he was wont to say to his intimates: 'I, myself, have the smallest share in myself.' From youth, onwards, there is abundant evidence that the saying expressed, unboastingly, the simple facts of his daily life." Preserved correspondence shows Cotton receiving, and answering, questions on nearly everything under the sun, from literature to law courts, numismatics to the nobility, buildings to burial fees. The great names and projects of the era borrowed from Cotton's library, and from Cotton: Sir Walter Raleigh for his popular *History of the World*, Ben Jonson and Inigo Jones for the lavish masques staged for the court. Furthering John Selden's research into cultures of the Orient may have been Cotton's whole purpose in acquiring various manuscripts in Arabic, Persian, Chinese, et al., languages which there is no evidence that Sir Robert himself understood.

Such thought for an audience beyond himself is evident throughout the library. Cotton enjoyed the activity of collecting, itself, and also sought to create a shelter for rare and endangered documents. But if any single theme could bind most of his sprawling, diverse collection it was *utility*. Whether seeking out material with a specific purpose in mind, or making every effort to match documents with those who could use them afterward, Cotton meant for his library to be used. Even among contemporaries, his collection was never significant for its volume. John Dee may have owned three times as many items, and other private libraries achieved similar or even greater scale. But Cotton was no hermetic scholar or gentleman ornamenting his den with unopened books, and much of the reason his collection endured when so many others dispersed is likely that his collection served more than his own ends. Money or passion could build a great library, but only purpose could sustain one.

A great deal of Cotton's utilitarian library was and is, somewhat counterintuitively, concerned with religious subjects. Given the circumstances of its foundation this was likely inevitable. Many of the manuscripts, as well as the whole project of collecting them, may be traced to the Dissolution of the Monasteries. A good deal of the state papers and official correspondence record the stages of that Dissolution, and of the larger English Reformation. Most important of all, Cotton lived his entire life in a time when the struggle over the church was inseparable from affairs of state.

Little suggests Sir Robert to have been very spiritually minded, personally. On the whole his professional and personal life seem those of a secular, even worldly individual. Jennifer Summit has pointed out that Cotton counted numerous Catholics among his friends and acquaintances, and even more notably, provided use of his library to more than one of them. One or two rumors claimed Cotton himself had secret Catholic sympathies, although, given his more extensive association with noted Protestants in government, it seems more likely that Sir Robert was simply a relatively open-minded man when it came to personal beliefs.

The official allegiance of the nation, however, was quite another matter. Church and state were then so entangled that the notion of a separation was practically inconceivable, even above and beyond the general aversion to innovation that characterized Stuart politics. Both Henry VIII and Elizabeth displayed partiality to Catholic forms even after the former's break from Rome, and the latter famously disavowed making "windows into men's souls," per Francis Bacon. But they were as committed to sustaining an independent English church as to an independent throne, and under the circumstances that ultimately meant a Protestant-leaning church. If in the end the Stuart dynasty did not share their determination, Sir Robert Cotton certainly did.

Cotton could and did show tolerance toward individual Catholics, in both his correspondence with foreign scholars like de Peiresc and his associations closer to home. He was simply determined that England never be their country, in a proprietary sense, again. In one of his essays, "Serious Considerations for Repressing of the Increase of Iesuites, Priests and Papists without Shedding Blood," Cotton argued against capital punishment of these persons—lest it create martyrs and inspire more.

Summit notes a parallel policy in his library, which contained not only monastic records but many saints' lives of the type destroyed under the more fanatical Edward VI, and even a holy relic. In among his cabinet of curiosities, Cotton preserved a small fragment of bone allegedly from the skull of Thomas Becket. In *Memory's Library,* Summit suggests that both fragment and manuscripts were being stripped of superstitious power through removal from shrine to archive. As with believers themselves, Cotton and his cohorts intended to prevail not through persecution but through patient, well-informed analysis. They could feel confident that history would vindicate their view, for the excellent reason that they would write the history. Cotton would, as usual, render every assistance; in a series of volumes eventually assigned to his library's "Cleopatra" shelves, Sir Robert assembled many letters and other papers documenting the history of the Reformation and, in effect, documenting the prehistory of the library itself.

It's possible that Cotton's library not only has origins in the English Reformation but, in some sense, began as a history thereof. One of James's earliest commissions of his "cousin" was a history of the church, and Graham Parry suggests that Cotton's collection "was assembled to some extent with this plan in mind." By 1603, his library was in fact already noteworthy among contemporaries, but collecting and organizing material for such a history may have been as specific a purpose as any Sir Robert ever had for his library as a whole.

As with most such plans he pursued, though, it was in the end as facilitator, rather than author. The previous year, James Ussher met Cotton on a visit to London, and when the latter found his ecclesiastical history project getting nowhere he handed it off to the young scholar and future archbishop. Or rather, handed charge of the project to Ussher; in both this and other endeavors Cotton provided liberal support for decades. He not only supplied Ussher with material from his collection, but sought out further items that could be of use and, when he couldn't obtain them, advised his friend where they might at least be examined *in situ*. Ussher's use of the library eventually lasted nearly 50 years, right to the end of his own life and well past that of its founder. One of the earliest library catalogs records his gratitude, of a pattern with nearly every other borrower's: "My most abundant supplies of manuscripts came from that noble Cotton library, which alone gave more help to the achievement of a history of the British nation than all others combined."

Some small sense of failure is still difficult to avoid, in reviewing Cotton's academic career. Cotton himself certainly felt an ambition to produce a larger work of history truly his own. At least twice he committed to such a goal, but failed to achieve it. Just possibly, though, in looking at Cotton's work and remarking the absence of a great history, one could be missing the forest for the trees. Summit proposes that the Cleopatra volumes are not only material for a history of the church but constitute, themselves, a sort of history by collage. Colin Tite has gone further, suggesting that the monastic chronicles in Cotton's library inspired him to prepare a version for his own day, through cut-and-paste rather than original prose. Tite points to the many volumes in which Cotton not only arranged original documents to form a chronological narrative, but frequently purchased or even commissioned copies when an important manuscript eluded his reach.

Whether this practice represented an innovative approach to authorship, or simply dedicated archiving, must ultimately remain a matter of opinion. It's worth considering that if Cotton did see his compilations as valid works in themselves, however, his idea has not been entirely without followers. Modern books like *Scotland: The Autobiography* have revived a similar concept of presenting a larger history entirely through period accounts. Robert "Bruce" Cotton might well enjoy some feeling of vindication from that.

In a larger sense of course, the greater validation of his life's efforts lies in his library, through which he created a legacy far more durable than any of those contemporaries who finished and published books. Even the work of those like Camden, who genuinely advanced the historian's profession, is today long since superseded by later scholarship. By contrast the original sources that Camden and others borrowed from Cotton's library have remained valuable ever since. Through Cotton's effort, many were not only circulated but published for the first time, in some cases preserving text that later perished in its original form. The greater part of the collection, meanwhile, endures as a source for research and surprises even in the 21st century.

EX LIBRIS
THE LINDISFARNE GOSPELS
Nero D IV

MANY QUALITIES mark the Lindisfarne Gospels as remarkable. Countless copies of the Four Gospels exist, but this one is the earliest surviving version in an English translation. Other illuminated manuscripts dazzle, but few match the Lindisfarne Gospels' technical achievements, or its rich blend of cultural influences. All of these things make Nero D IV an unquestionable highlight of the Cotton library. What may be more remarkable than any other feature of the book, however, is its own survival.

Most of the volume dates to the early 8th century. With some reason, the term "Dark Ages" has clung to this era, but it was also a period of great transition in Britain, and the Lindisfarne Gospels reflects this. Its pages reveal the legacies of Celts and Romans, and the more recent influence of Anglo-Saxons, and even traces of Coptic and other eastern cultures. Britain's repeated assimilation of newcomers and the cultural ferment that resulted were both, however, about to face one of their greatest challenges, the Vikings. In time the Danes became settled natives, like other invaders before them, but it was a long process. For many generations their place in society was frequently as pillagers, particularly of the rich monasteries that produced dazzling illuminated manuscripts. Vikings sacked Lindisfarne in 793, and again in 875.

The monastery's namesake work survived these years almost miraculously untouched by these visits. A century later, another hand transformed the Lindisfarne Gospels, and from a modern perspective enriched it. Yet the addition of an Old English translation above the Latin lines by a 10th century provost, Alfred, might as well have been a defacement if not outright blasphemy at many points between his own day and King James's endorsement of an Authorized Translation. Even into Tudor times, would-be translators suffered violent persecution. By then Old English was no longer a vernacular language, any more than the Latin it translated, but under Edward VI the Lindisfarne Gospels committed a new offense. C.E. Wright observes in *The English Library Before 1700* that, in Edward's campaign against "superstitious books," "the kinds of books specified several were just those that carried in the Middle Ages the richest illumination… the great gospel books and the psalters…"

Lindisfarne's great gospel book survived, again, thanks to Edward's brief reign, and the preservationist instincts that eventually inspired the antiquary movement and Sir Robert Cotton's library. The loss of the book's historically recorded ornamental binding suggests that its path from monastery to private ownership was not entirely gentle, however. (Its present binding dates from 1852.) No known source explains its journey from the north of England to a clerk of the House of Commons named Robert Bowyer. The Cotton library's receipt of the book from Bowyer is confirmed by Cotton's papers, but other early notes on the Lindisfarne Gospels are

Detail of The Lindisfarne Gospels

extraordinarily brisk; scholars presume that the acquisition marked a high point for Sir Robert but it is only a guess.

Whatever Sir Robert's thoughts, the book of Lindisfarne absolutely is a highlight of his collection, and its charmed avoidance of perils that robbed the collection of many other notable items is worth celebrating. Its artful combination of many types of pigment, gold leaf, and inventive calligraphy make it a masterpiece of craft. Unusually for the period, a colophon added by Alfred along with his translation records his own name, as well as those of the original illuminator and other often anonymous contributors. Its variety, meanwhile, captures a range of broader cultural influences that shaped the nation to which it now belongs. As Philip Howard writes in *The British Library: A Treasure House of Knowledge*, the Lindisfarne Gospels are, "in effect, a foundation document of English language, art, Christianity and history."

CHAPTER 4

The Insider's View

In allying himself with the Earl of Northampton, Robert Cotton prospered for more than a decade. By 1611, court-watchers regarded Cotton as a candidate to succeed the ailing Robert Cecil as secretary of state. Yet the game of power politics always carries a risk of being drawn into intrigues, and corruption. In choosing Northampton for his partner, Cotton essentially doubled down on his gamble.

Henry Howard was intelligent, and cultured. He was prepared to devote considerable effort to government service, as in his naval reform campaign. He was also an inveterate intriguer and morally flexible. Northampton's reaction to Cecil's death in 1612 provides a sense of the sort of person Cotton had made his patron; though Northampton had worked effectively with Cecil, he resented him deeply and eagerly speculated on the late courtier joining Queen Elizabeth herself "by an extreme whotte fieres side."

A sense that Northampton might betray anyone or anything in pursuit of advancement may be part of the reason he was, ultimately, frustrated in it. King James respected Northampton's talents and advice. But James—the addressee of Northampton's gloating remark—never really warmed to the man or to entrusting him with formal high office. If the earl could not win over James directly, however, he just might attach himself to one who could. When a rising young man named Robert Carr caught the king's eye, Northampton conceived a master stratagem. He would need to manipulate people, even those closest to him, like pawns. But that came only too naturally to Sir Robert Cotton's patron.

Northampton never misused Cotton himself, not in any substantive sense. If Sir Robert ever felt betrayed by Northampton, after scandals and arrests and the wreck of his promising career as courtier, it can only have been in a general sense of being let down by the earl's disregard for ethics. More likely, Cotton had always known well enough whom he was dealing with and saw it as just one more expedient, little different from his own sticky-fingered collecting or lucrative but neglected marriage. As long as one had the favor of the king, personal honor could quite easily withstand a few dings.

Northampton, unfortunately, took this attitude to an extreme. That seemed to run in his family. His older brother had plotted treason against Elizabeth, and his niece now proved a ready partner in his own scheme. An attraction between Frances Howard and Carr, the royal favorite, suggested a convenient chance to consolidate influence at court through a marriage alliance. The fact that Frances was already married to the Earl of Essex (the son of another notorious Elizabethan figure) seemed, to the Howards, a minor detail. Similar insouciance probably applied to the other key figure in this tangled ménage. While King James seemed entirely content to watch his favorite get in bed with the Howards, Sir Thomas Overbury was not. Overbury's friendship and possible romance with Carr was older, more intense and perhaps less secure. He vehemently opposed Carr's attachment to Frances Howard and applied all of his influence to blocking it. The Howards, accordingly, dispensed with Overbury as casually as they annulled Frances's first marriage. Northampton found an excuse to imprison Overbury in the Tower of London, and with his objections effectively removed, Frances Howard and Robert Carr wed in late 1613.

Up to this point Sir Robert Cotton was merely a spectator in these matters. He, too, seemed pleased by his patron bringing their faction even closer to the crown in one big happy family, though. By the beginning of 1615, Cotton was pursuing an even bigger matrimonial alliance for the Stuart court as his next project, collaborating with Carr, whom James had created Earl of Somerset. Cotton's involvement with negotiating and even lobbying for a marriage alliance with Catholic Spain may indicate how thoroughly he had pledged himself to *realpolitik*; the main reason for Cotton's curious turn to matchmaking may be its relevance to his work on crown revenues. Though the Habsburgs championed the Roman church that Cotton wanted kept well out of England, they were fabulously rich. James having taken little note of Sir Robert's points about economizing, Cotton gamely went to work promoting a match between Prince Charles and the Spanish infanta.

Unfortunately for Cotton, he was not only in deep with plots and plotters, but simply out of his depth. Over the course of 1615 everything began to collapse. The Spanish ambassador, Count Gondomar, proved nearly as capable as Queen Elizabeth had in stringing along suitors indefinitely. Meanwhile, rumors began circulating that Somerset's own marriage alliance was even more an amoral episode than already apparent. Sir Thomas Overbury had died in confinement a few months before the wedding he wished to prevent, and the new gossip claimed this was no coincidence. Between it and the failure of negotiations for the Spanish match, the king distanced himself from his former favorite. When rumor did not die out, James authorized a formal investigation into Overbury's death. The investigators quickly decided that popular rumor had substance.

Modern authorities generally regard the case against Somerset and his wife as politically motivated, and its evidence thin. Someone may have tried to weaken the interfering Overbury using poison, or even fully intended to murder him, and perhaps Frances Howard was involved. But perhaps not. Four men were nonetheless executed over the affair, and Somerset and his wife sent to prison for a short period. Cotton regarded the conviction of Somerset, at least, as a gross injustice, and for the rest of his life publicly stood up for Carr's honor. In private, he may have wavered, at least briefly. But by that point, Cotton himself was in need of friends and suddenly short of them.

Northampton had died the previous year, after an operation left his leg infected and eventually gangrenous. The late earl thereby eluded any personal involvement in the investigations that followed; his reputation, and Sir Robert, did not. On October 26 James approved a further commission to investigate both Cotton and his library. The official cause was alleged misconduct during the marriage negotiations; examiners were directed to search Cotton's papers for evidence "that Sir Robert Cotton, Knt. having amassed together the secrets of State, hath communicated them to the Spanish Ambassador…" Finding sensitive state documents in Cotton's possession was all too likely, as James and everyone around him already knew perfectly well. Discontent over the failed marriage negotiations had by this point begun to blur with the Overbury scandal, however, and Cotton being one of the few direct links between the two, some censure of Sir Robert allowed James to cover for the fact that he himself was one of the others. Rifling Cotton's library also offered the possibility of finding more substantial evidence in the Overbury matter, and in this object, Cotton seems to have been dangerously accommodating.

By one means or another Sir Edward Coke, Lord Chief Justice and head of the investigation, acquired letters from Somerset to Northampton discussing Overbury's imprisonment. Later suspicion accused Cotton himself of providing them. There is no question that the letters had been in his possession earlier. One theory suggested that, foreseeing a raid on his papers, he attempted to conceal them with a third party who then gave them up to Coke. Another possibility is that Cotton discretely provided the evidence directly. Given the signs that someone was certain to suffer for the scandal eventually, Cotton might well have concluded that he had no hope of saving Somerset and ought at least to save himself. Cotton was in fact arrested, too, that December. Any intentional cooperation on his part must have been a desperate cast, all the same, given that he had not only been close to Northampton and Somerset, but added dates to Somerset's correspondence in his own hand.

Letters were routinely undated in Cotton's day. But the precise timing of what Somerset wrote, and when, proved crucial to the question of his having plotted Overbury's death or having been a mere bystander. As Northampton's trusted aide, Cotton had access to all of the late earl's papers, including the letters. Conceivably, Cotton might have attempted to sort the letters from Somerset after Northampton's death, in order to prevent a misinterpretation from blackening his friends' names. Just as plausibly, he might have reordered the letters to disguise crime as coincidence. It's also possible that Cotton may not even have known, himself, but merely assembled documents into a narrative compatible with his own convictions, on faith, just as he did with various manuscripts in his library.

In both cases, no actual evidence suggests his deliberately falsifying the record, and any judgment must depend wholly on the mystery of Cotton's character. The Overbury scandal left that character in some question, whatever Sir Robert's own role may have been. His patron Northampton may not have plotted murder, but publication of his own letters revealed that he had practically pimped his married niece to Somerset using the crudest of terms, and Somerset had obviously responded. If Cotton's personal behavior was never on the same level, combined with such poor choice of associates it looked bad enough.

Hope Mirrlees argues that he realized it and attempted thereafter to do better, and that the crisis proved "the turning-point, spiritually, of Cotton's life." The conditions of his imprisonment had been relatively mild, and he was never formally tried. In June of 1616 he acquired a royal pardon by payment of a fine (or price) of £500. A worldly and flexible pragmatist might in the end have shrugged off the entire affair. But, for those open to seeing it, a kind of personal reformation is evident in Cotton thereafter. He returned to his wife, and he distanced himself from the game of chasing power and favor. His friend Arthur Agarde had once counseled him, "Be yourself, and no man's creature; but God's," and to a real extent, Cotton took this advice to heart after Northampton's fall. He did not permanently abandon politics, or patrons, or even the Howards, but when eventually he involved himself with the court once again he seemed more a cautious statesman driven by principle than an ambitious courtier driven by power.

Several years passed before even that rehabilitation, however, and after his constant activity during James's first dozen years, Cotton experienced a relatively quiet life away from court, Parliament and mistress. As ever, there remained plenty to do in his library.

By the time Cotton resumed a more direct role in politics in the early 1620s, his library had much of the form it retained for the next century. With allowances for limited if important losses and additions, the contents of the library were probably similar to what researchers encounter even today, although any comparison must be qualified; throughout its history "Sir Robert Cotton's library" has never had a single, clearly fixed definition.

In addition to his state papers, salvaged monastic records and other manuscripts, Cotton undoubtedly owned a collection of printed books. These were apparently dispersed later in the 17th century, however, almost without trace. In recent years, scholars like Colin Tite have re-identified a few. But if other printed books once owned by Sir Robert are somewhere among the holdings of the British Library, e.g., they are likely to remain unrecognized in the absence of any complete record of Cotton's print collection. To date, none has emerged. The facts that Cotton at least attempted to catalog his manuscripts, by contrast, and that his heirs determinedly kept those holdings together while the printed books were dispersed without fanfare, support the view of Kevin Sharpe and others that the manuscript library and printed books were always two distinct collections.

On the other hand, traditions of what constitutes *a library* press for a view that all of the texts Cotton kept under his roof were, in some sense, part of his library. If a visitor borrowed a printed book from Cotton, it would have seemed natural to think of it as on loan from his library, regardless of how Sir Robert shelved everything. Once established in Cotton House—as close to an official, physical, "Cotton Library" as has ever existed—manuscripts were shelved apart from other books, in a separate room that might offer a boundary for defining *the* Cotton library. But that room also housed an assortment of other objects that might consequently claim a place in the library, despite being documents in only a loose sense.

Like any gentleman collector of his day, Cotton assembled a cabinet of curiosities along with his more notable pursuit of books and papers. In addition to his perhaps-relic of Thomas Becket, guests could peer at Dr. John Dee's alchemical instruments, an enormous fossil fish, coins, potsherds, bits of statues and other scraps of antiquity. Most of this is easy enough to think of as distinct from a library, even if it shared the same space. But classifying Cotton's coin collection presents more of a challenge.

His coins were not only stored in the same shelves as the manuscripts, in bins or drawers along with other loose items, but also put to many of the same uses. Like his book collection, Cotton loaned coins in at least a few instances, and regarded both as material for historical research. Both Camden and John Speed made reference to the Cotton coins and their curator, in their histories; the former noted that Sir Robert "hath begunne a famous cabinet whence of his singular courtesie he hath often times given me great light in these darksome obscurities."

Cotton's coin collection even shared a similar background with his manuscripts. Like the dispersed libraries of England's abbeys and monasteries, scattered ancient coins received limited attention up until Cotton's day. He was one of the first to devote scholarly attention to the bits of metal turned up by a farmer's plow or caught in a fishing net. Though their texts were necessarily brief, coins were valuable, direct documentary records from Roman and pre-Roman Britain, for which other records were all but nonexistent outside of limited copies, with all their vulnerability to error and bias.

The same applied to the stone inscriptions Cotton gradually obtained. Beginning with his northern tour in 1599, Cotton eventually acquired 16 markers and monuments from Roman or early post-Roman Britain. Most of these were as heavy as parchment or coins are portable, and Cotton accordingly installed them at his Conington estate rather than any of his London homes. In some sense, though, even they may have belonged to his library; Sharpe suggests that, if nothing else, contemporaries esteemed all of Cotton's artifact collection as a complement and peer to his manuscripts.

Whatever else may have comprised Cotton's library, his manuscripts are its core. That core is nonetheless as odd an assortment, in its way, as the rest of his collections. For all the many purposes it served, Cotton's library of manuscripts is distinctly not a general purpose library and never has been.

Effectively cataloging Cotton's collection has been an ongoing goal through most of its history, and what organization Cotton himself achieved is little help in getting any broad sense of the contents. Colin Tite has suggested a system of six categories that is as good a beginning as anything: 1) Anglo-Saxon and later medieval manuscripts, 2) monastic registers, 3) material of religious content, 4) genealogical and heraldic material, 5) chronicles and other works of history, and 6) state papers. Sharpe, as well as the British Library, outline similar patterns to the collection, with Sharpe adding a distinct category for foreign material in light of the British origins and focus of most items.

The Cotton state papers, naturally, are the combined letters, records and other government documents that Sir Robert amassed through donation or (famously) private initiative. Genealogical and heraldic manuscripts are to some extent a subset or annex of this material, though they often served quite different ends. These manuscripts were a focus for some of the library's non-scholarly uses in Cotton's time, as were the monastic registers. The former category interested "new men" eager to discover pedigree for their family, as well as those with established ancestry they wished to show off; Cotton's later patron, the Earl of Arundel, once dispatched a plea all the way from a sojourn in Italy beseeching Sir Robert to compile a history of his family. The registers served more practical ends, in contrast, as the complexities of English land titles and laws made precedent as invaluable to a landlord as to a politician. Sir Robert's son and grandson both continued adding to the collection of these records, and all three deployed them in maximizing the value of their property in Huntingdonshire, in addition to lending them to fellow landowners. Jennifer Summit finds frequent loans of monastic registers among the early library records that survive.

Much of the interest in the Cotton manuscripts since its founder's time, though, lies in the first and third categories. Here one finds a majority of the jewels within the larger treasure: the spectacular Book of Lindisfarne, Cotton's beloved if elusive Greek Genesis, as well as the so-called Coronation Gospels that featured in another memorably disastrous episode. These and other biblical excerpts all belong to the religious category. They share it with saints' lives, and other stories Cotton considered worth preserving for fragments of valid history amid their "papist superstitions."

The more-or-less secular medieval manuscripts conceal riches, also, if more deeply. The first specific mention of *Beowulf*, one of the best-known items in the whole library, dates from long after Cotton's time. It's certain that he had the poem, but he acquired it already bound up with at least part of the compendium now labeled Vitellius A XV. Graham Parry remarks that "In the utilitarian atmosphere of the Cotton Library, records of Saxon church councils of details of Saxon lawmaking were more eagerly seized on than poetry that was in a barely comprehensible mode," and most of Cotton's habits support this notion. Cotton was an unusually prosaic man in an age when most educated people expressed themselves in poetry at least on occasion; the fact that much of the verse Cotton collected is found among the state papers demonstrates both points.

Despite which, his medieval manuscripts also include the "Pearl poems," including the wonderfully subtle tale of *Sir Gawain and the Green Knight*. C.E. Wright argues that "the loss of this MS would have affected the story of Middle English literature as vitally as the loss of the Beowulf MS would that of Anglo-Saxon." The evocative *Rune Poem* also owes Cotton for its survival, or at least for that of an Old English version, a fortunate preservation even though variants exist in other languages. So small is the grand total of surviving Anglo-Saxon text, in the world, that all of Sir Robert's manuscripts from that era are precious whether prose or poetry, epic or account-book.

If judged as one category, documents of medieval England are very likely the ultimate highlight of Cotton's whole remarkable collection. Five manuscripts of the Anglo-Saxon Chronicle, of seven now known, reached the present day through Cotton. As did laws, charters and even a map of the world as understood by King Alfred's England; a priceless biography of Alfred himself has not made it, but as with other losses after Cotton's time much of the text survives, thanks to his not only preserving manuscripts but eagerly circulating them.

Whether restricted to those manuscripts, or expanded to embrace coins, stones, bones and more, this element also belongs in any definition of the Cotton library that is to capture its real significance. The true value of the library was inseparable from what Cotton added to its holdings: its infrastructure, its organization, its connections, and above all its active lending. These things made the Cotton library, as an institution, worth preserving as much as even the rarest letter or most brilliant illuminated gospels.

EX LIBRIS
ANGLO-SAXON MAPPA MUNDI
Tiberius B V f56v

MOST OF THE MAPS in the Cotton library were, at the time of its founder, working reference material. Sir Robert's emphasis as a map collector lay squarely on maps from the mid-16th century onward; the majority were, given the state of cartography, contemporary information. Nearly every rule had its exception in Cotton's library, however. Maps were no different. One unusually old manuscript may be the most interesting Cotton map from a modern perspective. What's more, though it is an anomaly among the map collection, its history and features align very closely to the library as a whole.

The verso of folio 56 in Tiberius B V, sometimes called the Cottoniana, is an early 11th-century Mappa Mundi. In other words, it is a world map—of surprising accuracy—produced in Anglo-Saxon Britain. The concept alone seems an inherent contradiction, like a Bronze Age computer or a Victorian space program. The fact that much of the Cottoniana seems more like a modern map than like the symbolic diagrams of most contemporary *mappae mundi* is almost fantastic. It is all too easy to imagine Britain before the Norman conquest as a primitive and isolated country, the target of aggressive expeditions rather than sponsor of them. Yet the eventual fall of Anglo-Saxon Britain owed as much to bad luck as to any cultural shortcomings. The kingdom founded by Alfred the Great, who twice visited Rome, was very much a member of the European community, actively interested in its lands and learning.

Cotton's Mappa Mundi reflects this intellectual reach of Anglo-Saxon civilization, as well as the range of his own library. Much of its content likely derives from classical sources, as it preserves "Britannia" and other Roman province names; Cotton, with his coins and stone inscriptions, also sought to learn from legacies of the classical world. But the Anglo-Saxon cartographers improved on those models, particularly in Britain, of which the Mappa Mundi is "the earliest known, relatively realistic depiction" according to the British Library. Their map demonstrates a breadth of perspective encompassing the entire known world, alongside a deep knowledge of and interest in their own corner of it, and much the same can be said of Cotton's manuscripts. British, and in particular Anglo-Saxon, records are its greatest strength, but even the far corners of the Orient receive some representation.

Also like Cotton, the Anglo-Saxons were more closely engaged with their nearest neighbors. Cotton corresponded regularly with French scholars like de Peiresc. The Mappa Mundi itself, though very likely drawn in Canterbury, may actually be the work of an Irish scribe. Jim Siebold has studied the Cottoniana and other antique maps for many years, and suggests that an Irish monk produced the manuscript while attached to the court of Canterbury's archbishop. Siebold argues that "In the British isle of the pre-Norman period,

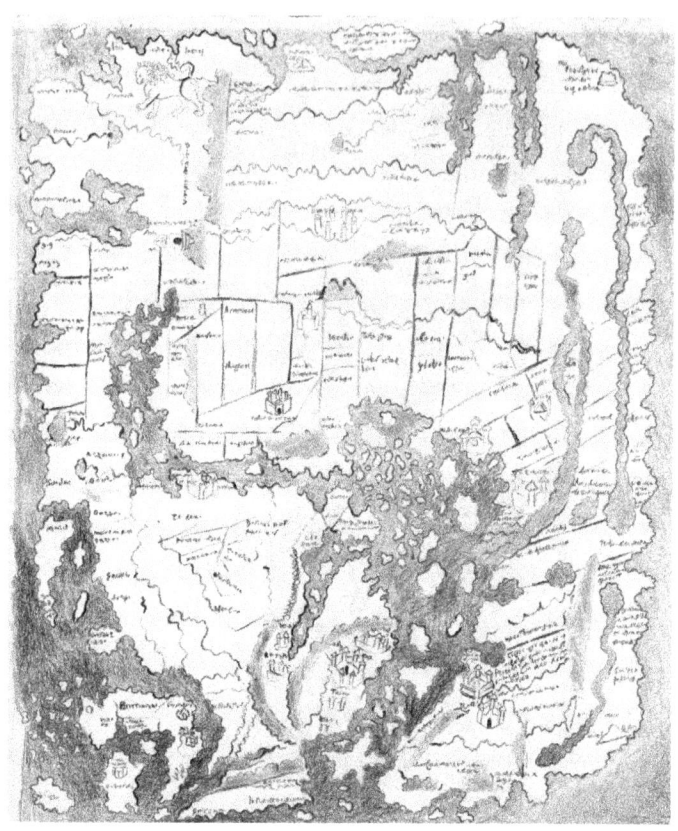

Anglo-Saxon world map from Tiberius B V

there is no school of learning art, or science comparable to that which sprang from the Irish Church... and the insertion of the name of Armagh, so rarely found in medieval maps, strengthens the view that there we have the handiwork of a student who was trained in Irish schools, or derived his knowledge from men so trained."

Whoever its primary author, over time the map was certainly updated by others, and in combination with its older sources, the result is a palimpsest recording centuries of evolving knowledge and culture. Latin names appear alongside others in Old English; Roman town symbols identify Anglo-Saxon cities; detailed and relatively accurate British islands border a Eurasia that hosts "Here There Be Dragons" monsters in its more distant corners. Yet the rough records of the past can offer interest and knowledge, long after their original value becomes obsolete. Cotton recognized this and valued the Mappa Mundi along with much newer maps that, now, are themselves relics; today's scholars continue to preserve and study his whole collection for much the same reason. The realms of the past are never fully explored, and in seeking to know them *every* map and diary remains potentially useful.

CHAPTER 5

Sorting Things Out

C ONTROVERSY HAS TARGETED Sir Robert Cotton throughout his library's history. Some quarrels were confined to his own time, as with Cotton's varied troubles stemming from politics. Other controversies, like his readiness to add items to his collection by all available means, have to some extent been perpetual. Cotton's practices in organizing his library have, by contrast, attracted criticism almost certainly never heard or even imagined by Sir Robert himself.

Anyone casually dividing up, cutting margins from or rebinding even the most inexpensive mass-produced volume in the modern British Library's holdings could hardly expect to last long as a public user, to say nothing of a librarian or curator. Yet Cotton did all of these things, regularly, to manuscripts recognized even in his own time as rare and valuable. Whether or not his compilations represent an attempt at updating the medieval chronicles he collected, in assembling those volumes he took liberties that understandably shock his inheritors.

The sometimes curious combinations he produced, like that which *Beowulf* shares with a letter, the fragment of a homily and various religious texts, were the least of it. Documents of different page size might receive a trim, to keep a bound volume's edges neat. Medieval manuscripts did not always have their own outer bindings originally, but those that did could retain them up to the 17th century only for Sir Robert Cotton to tear loose their leaves. In some cases he divided up the contents, either among multiple volumes in his own collection, or with a friend like Simonds D'Ewes, with whom Cotton split a 12th-century passional. Occasionally he stripped out part of a borrowed volume when finally pressed for its overdue return; a modern bibliophile might be at a loss to identify which part of such episodes appalls the most.

As fellow collectors often shared Cotton's practices, they do not appear to have drawn serious criticism, or even notice, from contemporaries. By the 20th century, however, much had changed. In 1931 the British Museum's keeper of manuscripts, Idris Bell, published critical remarks even in the context of an exhibit planned to celebrate Cotton's collection. Nearly every examination of Cotton beyond a few paragraphs has, in more recent years, noted the same charges. Tite's summation of them may be the most pithy: "the dissolution of the monasteries hugely disrupted the libraries of medieval England but so did Sir Robert Cotton."

Nonetheless, the same sources almost universally leap to Cotton's defense. Most of his "abuses," they emphasize again and again, were not regarded as such until generations later. By that time, Cotton's library had long passed into the care, or too often the carelessness, of others; Sir Robert may take the blame for any number of damaged or discarded medieval bindings that he had in fact delivered intact to his successors.

Cotton's still-considerable editing of his manuscripts can be viewed in a positive light, also, even if one regrets that it took place. Today one would hardly write titles, tables of contents and other notes directly into an Anglo-Saxon chronicle, but the many such additions in Cotton's own handwriting testify to close and active librarianship. By the standards of his time, Cotton was in fact a conscientious curator. He did send volumes for rebinding, but his notes to the binders were detailed, and even finicky. He split manuscripts apart, but primarily to reorder their contents within his own library rather than to resell them piecemeal and likely scatter their contents to parts unknown. If the prevailing notions of conservation that guided him were still primitive, this is easy enough to understand; libraries of Cotton's day were only just recognizing the blessing and challenge of collections large enough to demand a true system of library science.

In measuring Cotton's library, the figure most often quoted is 1,000 volumes. The number is obviously and inevitably a rounded approximation, given losses, acquisitions, reformatting and questions about the very definition of that library. But it provides a useful enough point for comparison with other collections. By the early 17th century, much larger libraries existed. In England, Dr. Dee and Lord Lumley may each have owned 3,000 volumes, while Cotton's friend John Selden acquired more than 6,000; the great French collector Jacque de Thou could boast 8,000 books in addition to 1,000 manuscripts. All of these were private collections, however, and for long after the depredations of Henry VIII and his son, such institutional libraries as existed in England operated on a much smaller scale. *The English Library Before 1700* assigns the Cambridge university library but 1,000 printed books and 400 manuscripts as late as 1649, next to which Cotton's holdings appear eminently respectable.

All of these collections were lavish, meanwhile, compared with those of just a century earlier. Before the printing press transformed European publishing, a few dozen books could constitute a substantial library. The emergence of far larger collections during the Tudor era challenged long-held assumptions of archivists and librarians. Even a few shelves of books call for some degree of management, compared with a single chest. One thousand volumes might demand almost a revolution in record keeping, at least when many of them were diverse compilations of previously distinct manuscripts, and when they served not only one private owner but a sizable audience of active borrowers.

Cotton's own library management never quite reached the level of a formal system, let alone a revolution. Sorting, cataloging and loan records all remained works in progress through the end of his life. To some extent all of these have remained incomplete into the modern era, though, and—for better and for worse—Sir Robert Cotton's tenure as the collection's first librarian left indelible legacies.

After Cotton passed from the scene, his early successors reported "bales" of documents loose in boxes and drawers, still awaiting binding. But of the many bound volumes completed under Sir Robert's watch, few have been broken up since— intentionally, at least—and these compilations are probably his most extensive legacy as curator. Criticism of the mechanics aside, the most basic interpretation of that legacy remains a matter of debate. Some scholars like Jennifer Summit see a loose but consistent attempt at topical and chronological sorting, furthering the library's role as a working reference collection by combining items likely to be used together. Given that Cotton acquired manuscripts over the course of decades, however, any system he had in mind was likely disrupted by practical execution. Volumes like Claudius A IV are difficult to account for as part of any rational scheme. Between its covers one finds letters from three 12th-century popes; statutes of Queen's College; a treatise on the calendar; a work on the city of Jerusalem and relics unearthed at Constantinople; and John of Caen's *Abbreuiatio Decreti Gratiani*. Kevin Sharpe is by no means alone in declaring that "Often it is hard to see any logic in the compilations."

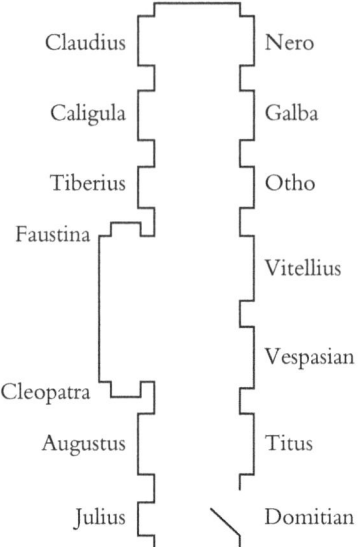

Plan of the Cotton library in Cotton House
Based on research by Colin Tite and others

The same might be said of Cotton's system of shelving, which may be the most distinctive of his legacies. Had Sir Robert employed simple numbers, or some other purely utilitarian system, the Cotton library and its history would be just as remarkable. The system he devised holds a certain fascination, nonetheless. The fact that Cotton's copy of Bede's *Historia Ecclesiastica* is part of Tiberius C II, and that many records of the Society of Antiquities appear in Faustina E V, adds a touch of both the personal and the exotic to even the humblest volume in the collection.

Cotton manuscripts are cataloged by their historical place on a particular bookpress, or set of bookshelves. Each press was identified by a bust and the name of a figure from antiquity, with individual shelves assigned letters, and individual volumes numbered in shelf order from left to right. Vitellius A XV, e.g., which includes *Beowulf*, was the fifteenth volume on the top shelf of the Emperor Vitellius press. (Distinct and much later cataloging systems identify coins, as well as most charters.)

No one is entirely certain how, or why, Cotton instituted the "emperor system." Some precedent (naturally) existed for the practice in Roman, as well as medieval libraries, though Sharpe suggests it was "out of fashion" by Cotton's day. Colin Tite points out a series of portraits of the early Roman emperors that King Charles I received in 1628, around the same time Cotton was installing brass busts of the same emperors in his library. Given Cotton's interests and allegiances, the selection of Roman emperors still seems mildly odd, and even grotesque in the case of Caligula or Nero. Only a collector's completist instinct seems to justify honoring such monsters. The additions of a later emperor's wife (Faustina), and a Ptolemaic Egyptian pharaoh (Cleopatra), seem to defy any logical pattern at all.

Faustina and Cleopatra may in fact have joined the first dozen Roman emperors after Sir Robert's time, and, if so, represent a successor's (still odd) completion of the system. Like so many of Cotton's plans he left incomplete the reorganization of his library. Unlike his histories of Huntingdonshire or the church, he did make a considerable start, at least. His various heirs were able to complete and preserve to the present day the emperor system, and, although his own surviving references to it amount to no more than a few scraps, it was definitely Cotton's design.

As far as organization is concerned, ad-hoc lists and rough notes appear to be as far as Cotton ever got, in general. Viewed as a whole his loan lists were extensive, and provide much evidence of the library's early activity. But Cotton never prepared any unified, formal circulation ledger. In auditing the lists from Cotton's day, Colin Tite has found overlapping entries in some, gaps in others; he suggests that while Sir Robert was indisputably a generous lender, his leniency with borrowers may not always have been intentional. Tite concludes that "The confusion could be considerable and Cotton was not always certain where his books had gone." The judgment is entirely plausible. The Cotton Genesis was far from his only volume to go astray, and many escapees never returned. The modern name of the Utrecht Psalter, another early masterpiece of illumination, disguises its history as a Cotton manuscript. Others alienated from the collection have resurfaced as far afield as the National Library of Australia.

Merely keeping track of items within the library's own walls must have been an uncertain business. The size and diversity of Cotton's collection easily warrants a detailed, extensive catalog, but here, too, nothing in Sir Robert's lifetime made progress beyond the incomplete draft stage. Relative to the library's other organizational wants, however, this deficiency may have been both less of a hindrance to contemporary users, and more understandable in the context of subsequent events. As will be demonstrated, inadequate cataloging has been a kind of perverse tradition in the Cotton library's history. That tradition continues even today, long after custodians obtained the advantage of technological and human resources likely never imagined by Sir Robert, even in his days dreaming of a Queen Elizabeth Academy.

The library under Cotton was, in comparison, a skeleton staff at most. What assistance Cotton had was usually contracted as needed for specific tasks. He regularly purchased the services of binders, and sometimes of copyists. A number of headings and contents lists in unidentified handwriting may imply that he hired clerical help, as well—though the early library always had something of a cooperative character and these could have been the volunteer contributions of borrowers.

Eventually Cotton did appoint a more or less formal library staff of one. Richard James brought to the job a decidedly novel background. Around 21 years Cotton's junior, at least one rumor suggested he was actually his employer's bastard son. Such gossip seems to accompany nearly every significant figure of the era, but in Cotton's case it's plausible, and Hope Mirrlees finds a reference by Sir Robert's legitimate son Thomas to an unknown

The library in Cotton House
Reconstruction by John Ronayne, used with the artist's permission

"brother" in a 1621 letter. Whether or not James's real father was Robert Cotton, his legal uncle, Thomas James, was the first librarian of Oxford's Bodleian library. Richard himself studied at Oxford's Exeter College and Corpus Christi College. He also traveled widely as a young man. His wanderings took him as far as Newfoundland, and later Moscow where he served as part of a royal embassy and made extensive notes on Russian language and culture.

Richard James officially met Sir Robert around 1625. He secured the post of librarian soon thereafter. Merit or nepotism might account for the appointment, as might the prospect of new acquisitions; James shared with Cotton both interests and habits, and adopted similar eagerness in expanding the library collection as already noted. Even as manuscripts strayed out of the Cotton library, others "strayed in" courtesy of James's connections with Corpus Christi and the Bodleian. For his part, James made use of the library's holdings for research and writing, mostly Protestant polemic. As librarian he also made significant contributions to the reorganization begun by his employer, and, surviving on several years after him, prepared the first real catalog to reflect the emperor system. Though incomplete—like every Cotton catalog to the present day—the 1638 co-production of Sir Robert and Richard James remained the best guide to the library for half a century.

In Cotton's own lifetime, the best and most important guide to his library remained Sir Robert, himself. If his documentary records were haphazard, they were also to some extent beside the point. As a private collection, one did not access Cotton's manuscripts without Cotton, and with Cotton one had a deeply knowledgeable research librarian. Eventually, Richard James shared in many responsibilities, but it was still first and foremost Cotton's library. He built the collection. He consulted it. He involved himself in all the details of its management, makeshift though that sometimes was. James became a live-in librarian, but both he and the library still resided in Cotton's own home.

Cotton House is now long gone. Its former location has been built over entirely by the modern Houses of Parliament. Thanks to the library, however, literate visitors frequented it for decades and impressions they left provide a fair sense of what they encountered. Colin Tite has studied these, along with architectural drawings of the house prepared around 1700. By combining these sources and a modest amount of conjecture, he prepared a reconstructed tour, later published as part of *The Panizzi Lectures 1993*.

The house itself, Tite records, was a four-story, 21-room building. The library, at any rate the main library, occupied a long, narrow room on an upper floor. Approximately 37′ by 6′ with the only windows at the far ends, the room must have felt rather confined. Although various items from Cotton's cabinet were on display, Tite suggests that the library room was, ultimately, "storeroom rather than a study." Heavy oak bookpresses, perhaps set into niches in the walls, lined each side. Busts of the 12 Caesars identified most of these, probably following chronological order around the room. Beginning with Julius, opposite the door, successive emperors would have followed up that side and then back down the other, ending with Domitian; as the Domitian volumes don't extend beyond "A" it was presumably a single shelf, perhaps mounted over the doorway. Scholars' best guess about Cleopatra and Faustina is that they faced one another within a small alcove, between Augustus and Tiberius.

Caesar, Cleopatra, et al., aside, Cotton's installation of his library in this modest chamber was likely driven by practical considerations. Yet, for what it's worth, the room also had its own interesting history. Tite finds evidence that Cotton House was once known as "The Lady Pewe," from a tradition that it housed "at one time an ancient oratory in the Palace of Westminster known as the Chapel of Our Lady of the Pew and used by King Edward the Confessor." The library room, he suggests, was the former royal chapel itself.

Cotton may have appreciated the resonance between a medieval king's chapel and the themes of his own library, but the great attraction of Cotton House for its home base was something much simpler: location, location, location.

Cotton House, and perhaps a few other homes, extended north from the old Painted Chamber (also since destroyed), a part of the original Palace of Whitehall. South of that stood the House of Lords, while the House of Commons met a short distance in the other direction. Beyond these, courts, archives and other government offices were all accessible with only a brief walk. If a longer trip beckoned, a green space later known as Cotton Garden spread east down to the Thames—an enviable amenity

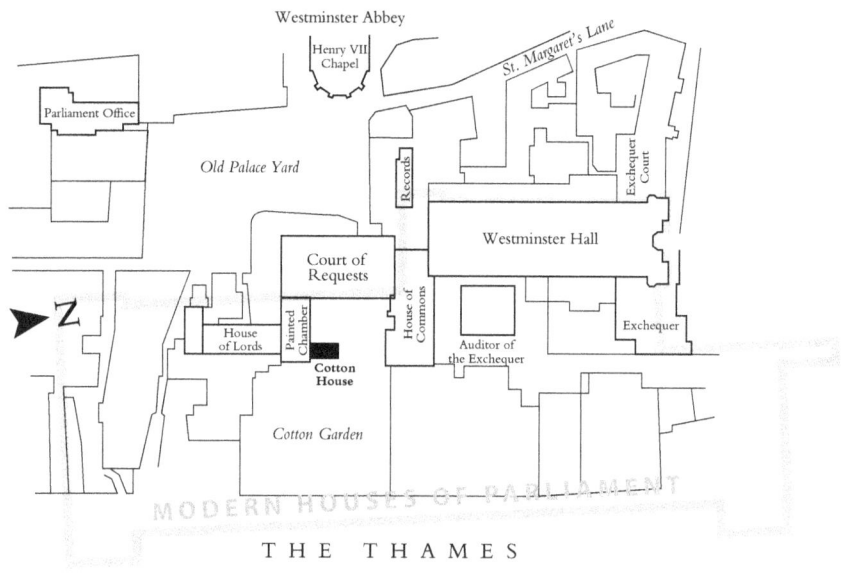

Cotton House in Westminster c. 1625
Based on research by Colin Tite

when traveling by boat was as much as possible preferred over London's winding, crowded and muddy streets.

C.E. Wright among others has speculated on the attractions of this address for Cotton, who might almost raid the state papers simply by reaching his arm out the window. Sir Robert collected all his life, and probably appreciated the opportunity. But by his arrival at Cotton House in 1622 much of his eventual library already accompanied him, and he had obviously experienced little inconvenience acquiring state papers for it from homes in Blackfriars, or the Strand. His decision to settle in the very heart of government probably owes much more to the persistence of his other passion, politics.

The disaster of the Overbury scandal cast a shadow on Cotton for six years, but by the 1620s he was re-emerging. Kevin Sharpe describes him as "a leading figure" of the 1621 parliament, despite Sir Robert's having no seat. Cotton was at all events aspiring to rejoin the leading players, having allied himself to a new patron, Thomas Howard. A more principled figure, as well as a major collector and connoisseur himself, the 14th Earl of Arundel was generally a much better match for Cotton than Arundel's late uncle Henry Howard, Cotton's great but flawed earlier patron. Cotton obviously trusted Arundel; in 1622, he helped him acquire the office of constable and then develop it as a power center through disused precedents.

Two years later, Sir Robert Cotton returned to Parliament as a member, for Old Sarum. At 53 he was back in office, older but better prepared. In Arundel he had the backing of a promising new patron. In Cotton House he had a firm claim in solid, physical form to returning himself and his library to the center of Stuart government. But, as history had shown, and would soon remind him, the center of a Stuart government was often a very stormy anchorage to call home.

EX LIBRIS
CODEX PURPUREUS FRAGMENT
Titus C XV ff 2r–5v

The Cotton library, today, includes many fragmentary items. More than a few of them came to that state only after arriving in the collection—but not all of them. Four leaves now part of Titus C XV were alienated from their parent volume long, long ago, before most of the library's manuscripts had even been written. Yet even this brief excerpt must rank as one of the collection's treasures.

The Codex Purpureus Petropolitanus is, or was, an ancient and lavish copy of the Four Gospels in Greek. Scholars have suggested multiple sites for its origin; some propose the imperial scriptorium at Constantinople, while others link it with Antioch. Regardless of its original authors, it is assuredly imperial in its grandeur. Written with gold and silver inks, the words of the gospels glimmer and shine, all the more so against rich purple vellum. This type of dyed manuscript, a *codex purpureus*, may once have been produced exclusively for emperors. By the 6th century when craftsmen were preparing the Petropolitanus, the imperial purple was not so formally exclusive, but the technique's arresting appearance—and expense—kept it associated with emperors long afterward.

In contrast, the present state of the Petropolitanus testifies to the Byzantine empire's eventual fall. Some time in or around the 12th century, someone split the manuscript apart and many of its leaves vanished. Historians regard this period as the empire's peak, but a peak may also signify the beginning of a decline. Western Crusaders' sack of Constantinople in 1204 also proved a signpost toward Byzantium's erosion; it's at least possible that the Petropolitanus was among the treasures that Crusaders broke up and carried away. In any event, most of the manuscript remained lost until the late 19th century. After the missing majority's rediscovery, the government of the czars purchased it, and today the core of the manuscript belongs to the National Library of Russia. (The library's home of St. Petersburg provides the codex's modern name of Petropolitanus.) Yet at least nine other collections including the British Library possess one or more fragments.

When and how Sir Robert Cotton acquired one of those fragments remains a matter of guesswork. The same can be said of another, smaller fragment in Titus C XV, which despite a plainer appearance may be almost as remarkable as the *codex purpureus*. The volume's first folio is a collage assembled, presumably by Cotton, from two manuscripts. A decorative border, originally from a 15th-century breviary, provides a frame. Within the frame, Cotton has placed a very old fragment of papyrus, roughly 2.5 × 5″.

The British Library's Sarah J. Biggs has recently noted that, having arrived as one of the founding collections, this fragment "may well be the first papyrus to enter the British Museum." Its history in England may go much deeper still. Robert Babcock has identified the papyrus as a fragment of

Pope Gregory the Great's *Forty Homilies on the Gospels*, from the late 6th or early 7th century. Babcock suggests the manuscript originated in France or Italy—"raising the tantalising possibility that Gregory himself may have been responsible for its commissioning," per Biggs—but that it may already have been in England for centuries when Cotton acquired some portion of it. Acknowledging that "At this point we are into the realm of educated guesswork and speculation," Biggs adds that "it is not impossible that the codex could have come over with early missionaries sent to England by Gregory. It could even be the case that it was an early copy of the *Homilies* (completed in 592-3) brought over by Augustine of Canterbury when he arrived in Kent in 597."

Cotton seems to have perceived some sort of significance to the papyrus, at least, given its careful placement within a decorative frame. Its placement within Titus C XV, meanwhile, suggests another significance that he may not have intended but might nonetheless appreciate. The combination of papyrus fragment and codex purpureus fragment creates a curious thematic (as well as phonetic) juxtaposition. Whether or not Cotton personally removed the *Homilies* fragment from a whole folio, by associating it with the long-fragmented Petropolitanus he seems to say "yes, it's true, I did rearrange and collage manuscript pieces… but don't forget that plenty of them were already *in* pieces long before my time."

CHAPTER 6

Enemy of the State

WITHIN A FEW YEARS of the Earl of Somerset's implosion, so nearly fatal to Cotton's own political career, King James found a new favorite at court. George Villiers would provide a different sort of nemesis for Cotton, though in the end, one every bit as hazardous as the latter's involvement with Somerset. Beginning in 1616, James raised Villiers rapidly through the peerage. By the time he became Duke of Buckingham in 1623, Villiers was the highest-ranking person in England outside the royal family. But such extraordinary privilege bred controversy, and eventually Sir Robert found himself and the duke on opposing sides.

The origins of the conflict appear somewhat arbitrary, from the distance of four centuries. By an exacting standard Buckingham was probably corrupt, but no more so than the typical official of his day. Opponents were generally as interested in sharing the duke's influence in the government as they were in reforming it. To the extent that they did have other grievances, Buckingham was largely a lightning rod for any and all discontent; as Roger Lockyer observes, for centuries "part of the function of a favourite was to shield the monarch from blame for the actions of his government…" By performing this role in a particularly high-handed manner, Buckingham inflamed frustrations among less-favored courtiers all the more. The Earl of Arundel numbered among these, and eventually, both Cotton and his patron earned Buckingham's enmity.

The subsequent feud still seems, on some level, needless. Given Cotton's readiness to offer his library and friendship to interested persons of varying creeds, nationalities and agendas, Buckingham should in many ways have fit easily into the same circle. The duke shared the interest of both Cotton and his patron in antiquities. He collected paintings and sculpture, books and manuscripts. Also like the other two, Buckingham was much more than a dilettante collector. As chancellor of Cambridge, he made plans for a splendid new university library; in 1617 he was even part of a brief attempt to form a new Society of Antiquaries. Rising to power in the years that followed, Buckingham had every reason to take advantage of the experience of Sir Robert Cotton, still well regarded by King James even during his time in the wilderness.

While James was alive Buckingham did just that. In the first years of Cotton's return to active politics, the statesman and favorite cooperated effectively amid renewed tensions with Spain. Having been burned once, himself, Cotton readily supported Buckingham in breaking off further negotiations for a marriage alliance in 1623. When controversy followed, Cotton provided further cover for the duke by drafting "Proceedings against ambassadors who have miscarried themselves," a manual for shifting blame onto Spain's negotiators. Cotton also volunteered candid advice that a larger solution to the favorite's problems, and those of the crown, ultimately lay in earnest, inclusive collaboration with Parliament. A considerable evolution from Cotton's early views, it was the lesson of hard-won experience. Though no program could offer a painless escape from all of the problems facing English government, this counsel might have spared all parties a good deal of trouble if accepted.

Unfortunately, if any favorite might have won King James to such a course, it was not Buckingham. Though willing to seek help from Cotton when in over his head, at least early on, his default instinct was always solidarity with his royal patron above all else, ironically recalling Cotton's own habits in the years of Northampton. The prospects for compromise grew even more remote after Charles I succeeded his father as king in 1625. If any Stuart monarch might have listened to the warnings of Cotton and others, it was certainly not Charles. Where James had been insistent on unilateral authority in theory but shied from confrontation in practice, Charles seemed determined to see hostility in even the most loyal critics, and to respond in kind.

The new sovereign's very first significant interaction with Cotton seems impossible to explain except by perverse, malicious partisanship. Though Arundel's criticism of Buckingham had hardened into a feud by the mid-1620s, and the favorite of the late James had surprisingly preserved his standing with Charles, the coronation might have seemed the occasion for a new start, at least in form.

Both Sir Robert and his patron were prepared to receive Charles I with honor and goodwill. They invested much effort in a literal reception for the new king, in fact. On the day of the coronation, Cotton House as well as the garden and stairs leading to the Thames were gaily decorated in expectation of greeting Charles's arrival, by barge, and procession to Westminster Abbey. Cotton had every confidence that the court knew of the plan and favored it. In addition to the decorations, he invited guests to witness what should have been a proud moment for both him and his library, from which he had retrieved an ancient copy of the gospels for the coronation oath. The small, illuminated gospel book had, he believed, served in the same ceremony in ages long past.

Subsequent events became a legend of Cotton's life owing to a serious misconception on his part. He erred as a librarian, and was likely mistaken about the "coronation gospels'" origins; the history of Tiberius A II in other coronations was probably limited at most, if not entirely apocryphal. This was only a modest error, nonetheless, not subjected to serious skepticism until long after Cotton's time. The gospels' expected role in the coronation of Charles I met a far more sudden and dramatic exposure. As 8 a.m. approached on February 2, 1626, Sir Robert Cotton stood with his guests watching the royal barge approach up the Thames. His home and garden made up into a reception fit for a king, Cotton must have welled with anticipation as the barge drew near. Then, disaster cruelly disabused him of everything he had hoped and arranged for.

Cotton's friend Sir Simonds D'Ewes stood among the guests at Cotton House, and afterward recorded the catastrophe: "…the roiall barge bawked those stepps so fitlie accommodated… we saw the King's barge pass to the ordinary stairs… where the landing was dirty… and the incommodity was increased by the royal barge dashing into the ground and sticking fast." Charles and Buckingham had to leap across mud to disembark—perhaps at Parliament Stairs—which only emphasized their determination to avoid Cotton and Arundel's scrubbed and carpeted reception. If in doing so they looked somewhat awkward, Cotton was presumably mortified, helplessly watching his own snub from a short distance away.

Even at this stage, Cotton seemed unwilling to believe the new reign could treat him so badly. D'Ewes describes how he dutifully showed up at the abbey doors, gospels in hand; "he and it were contemptuously thrust aside." His public humiliation complete, Cotton must have despaired for both his own prospects and those of the nation under a king and minister such as these. Yet, perhaps after a long sigh, he no doubt resigned himself to making the best of things, somehow. There was nothing else for it, in the end; Charles was king and that was that.

A quarter-century later, the victors of England's Civil War ultimately decided that the authority of Charles I as king was not, after all, final and beyond question. Few men of Cotton's generation were ready to conceive of deposing a king, however, let alone executing one. One may take for granted that no such thought ever entered Sir Robert's mind.

Modern authors have speculated on what Cotton would have done had he lived during the Civil War. One has written that in the end, he "would probably have ranged himself, at last, with the Cavaliers," while another has confidently declared that "Cotton would no doubt have sided with Parliament." While offering no clear answer on this "what if" scenario, the range of their conclusions perfectly demonstrates the reality of what was: for Cotton, the very concept of a choice between crown or Parliament was invalid.

In evaluating his political career, Cotton comes across as a Jacobean Cicero. Like the influential senator at the end of Rome's republic, Cotton stood in the very middle of a constitutional system buckling and splintering under strain, yet never saw any possible solution but voluntary moderation of the competing forces. The relatively respectful and effective interplay between Elizabeth and her parliaments during Cotton's early life always remained his model of how English government worked. As political relations deteriorated under the Stuarts he did not see a failure of the system; the system was perfect, and the need for change lay not with it, but with the people within it. Those people certainly included men like Buckingham, and possibly even the king, but the king could not be replaced no matter how poor his judgment. If Buckingham proved wholly resistant to reason, one might try to persuade Charles to dispense with the favorite's counsels, but Charles himself was the keystone of the constitutional structure. The duty of parliamentarians and other supporting pieces was, as Cotton saw it, to offer the sovereign good advice and perhaps to argue forcefully for it, but never to *oppose* him; one might as soon speak of opposing the ocean.

This conviction should have been enough to confirm Cotton as a model subject and invaluable support to the throne, rather than an enemy. That it was not seems, ultimately, directly traceable to Charles's fundamentally contrary view of England's constitution. For Cotton, the nation's leading subjects had a duty to serve the king, but that duty included playing their role in informing and shaping policy. For Charles, by contrast, everyone else's duty began and ended with supporting his decisions, including decisions about who did and did not have any business offering counsel. As Charles demonstrated later in his reign, he viewed Parliament as quite unnecessary. In his view, if parliamentary critics disapproved of Buckingham's influence in government, this by itself represented opposition to the crown. Merely associating with such critics was enough to merit royal enmity. Some recognition of political realities limited active persecution, but if a man like Cotton was not with the king's party exclusively, he was not welcomed there at all.

Cotton would not and could not serve on terms such as these; the king's role was foremost in the constitution but the other parts were also essential. More than the difficult relations among Cotton, Arundel and Buckingham, indeed more than any personal factor, Cotton's refusal to entirely reject any faction focused the displeasure of Charles I on him, and on his library.

It's difficult to say which, of the two, the king resented most. Though Charles's first act of displeasure was a blow to Cotton personally, over the years that followed the library very likely proved the greater irritant. As with Cotton's possible choice of allegiance had he been pressed, opinion differs on his individual importance in the widening political schism; a few sources see his role as critical, and nearly the spark that ignited the conflagration of civil war, while general histories of the period typically make no mention of Cotton at all. Whatever his own direct significance, Cotton was in contact with many of those gradually moving toward more overt opposition to both Buckingham and the king. What concerned the latter pair considerably more, however, was that Cotton not only met such men but seemed to provide a base for them to coordinate and conspire.

Any outright conspiring at Cotton House was, given Cotton's own loyalties, likely negligible. Yet his home did serve as a kind of informal meeting place for parliamentary leaders, if only because like Cotton himself it was at the service of one and all, but, being rejected by the crown's party, became associated with critical voices by default. The critics in Parliament, in contrast to their opponents, gladly made use of the convenient store of precedents Cotton made available. Being so near at hand, library and librarian became once more the center of an intellectual circle, now providing not only valuable historical information but a space where one might regularly meet fellow travelers in person as well, and freely discuss the issues of the day. Hugh Holland, a fellow courtier and close contemporary, described it as "a kind of universitie." Though his petition for royal backing was long abandoned, Cotton had come remarkably far in achieving his dreamed-of academy, after all.

Unlike Elizabeth and James I, however, the government of Charles I was far from uninterested in Cotton's antiquarian "universitie." Within a year of spurning its coronation day reception, Buckingham proposed shutting it down entirely. Many authors have noted that the Cotton library supplied ammunition for battles of precedent in which the crown suffered its share of losses, and already in the previous reign the king had demonstrated a wariness of this threat. In 1621, James's government took the extraordinary step of banning Francis Bacon from the library following his fall from favor. In advising that the library be closed to everyone, Buckingham's logic may have been even more brutally simple. The library drew critics together at Cotton House—so shuttering that library presented an obvious way to disrupt those critics. In a sense, any corresponding persecution of Sir Robert was only collateral damage.

Whatever the thinking behind Buckingham's suggestion, Charles was not quite ready for so direct an assault. It may have seemed unnecessary given the events that followed the unspoken but obvious warning delivered earlier in 1626. Within weeks of Charles's coronation, he found cause to imprison Arundel in the Tower for several months. Cotton himself failed to win a seat in Parliament at that year's election. Under the circumstances, Charles may even have entertained a thought of permitting Cotton some voice at court after all, having firmly demonstrated whose word would be final. When Sir Robert joined others in opposing a new, debased coinage that Buckingham defended, Charles eventually withdrew the coins. Further consultation with Cotton followed, on familiar topics: naval reform, and revenue-raising in the form of a forced loan.

After two years this brief rapprochement was interred, along with Buckingham, both arguably the victims of an assassin's knife. Charles and parliamentary critics had continued to spar over Buckingham's outsized power, and in early 1628 Cotton felt compelled to take a direct part. That January he released what was essentially the only work published under his own name in his lifetime, *The Danger wherein this Kingdom now Standeth, and the Remedy*. The remedy, at its simplest, was a reduction of the overly powerful Buckingham, and the fact that Cotton took such a dramatic step in publicly proclaiming his cause reflects a sense of urgency that prevailed generally. Over the months that followed, mounting outrage erupted into murder on two occasions, with wildly different consequences.

The first nearly shocked both sides into an armistice. When a mob killed Buckingham's astrologer in June 1628, remarkably the subsequent reaction was primarily for order and calm rather than for vengeance. In late August, however, a soldier named John Felton fatally stabbed Buckingham himself in Portsmouth. Thereafter the king, at least, was done with compromise. Felton claimed that Parliament's condemnation of Buckingham had convinced him to destroy the duke for the good of the nation. After Felton's radical interpretation of parliamentarians' rhetoric, any further impulses toward moderation that they may have felt were likely to do little good.

Cotton had contributed materially to that rhetoric, and Sharpe writes that when news of the assassination reached Sir Robert, "Evidently Cotton did not receive it with displeasure." If uncharitable, this was an understandable, human reaction, and for all of his virtues Cotton was always very human. In a personal sense, Buckingham had humiliated him at the coronation, and had been at the back of most if not all the rumors about a royal move against Cotton's library that had circulated during Charles's reign. Charles himself had a role in all of this, of course, but Cotton could never actually turn himself against the king. As throughout history, a bad adviser offered a convenient proxy, and from that perspective Cotton might well have hoped that other and better counsels might finally prevail with Charles. Buckingham's removal from the scene, however deplorable the means, must have seemed an irreversible turning point. The time had come when Cotton and others who had been voices of warning, for so long in vain, must win the king's attention.

In 1629, nearly half a lifetime after first attempting to contribute his books to a formal national library, Sir Robert Cotton once again pledged to the nation the collection he had developed into an informal substitute. His second attempt was rather less direct than the petition of earlier, happier days. Cotton's last will bequeathed ownership of the library to his son, but Colin Tite finds significance in its confirmation of a now-lost indenture of 1629 that pledged the library "by feoffment to continue for the use of Posterity." Tite suggests that the indenture was, effectively, a promise of the library's continued availability as a private resource open to the public, issued as a legal document perhaps as "an attempt to protect the collection from potential enemies."

Cotton probably sensed by then that the library's potential enemies had not, after all, gone extinct with Buckingham. Contrary to his hopes, the larger hostilities between crown and Parliament certainly had not. Critics' animosity toward Buckingham may have been in some measure arbitrary, but policy differences between them and the crown Buckingham had served were real and growing wider. Amid those circumstances Cotton and his library, both, remained targets for a king who likely regretted the occasions when he ignored the late favorite's advice, much more than the many occasions he endorsed it. In 1626, Charles had demurred at a full-out assault on the well-connected and astute Cotton in the absence of even a minimal pretext. By 1629 he may well have regretted that concession to legal niceties—but he had a pretext anyway. Royal agents had discovered an incendiary political tract, titled "The Proposition... to bridle the impertinence of Parliaments," circulating among several critics of the court. The source of this wicked pamphlet, they informed the king, was Sir Robert Cotton. Charles wasted no time in ordering a full investigation.

Among flimsy pretexts for persecuting an opponent, the resultant affair of "The Proposition...to bridle the impertinence of

Parliaments" is the very archetype, rich with double standards and ironies. Declaring a scandal over something seditious discovered in Cotton's library seems inevitably arbitrary, first of all, given the large and varied contents of the collection, as well as the fact that by 1629 its books had been open to public inspection for decades. Just as important, Cotton made no secret of his own critical views. Two years earlier an essay he had composed on "The life and raign of Henry the Third" had prompted a kind of trial-run scandal, alleging that its analysis of how overly influential favorites can lead a monarch astray were intended to disparage Charles and Buckingham. Cotton insisted that he had written the essay years earlier as private advice for King James, and certainly not authorized its anonymous 1627 publication; even if he had, it would have been strange indeed to charge Cotton over a work of history that *might* be applied to current events when he addressed them, directly, many times. As neither "Henry III" nor *The Danger wherein this Kingdom now Standeth* had merited formal action against him, the precedents for a Cotton library scandal were distinctly awkward.

Perhaps this explains in some sense the bizarre option finally seized on, by the crown, to close down Cotton's library. Its very absurdity made it difficult to counter with reasoned arguments because they were plainly beside the point. For Charles I to express dismay at a tract arguing for autocratic government, and at Sir Robert Cotton's alleged endorsement of it, was obviously disingenuous in the extreme. The crown's audacious adoption of this line, anyway, made the details largely irrelevant. "The Proposicion for Your Majesties Service... to secure your Estate and to bridle the impertinence of Parliaments" was not Cotton's work at all, but that of Sir Robert Dudley (the son and namesake of Queen Elizabeth's paramour). Like Cotton's "Henry III," it dated from the reign of King James, with whom Dudley sought to curry favor by flattering James's frustration with parliamentary interference. Though Charles obviously shared his late father's views in this regard, he piously declared that "the meanes propounded in this Discourse for effecting thereof are such as are fitter to be practised in a Turkish State than amongst Christians, being contrary to the justice and mildness of His Majestie's Government…"

Having established this standard of complete nonsense, Charles found nothing problematic in championing "justice and mildness" by dispatching several men to the Tower over an invented thought crime. The privy council ordered Cotton's arrest on November 3, along with his librarian Richard James, friend and fellow critic John Selden, and three other men. All had allegedly received or distributed a copy of the contested tract; in all cases, their only real offense was participation in the critical caucus loosely tied to Cotton's library. Tellingly, the library itself received much sterner detention than did its keepers. The crown promptly placed an armed guard at the library door and made plans for a search of its troublesome contents. Sir Robert, by contrast, was one of the first of the group released, and soon even taking part in government service once more. By April 1630 his name was among those appointed to a commission on exacted fees.

While the crown's vacillation between persecution and rehabilitation might appear mystifying, one must recall that here at least the Stuarts were merely following established customs of the time. Elizabeth, too, regularly alternated between rewarding and imprisoning many of those closest to her, and at least one spell in the Tower was almost an essential badge of significance at court. By the late 1620s, Cotton had long since achieved the prominence that invited this carrot-and-stick approach, and might almost have taken it in stride.

Yet Cotton's own quickly restored freedom gave no comfort when his library remained under lock and key. Cotton himself retained limited access to the manuscripts; if the privy council's mood was favorable, Sir Robert might be able to visit his library briefly, under supervision. But the library was completely shut down as any kind of resource for the scholarly or political communities, which had always been Cotton's priority far more than simply amassing treasures in a vault.

Cotton petitioned for the library's return. He pleaded that the manuscripts would be damaged by neglect—prophetic, in fact, but perhaps an exaggeration after scarcely a year. He complained that having a significant section of his own home blockaded was tremendously burdensome. This point was undoubtedly valid, at least, but it made no difference. Nothing did. Sir Robert's son Thomas, who had followed his father into Parliament, makes his first significant appearance in the library's story aiding his father's repeated petitions to the crown. After the future Charles II was born in May 1630, King Charles announced a general pardon. The Cotton library was exempted, however, and remained under indefinite ban.

In the same month of the not-completely-general pardon, Cotton did enjoy one small piece of genuinely positive news as a librarian. His friend Sir Edward Dering wrote from Dover Castle, sending thanks for the loan of two books that would follow soon, along with the gift of another manuscript: "I have heere ye charter of K. John dat. at Runninge Meade: By ye first safe and sure messenger itt is yours. So are ye Saxon Charters as fast as I can coppy them: but in ye meane time I will close K. John in a box and send him." Dering was, in other words, donating to Cotton's library a rare 1215 copy of Magna Carta, revered by Cotton's generation and those since for its declaration of limits to a sovereign's authority.

Adding a second copy of this priceless charter to his collection may have cheered Cotton at least briefly, despite the ironies.

He was still an avid collector and student of history. For these same reasons, though, the uncertain state of his library gnawed at him for most of two years. The evidence suggests his anxiety drove Cotton into a steep physical decline. Friends commented on his changed appearance; the 60-year-old Sir Robert suddenly seemed old and stooped.

The impression of a broken man may have inspired a crude extortion scheme aimed at Cotton in June, but the perpetrators were sorely mistaken in expecting an easy victim. Cotton demolished their alleged evidence against him, so thoroughly that the plot's ringleader finally submitted a formal and detailed confession to the offended baronet. Cotton's intellect was still as vital as ever. It was his heart that had been wounded by all of his troubles.

A remarkable document preserves a glimpse of the usually private, businesslike Cotton pouring out those troubles for once, if only on paper. In his contribution to *Sir Robert Cotton as Collector*, Nigel Ramsay examines a manuscript now among the Bodleian Library's collection, filed as MS. Smith 28. It is one of Cotton's few surviving personal papers, apparently a plea from Cotton to the crown for redress. MS. Smith 28 goes beyond other petitions from Sir Robert and his son, however, becoming more a personal defense by Cotton of his entire life. Cotton offers a point-by-point summary of more than a dozen services to the Stuart dynasty: the sale of baronetcies, naval investigations, defense of Mary Queen of Scots's reputation, consultation on finance and currency, and more. The document might easily be an expression of outrage at its author's shabby reward for such consistent labor on behalf of Charles and his family, but the tone is instead one of prostration and pathos, as well as some entirely understandable measure of self-pity. Ramsay notes that the manuscript is difficult to read and suggestive of someone writing amid considerable stress; though the document is undated his conclusion that it dates from the closure of Cotton's library is persuasive.

Ultimately, Cotton's self-defense has the air of a man writing as much to himself as to any external audience, asking hard questions about his life in anticipation of a greater judgment. Cotton was clearly sunk deep into morbid reflections by 1631. On May 4, he signed his will. It echoes the sense of tired exasperation evident in the petition for redress. In bequeathing the library to his son and grandson, Cotton's will refers to "the manuscripts books and antiquities and other collections in my studies being my labors for forty years." During his last illness, Cotton made no secret that he blamed the unjust loss of his library for the flight of his health. His library was the great passion and accomplishment of his life, and witnessing the inescapable power of the crown declare it outlawed had finally worn Sir Robert down.

Whether persuaded by any of the plaintive petitions from Cotton House, or simply by discomfort at finally realizing what he had done, Charles did attempt to relieve Cotton's despair at the last hour. John Rowland reached Sir Robert's bedside in time to share "that at length, his mediation had been successful, and the King was reconciled to him." Cotton, however, was driven so low that he responded to this emissary from the throne with sad and uncharacteristic frankness. "You come too late. My heart is broken."

Sir Robert Cotton died May 6, 1631, of what even the most levelheaded modern physician might concede was as much as anything simple grief for his library. Cotton had dedicated his life to two purposes above all else: sponsoring the study and reappraisal of the past, and loyally serving a government in which one individual could act independently of any critical oversight.

Though Cotton could never countenance it, the two were ultimately incompatible, and the tension had destroyed his ambitions again and again.

Cotton had salvaged much of his library, originally, from the consequences of royal absolutism. When his proposal for a great research academy was ignored, and the Society of Antiquaries itself was suppressed, Cotton gradually made his own library and home into credible successors. Yet, at the last, King Charles's and his ministers' intolerance for criticism crushed Cotton's private initiative as well.

Perhaps, had Cotton censored his own efforts, he might in some sense have protected his library and person. Yet it would have been a pyrrhic victory. Cotton always managed his library as not only a collection but a resource to be used, in the service of historical study, religious reform, and, ultimately, good government. A strictly nonpolitical library might still have been useful but it would not have been the Cotton library. Instead, Cotton tried over and over both to be loyal to the king and to work constructively with all parties; in trying to avoid choosing one side or the other, he repeatedly risked the ruin of all he had worked for and of his own life and career. Mortality ultimately spared Sir Robert Cotton from being forced to take a side. Neither the nation, nor the library he left behind, would find any such reprieve from the trials ahead.

PART TWO
INTERREGNUM

CHAPTER 7

War and Peace

Survival is the great theme of the Cotton library's story. Sir Robert Cotton created his library by gathering up the endangered pages of English history, preserving them from neglect or outright destruction. Through four centuries since, the collection he founded has endured war, fire, politics, venality and the march of time itself. In outlasting its founder at all, however, the Cotton library survived what might have been the greatest crisis of its existence.

Amid the adventures that preceded it, and those that followed, the aftermath of Sir Robert's death is easily overlooked. It was in some sense a dog that did not bark, yet that should not diminish its significance. A large private collection rarely faces any peril more serious than its founder's death, for the simple reason that few of them survive to face others. Irwin Raymond's *The Origins of the English Library* introduces over and over the most magnificent collections, only to end their stories with one baleful word: "dispersed." Much of the Cotton library originated in such dispersals. The fate of Dee's collection, of Prince Henry's, of so many that Cotton mined must have foretold a similar fate for his own, and might have haunted his last years if not for more immediate problems. Instead, Sir Robert died protesting in vain his library's captivity as a political hostage; a collection's prospects for long outlasting its owner, in such a circumstance, should have been worse than even the pitiable average.

That the Cotton collection beat the odds is a tribute to many people, but the two names listed first must be Sir Thomas Cotton and Sir John Cotton. Where a collector's family so often breaks up a painstakingly assembled treasure—become more an expense and a burden than the delight that its founder knew—Sir Robert's son and grandson preserved his library, despite difficulties far beyond those to which most inheritors capitulate.

No one could sustain everything that Sir Robert Cotton meant to his library, admittedly, and his immediate heirs did not. The library that he worked so hard to make the center of the nation's government and politics receded from prominence. Sir Thomas and Sir John were less free with lending policy, as well as more active in seeking overdue items' return. Those who had known Sir Robert did not always appreciate his successors' differences; Sir Thomas's refusal to loan out an irreplaceable volume of Saxon charters to his father's old friend, Sir Simonds D'Ewes, may have played some part in D'Ewes criticizing him as "unworthy to be master of so inestimable a library." This was unfair, however, as well as ungrateful. No matter how much he resented being required to view an item *in situ* that Sir Robert would have simply handed over, D'Ewes ought to have considered that if not for Sir Thomas, the library might have remained locked up and out of reach entirely.

One might be forgiven for imagining the blockade of the Cotton library expired along with its founder. King Charles was too late in retracting the opprobrium that had so troubled Sir Robert, but the release of his library might logically have followed all the same, either because royal clemency extended to his son or because royal displeasure presumably did not. Yet the library remained locked up.

If Sir Thomas entertained hopes for a reversal of Charles's established policy toward the master of Cotton House, they were short-lived. They may indeed have been stillborn, if history accurately records the words of Charles's last emissary to Sir Robert. Arriving after the dying antiquary had passed on, Lord Dorset allegedly promised Sir Thomas that "To you, His Majesty commanded me to say that, as he loved your father *so* he will continue his love to yourself." Even very mild cynicism might have prompted more pessimism than hope at such an ambiguous promise. Thomas Cotton had reason to be more than mildly cynical toward the friendship of politicians, particularly when they were Stuart kings.

Sir Thomas and his own heir, Sir John, were so alike in habits that in the story of the Cotton library the father's era blends seamlessly into that of the son. In many ways, both men closely resembled Sir Robert, also: university education, marriage to a daughter of the elite, appearances in Parliament, general character of sociable, forthright men. In politics, however, both of the later Cottons diverged considerably from the pattern. Their relatively quiet and brief parliamentary careers have the character of a duty or class display, resolutely discharged and then left behind, compared with the constitutional crusading of Sir Robert. Neither Thomas nor John Cotton sought position at court, or in government. Though Sir Thomas married into the Howard family via his first wife, Margaret, he made no attempt to succeed his father as client of the Earl of Arundel or any other patron.

Sir Thomas was not without an interest in political affairs. Jason Peacey, writing in the pages of *The Library*, has revealed that Thomas spent eagerly on the pamphlets and early newspapers chronicling and arguing the dramatic transformations in English government of the mid-17th century. Unlike his father,

Thomas Cotton simply preferred to read the news rather than feature in it. Given how a life of news-making had rewarded Sir Robert, his son's and grandson's choice to shun London and political ambition in favor of country estates is hardly surprising.

They did not and would not abandon Sir Robert's greatest passion and accomplishment, however. They took pains to sustain the Cotton library, at least as a legacy owed to posterity. Its availability to contemporaries was reduced, but then they lived in confused times—as amply demonstrated by the Cottons' tortuous path to regaining control of their library. Before the month of his father's death was out Sir Thomas petitioned the crown once more to release the collection. Seemingly no logical grounds for its further detention existed, to the extent that any had ever done in the first place. Yet king and council had chosen a course of action on the Cotton library, and, as can be the way with official decisions, seemed set on seeing it through whether or not any valid reason remained. The privy council had already conducted searches of the library and commissioned some sort of report on its contents; Charles responded to the latest petition from Sir Thomas by insisting that the library be cataloged before any further actions.

The privy council catalog of the early 1630s was arguably an outgrowth of the crown's initial hopes of finding incriminating evidence against Sir Robert or his associates. Through all of their searching, they never did. Even among the horde of state papers they could not find certain evidence of anything unlawfully in Cotton's possession. Absent this, the cataloging project seems to have had no clear motivation except bureaucratic obstinacy. Sir Thomas very plainly considered the whole situation ridiculous. Kevin Sharpe writes that, ordered to call in loaned items for the catalogers to examine, Sir Thomas "followed the letter of the Council's orders [but] did so in the spirit of his father." More than a year after Sir Robert's death, his son had to ask permission to take a few items from the family's collection; asked when he would return them Sir Thomas replied "When I shall thinke good, or not at all… for they are my goods as truely as this cloak upon my back."

Control of the library probably returned to the Cottons through this kind of cynical, gradual, unofficial but effective reassertion, as much as through formal action. Notably, throughout its years-long custody over the library, Charles's government never removed either the collection or the Cottons from Cotton House. It was still possible to cut off access to the library in such circumstances, but only through focused effort. Very likely, Charles and his government were already losing the necessary interest after just a few years. As relations with Parliament approached a complete breakdown, royal interference with the Cotton library was likely abandoned as anything more than the most vestigial formality.

By the time that the English government ceded back its last claim on the Cottons' library, much had changed, including the entire shape of that government. In 1640, Sir Thomas sat in Parliament for the last time during the aptly-remembered "Short Parliament." Charles, finding the pressure for reforms greater than ever and his patience, in contrast, diminished, quickly dispersed Parliament yet again. His opponents' own patience with such tactics then ran out, and by 1642 England's governing class was ranged into opposing sides and commencing open warfare.

Most of the larger events that followed may be excluded from this narrative. For the Cottons and their library the Civil War mainly meant another decade similar to the one preceding it, i.e. awkward, uncertain coexistence with the government of the day, managed at arm's length as much as possible. Sir Thomas had little incentive and evinced correspondingly small enthusiasm to rally to King Charles—but he was scarcely more enthusiastic toward the parliamentary rival government.

Conscripted to harass his royalist neighbors, Sir Thomas demurred, citing ill health. His ailments were not entirely invented, in point of fact, but the Committee of Sequestration adopted a with-us-or-against-us line every bit as firm as the dynasty they were opposing. The committee assigned Sir Thomas various fines, then proceeded to help themselves rather than await likely further noncooperation. Through 1643, parliamentary troops made repeated raids on the Cotton estate in Huntingdonshire. At one point soldiers even intruded on the second Mrs. Cotton, whom Sir Thomas had married after Margaret Howard's early death; Edward Edwards asserts that the intruders forced their way into Lady Cotton's bedroom, "broke open her drawers and trunks, and carried off what they thought meet."

Precisely how much of a threat the Civil War meant for the Cottons' most valuable property—from history's perspective—is difficult to say. Many sources suggest that Sir Robert's old friend John Selden played a key role as proxy for the family, maintaining and defending the library in their absence. Sir Thomas was certainly making himself scarce, away from London through most of the period. (In *Sir Robert Cotton As Collector*, David Howarth charges that Sir Thomas even "abandoned his wife in an advanced state of pregnancy, to decamp with the rest of his household to a property at Eyworth in Bedfordshire.") Presumably the same was true of John Cotton, by then a young man but equally inclined to the country in his later life, even after peace returned. Selden, by contrast, remained both geographically and politically closer to parliamentary leaders while still keeping up a friendship with the Cottons.

Records show that their library not only remained unmolested, but even resumed limited activity during the war years.

Selden himself borrowed books, as did Archbishop Ussher. In the absence of the Cottons, and Richard James who had died in 1638, Selden and William Dugdale must indeed have been as much as the collection had in the way of guardians during the 1640s. A young antiquarian in the mold of Sir Robert and his circle, Dugdale had recently arrived in London and promptly befriended their surviving number. He later claimed to have assisted Selden during these years in sorting and binding many loose papers left from Sir Robert's and Richard James's efforts.

Colin Tite has poured a measure of cold water on some of the details of Selden's custodianship of the library, including a later tradition that Selden had a personal key to the still officially sealed collection. Tite nonetheless asserts that "the risk of confiscation or damage must have been real" for the library, and that Selden did provide important protection through the Civil War and early Commonwealth. As the Cotton library did survive, along with various others that Selden allegedly intervened in favor of, one may conclude that his influence with parliamentary forces was powerful indeed, or else that the threat was in reality less than dire. People at the time certainly worried, though, and with reason. The Cottons' other property did suffer substantial losses. A threat of similar "visitations" seemed real enough for the provost of Queen's College to actively solicit Selden's aid, in 1648. The example of George Thomason, moreover, suggests that Parliament was not always easily deflected from a potentially valuable store of documents. A contemporary of Sir Thomas who shared his appetite for war-era tracts and periodicals, Thomason created a vast archive documenting the origins and fortunes of the conflict. His collection also survived, and is today revered by historians. Yet during the war he perceived sufficient danger of its being seized or destroyed to move it repeatedly between various hiding places.

The Cotton library would certainly have been of at least

as much interest. By the Civil War, it was the property of Sir Thomas Cotton—a man parliamentary leaders found untrustworthy and uncooperative—as well as still formally impounded by the government of Charles I, against whom they were in open revolt. In such circumstances, the library's security cannot have seemed readily taken for granted.

Despite frequent absenteeism, Sir Thomas did not take the library for granted, even after the danger might have seemed past. In 1650 the Cottons finally regained free and clear title to the collection and its chamber in Cotton House, which King Charles had ordered closed more than 20 years earlier. By then of course, Charles's effective authority had ceased some time before, as more recently had Charles himself. On January 30, 1649, Charles I died, executed by a military dictatorship that had ultimately supplanted both crown and Parliament. Notably, during the trial that finally condemned him, Charles's captors had lodged him in a nearby home that they had discussed seizing for such use at least once during the war. They placed the captive king in Cotton House. In a small irony, the man who had locked up the Cotton library found himself imprisoned by it.

Sir Thomas himself was back in Cotton House during at least part of the dramatic trial. If he indulged in any twinge of grim satisfaction at events that would have horrified his father, however, he did not take reassurance from them. The next year found Sir Thomas once more lying low in Bedfordshire, and his library along with him.

For a decade after its release from house arrest, the Cotton library's trail goes relatively cold. Its master watched events from the countryside, likely counting up his losses from the war years, and wondering what would happen next in the mystifying new England of Lord Protector Cromwell. For the library itself, speculating with even this much precision is challenging. Scholarship of recent decades has traced the collection's history in sometimes incredible detail, but holes remain, and the exile from London during the Commonwealth is one of them. In 1650, Sir Thomas removed all or nearly all of his library to Stratton in Bedfordshire; in 1692, Richard Lapthorne described a visit to Cotton House and a resident collection once again reunited as completely as it has ever been. In between, the records provide clues but no firm conclusions.

Very possibly, the bulk of the Cotton manuscripts and related artifacts simply sat in chests and storerooms at one or another country manor for a number of years, ironically closed up even more effectively than during their long formal captivity. For the Cottons' legacy to history, the 1650s' most noteworthy event was no more than tangentially related to their library. James Howell, another man of letters inspired by the library's founder, saw Sir Robert's many warnings of constitutional crisis vindicated by events, and freshly relevant in post-monarchy England. In 1651 Howell produced a book from many of Sir Robert's tracts and essays, most previously unpublished. Though *Cottoni Posthuma* is not counted among history's great influential texts, it was a fitting minor tribute, as Howell in a sense repaid the same service that Sir Robert had performed for so many writers and thinkers before him.

Otherwise, the next significant date for the Cotton family treasure is that engraved on so many of Britain's literal crown jewels, 1661. The nation's experiment with uncrowned rule had effectively died along with Oliver Cromwell, three years earlier. The remaining men of influence then decided, more or less, to tiptoe quietly away from the remains, summon back king and Parliament, and ask them to please have another try and see if they couldn't work out a way to cooperate after all. Remarkably enough, it actually worked. He would have been suspicious of many of its details and horrified at all of its origins, but had Sir

Robert lived to see it he might have been justified in feeling that, in broad outline at least, the restored monarchy under Charles's son finally achieved the stable coexistence that he had insisted all along was the solution.

Much credit for that achievement belonged to Charles II, the one sovereign of his dynasty who mastered both wise pragmatism as a politician and likability as a person. In guiding a way toward reconciliation and out of the shadow of his executed father, the new king exercised both qualities, in ways large and small; an instance of the latter offered one further, subtle vindication to the late Sir Robert. Three decades earlier Charles I had spurned Sir Robert's coronation reception along with the ancient gospel book Tiberius A II from his library. Colin Tite finds that "It seems likely that the anecdote was told to Charles the Second... he sent—before he had been many days in England—a confidential servant to borrow the book from Sir Thomas." A fly-leaf still records the loan, made perhaps with mixed feelings but a sense of honor and satisfaction certainly prominent among them.

EX LIBRIS
THE LIBER VITAE
Domitian A VII

OCCASIONALLY AN INDIVIDUAL may be so heinous that people may speak, figuratively, of his or her name being "struck from the book of life." The corollary of entering names into the book of life in the first place is considered only rarely, if ever. Yet it is this action that, historically at least, has a much more literal reality. One of the best surviving examples is the Durham Book of Life, or *Liber Vitae*.

Cotton manuscript Domitian A VII begins with excerpts from the Four Gospels. But its greatest interest has for more than a millennium been found in the pages and pages of names that follow. Some time in the 9th century, scribes began recording the names of people associated with their church, perhaps Lindisfarne or Jarrow, though the book's original sponsor is unknown. By the early 12th century it had arrived at Durham Cathedral Priory, with which the book remains most strongly associated. For more than 400 years Durham's brothers extended and expanded the great registry of names. They filled its pages with generations of churchmen, nobles, and royalty, as well as thousands of the ordinary people otherwise nearly invisible today.

The exact significance of the book they produced has evolved, even as it has continued to inspire reverence of one sort or another. Originally, as the British Library's Julian Harrison explains, a name's entry in the *Liber Vitae* recognized someone important to the church; "all the members of the monastic community of Durham and its predecessors, together with lay benefactors and others associated in Durham's prayers," were in some sense remembered in perpetuity. In the 16th century, however, Durham Cathedral itself was in some sense struck from the rolls, dissolved at the prompting of Henry VIII along with all of England's monasteries.

For the antiquaries who gathered up the monasteries' scattered archives, the *Liber Vitae*'s pre-Reformation function as ledger for monks chanting eternal prayers was a relic of the past and its "papist superstition." They nonetheless valued it greatly *as* a relic of the past. Sir Robert Cotton can have felt no small pleasure in seeing its pages, the oldest of them already ancient by his day, enclosed in a red leather binding emphatically declaring the *Liber Vitae* a part of his library. For Cotton and his fellow antiquarians its names represented not piety or religious merit, but a rich mine of historical data. Scholars since have shared much of their interest. The names themselves provide a vast demographic record: family relations, societal structure, the migrations of different ethnic and cultural populations across centuries. The writing, meanwhile, offers an invaluable history of how spelling and letterforms themselves evolved from before the Norman conquest up through the Tudor dynasty.

As a result, the *Liber Vitae*'s survival of the Cotton library's varied misfortunes has been particularly merciful. Other houses produced their own "books of life," but only two comparable *libri vitae* from medieval Britain survive today. In recent decades, multiple institutions have worked to preserve the contents of Domitian A VII, and to expand their accessibility. Today, scholars can consult print replicas and online projects, including a digital facsimile hosted by the British Library's web site since 2013. Despite the dissolution of Durham's monastery centuries ago, the survival of generations of its benefactors' names in perpetuity seems, today, more assured than ever.

CHAPTER 8

Declassification

THE RESTORATION SEEMS a natural moment for the Cotton library's own return to London. Even if nothing confirms its restored presence in Cotton House until some years later, it's easy to imagine Sir Thomas weighing the general sense of renewal, as well as the conciliatory gesture of Charles II, and concluding that if the library were ever to reopen it may as well do so.

If the library did not move back from Bedfordshire within a couple of years of the Restoration, it had to await a second new regime. Sir Thomas Cotton died May 13, 1662, almost two years exactly after Charles II returned to England. The second Cotton baronet had lived through difficult times, and had done well in protecting his family's legacies. If he did not live to see them completely restored from their years in the wilderness he left a more than capable successor to carry on the work in the person of his son, John. The third baronet enjoyed longevity far surpassing his father or grandfather. Under his management the family library resumed some of its old role, and eventually greeted its second century.

Few things would be exactly the same as before war and regicide, and this applied to the Cotton library as well. The old guard of early days and the Society of Antiquaries was effectively all gone. Sir John had known his grandfather, but was only 10 when Sir Robert advised an emissary from Charles I that he had come too late. The scholars and artists and courtiers of Elizabethan and early Stuart times, who had formed a loose but active network about Sir Robert and his library, had passed from the scene; the tradition of Cotton House as a center for their disciplines had been broken.

Other centers had emerged in its place. The most prominent among them was the Bodleian Library. One of the first transactions in Sir Robert's career acquiring and sharing books was his gift of a dozen volumes to Sir Thomas Bodley, around 1602. Today's British Library notes its significance as the "first major donation of manuscripts to the Bodleian Library at Oxford," and Cotton's generous early role in the project is a somewhat bittersweet exploit. The recipient of that small gift flourished, even as Sir Robert's own attempt at a British national library suffered persecution and decline. The Bodleian emerged from civil war with its more formal links to intellectual activity largely intact, and its more general focus better adapted to a much-changed society. For the next hundred years, it, not the Cotton collection, was the unofficial national library in England. Sir Robert had indeed planted a seed that grew into a great institution, yet it was not the one to which he had given his name and so much of his care and effort.

The Cotton library was, nonetheless, down but not out. It still had a magnificent collection. Its home was still amid the heart of national government and other leading institutions, at any rate after its return from provincial exile. The latest scion of the Cotton family still cared for the library, and the vision his grandfather had for it, and in time Sir John's library began to assemble a new circle of its own.

Sir William Dugdale was probably the herald of the new order. Aspiring to the old antiquarian tradition of Sir Robert, et al., Dugdale arrived on the scene at a time of transition, and his career marks a passing of the torch from their generation to his. In 1638 the young Dugdale contacted the octogenarian Sir Henry Spelman, a founding member of the Society of Antiquaries. Spelman readily shared the benefits of his reputation and contacts, providing Dugdale entrée to all the great London archives, including the library of the Cotton family. Dugdale repaid him in the old cooperative tradition. He took up Spelman's incomplete project on provincial councils in England, and in the decade that followed did the same service for other antiquarian interests. The future Sir William dug deep into monastery records preserved in the Cotton collection and elsewhere, eventually making significant contributions to scholarly appreciation of charters and monastic history in general.

Dugdale's arrival was also well-timed from the Cotton library's perspective. The well-recommended young scholar probably seemed a godsend to Sir Thomas, beset by so many concerns at the time, and Dugdale's letters indicate that he was acting as unofficial secretary for the library as early as 1640. In February he apologized to Sir Simonds D'Ewes, "in despaire to obteyne the bookes of Sr Tho. Cotton wch you desire." The next month he was by contrast "very much pleased to heare... that Sr Thom. Cotton's coynes are in your hands..." Dugdale claimed, as noted, to have organized and bound many of the collection's loose documents, and for what it may be worth he had little need to exaggerate his service as a librarian. His correspondence is a record of diligent inquiries and responses on behalf of Sir Thomas, and later Sir John, stretching nearly half a century. Toward the end, he even completed his long quest for the Cotton Genesis and witnessed its reunion with the Otho shelf.

Dugdale also witnessed a revival for the library in a broader sense, which might be all the more impressive given its reduced accessibility. In the first confused years after Sir Robert's death, an old friend like D'Ewes could still borrow a treasure with few demands about its return, at least sometimes. Gradually, however, Sir Thomas introduced more restrictive policies. The library began requiring signed records for loans, and even bonds posted against their return, sometimes as much as £100 per volume. Under Sir John, such bonds became routine, and almost no loans issued without his express permission. Despite his infrequent presence in London, well into old age Sir John required his librarian to relay every loan request in writing, for his personal inspection. The old library had been a remarkably open "kind of universitie," but that of the later Cottons strongly encouraged users to examine materials in Cotton House, and the door was not always open to non-credentialed visitors.

Visitors persisted anyway, as the Cotton library remained a valuable resource. Kevin Sharpe suggests that the nation's quiet counter-revolution generated a return to the politics of precedent, and a corresponding revival in demand for Sir Robert's great encyclopedia of how things were done before. The library's days as an important resource in contemporary politics were waning, all the same, and further revolution before the century's end likely made such a revival short-lived. The collection always had far more to offer than political trump cards, however. In the meantime the university libraries' shortcomings, relative to open private collections, had by no means been eliminated even at the rising Bodleian. If the Cotton heirs kept their own library's door closed more than in times past, their librarian in the person of Dugdale still prioritized the sharing of information and not just the husbanding of volumes. As in Sir Robert's day, generosity continued to repay itself, and records show occasional donations to the library continuing through the 17th century.

At least one of those, a gift of manuscripts from John Marsham in the 1670s, may have been thanks (or trade) for information about the collection as much as for information within it. The catalog prepared by Sir Robert and Richard James was never complete—or published—and the need for updated resources only grew. The catalog prepared by Charles I's commission, probably never intended to aid consultation of the library, appears not to have done so to any great degree. Today it cannot even be identified with certainty among the few early manuscript catalogs known. Dugdale probably produced the next significant update, perhaps in the 1660s or '70s. His exact contribution to the perennial cataloging project is uncertain, although—given the length of his involvement with the collection—it's difficult to imagine he would not have at least attempted to prepare such an essential aid.

By the 1670s, in any event, several "classified catalogs" were circulating among English literati. Colin Tite has studied the six surviving examples of these catalogs, and they highlight the interesting contradictions of the library in this period. Each of the catalogs is handwritten, probably copied from notes by Dugdale or some other common template, but no two copies are entirely alike. Tite asserts that they "show no sign of having been produced centrally," and that some or all may have been copied piecemeal from partial references as and when they were available. The classified catalogs are decidedly not formal, published documents; access to them was probably dependent on making the right connections, perhaps helped along with an appropriate quid-pro-quo like Marsham's gift of books.

The entire enterprise of the classified catalogs has a distinctly underground quality calling to mind Russian *samizdat* of a much later era. Though a more relaxed political climate had prevailed in England since the Restoration, the Cotton library continued to prefer operating off the record and out of the spotlight—despite which, people continued to find and use it. The privately circulating, hand-copied catalogs of the 1670s are at once a testimony to resurgent interest in the library, and to the library's evasiveness. Scholar Thomas Gale went to the trouble of acquiring one, as did his friend Samuel Pepys, whose Cotton library catalog remains with his own preserved collection to this day. Half a century after Sir Robert Cotton died, disappointed in efforts to keep his library a leading resource for open intellectual inquiry, a new generation of inquirers was trying to dive back in, and obstruction by the crown seemed at an end. The library might yet look forward to a new buzz of productivity if someone could just overcome a few of the restrictions now imposed from within.

After William Dugdale's death in 1686, Sir John found his replacement in Thomas Smith. As prospective evangelist for exposing the Cotton library to wider audiences, Smith would seem a distinctly odd fit. He often appears cantankerous and hermetic, and once replied to a loan request with the acid advice that "Mahomet must condescend to go to the Mountaine." If this made him a misfit as the librarian who would finally convert the cautious Sir John, however, it was paradoxically a match with most of Smith's life. Out of all the nonconformist or ill-starred characters in the Cotton library's story, the most hopelessly awkward misfit was, indisputably, Thomas Smith.

Like his predecessor Richard James, while a young man Smith had traveled as a chaplain with embassies overseas, visiting France and Constantinople. An Oxford graduate, he eventually served in various high-ranking posts at Magdalen College including bursar and vice president. Unfortunately, Smith's gifts as a scholar were matched by a gift for always being the odd man out. In 1685, Charles II died without issue, leaving the throne to his Catholic brother James. Despite widespread suspicion, King James II was by no means plotting to roll back the entire English Reformation. But he did loosen up some of the government's avowedly Protestant-only policies. At Magdalen, he attempted to go further and actively remake the school as a Catholic college. Smith, an episcopal priest, was out of a job.

James's attempted "Catholicization" of Magdalen met considerable opposition, and Smith soon regained his post. Meanwhile general discontent with James continued to mount. Only a couple of years into the new reign, William of Orange invaded and sent him packing, then with Parliament's consent took over as co-sovereign alongside James's Protestant daughter Mary. Yet the "Glorious Revolution" left Smith still an outsider. Like Sir Robert Cotton in the time of James's father, Smith remained fixed in his belief in a king's rightful authority, even though he had personally suffered under it. Smith could not bring himself to pledge allegiance to William as king, no matter what Parliament declared. This refusal, frequently combined with religious nonconformism, made "non-jurors" like Smith into outcasts. In an article for *British Library Journal*, Eileen A. Joy writes that George Hickes, an acquaintance of Smith and a fellow non-juror, "was, on occasion, a wanted man" and forced to live and work in hiding. Back at Magdalen, in turn, Smith was once more an unwanted man.

It may in part have been Smith's experience of persecution that (in addition to his consequent willingness to work unpaid) endeared him to Sir John. By his 60s the third Cotton baronet had witnessed many reversals for both his family and his country, and become deeply cautious, even suspicious. When Smith first proposed to organize and then publish a new catalog of the Cotton library in 1687, Sir John's reply was full of dark foreboding:

"Truly, Sir, we are fallen into so dangerous times, that it be more for my private concerns, and the public, too, that the library should not be too much known. There are many things in it, which are very crosse to the Romish interest, & you know what kind of persons the Jesuits are."

Even after the "Romish" James's ouster, Sir John remained wary of publicizing the contents of his library. Smith later ascribed this to modesty on the baronet's part, and reluctance to show off his collection in such a way when many other great libraries had yet to approve such a step. Neither Sir Robert nor Sir Thomas had seen fit to publish a catalog, and Sir John hesitated at such a departure from precedent. Smith himself would have to remain library users' main guide. Given Smith's growing reputation as an exacting gatekeeper, it seemed that Sir John was influencing him more than the other way around, and that hopes were dimming for either a "declassified" catalog, or library.

Typical of Smith's luck, when he finally realized the design that is his greatest legacy, it owed much to the meddling of perhaps his greatest nemesis, Humfrey Wanley.

Various factors eroded Sir John's resistance to a published catalog. The years passed by with no further regime change, and England seemed made reliably safe for documents "crosse to the Romish interest." Meanwhile Sir John himself was growing elderly, and perhaps tempted to leave one further legacy of his own to the family's library even if it deviated from precedent. Above all, however, Sir John lifted the ban on a published catalog of his manuscripts because it was no longer in his power to maintain it. By the early 1690s, the threat of an independent Cotton library catalog was growing unstoppable, and Humfrey Wanley was pushing eagerly to make threat into reality.

If Smith is the Cotton library's great misfit, Wanley is, in comparison, its great dark horse. A young and ambitious man, he shared many of the old antiquarians' interests but came by them largely on his own, independent of the remaining heirs to the old days. Wanley apprenticed as a draper, originally, before practically willing himself into the role of a formidable scholar. By the early 18th century he offered an impressive résumé as a potential future librarian for the Cotton collection. Before he even moved to London, Wanley was already aspiring to become the Cotton library's first formal cataloger.

Wanley's challenge to the Cotton library's seclusion sprang from another, larger project, initially. Bernard's Catalogue began at Oxford in 1692, as a survey of the Bodleian library's manuscripts. By the time Wanley was pushing his way into bibliographic circles two years later, the project was turning into something much grander: an effort to document the medieval manuscripts of the whole nation. Even for a team, this was likely more than an entire lifetime's work, but certain archives offered obvious places to concentrate first. The fabled shelves of Cotton House were inevitably ranked high on their list.

The threat posed by Bernard, Wanley, and his fellow researchers placed Sir John Cotton in an awkward position. Declining to publish a catalog himself was one thing; overtly opposing someone else's attempt was another, particularly when that someone represented Oxford. Sir John might, even so, have attempted to discourage them by more subtle means. But even if he kept Wanley and his associates out of the library entirely, they could simply turn to another avenue—the several classified catalogs would reveal much of the collection's contents to anyone determined enough to track one down. All of these manuscript catalogs were in some way incomplete or otherwise flawed, which conjured the dismaying prospect of a published independent catalog that was full of misinformation, besides. Sir John could instead have simply given in, and let Bernard's men do what they might, or even aided them. Absent someone close at hand offering one further option, he might have done so. But Thomas Smith had been advocating that the library publish its own catalog for years, and under the threat of someone else preempting them, Sir John finally gave Smith his assent.

Despite having been Cotton librarian for several years, Smith had probably honored Sir John's wishes and made little attempt at starting a new catalog before the sudden reversal in 1694. Eileen Joy suggests that Smith's catalog, published two years later, was mostly compiled in the space of months; she notes that Smith himself acknowledged a debt to his predecessors, including James and Dugdale, and that the sheer size of the collection probably made reuse of old lists unavoidable given the race to publish first. Nearly all serious students of the Cotton library agree that Smith's 1696 *Catalogus librorum manuscriptorum Bibliothecæ Cottonianæ* has the character of a rushed work. Many items receive only minimal description, if any, and undoubtedly the same sort of human errors that characterized all of the previous catalogs abound.

Yet, for all of their awareness of its faults, Smith's catalog has continued to claim such scholars' attention for most of the three centuries since. As the first formal, public catalog of the Cotton manuscripts, it was a landmark achievement even if its advance was evolutionary rather than revolutionary. Working just ahead of major events in the library's history, Smith recorded much that might otherwise have been lost. Introductory essays provide background to the collection, including the first real biography of its founder; Hope Mirrlees remarks that Smith's Cotton biography is not only written in Latin but despairingly humorless, but it still preserves memories that could have perished with the aging Sir John. Beyond that, the catalog itself is a snapshot of the library as left by the Cottons, from whose ownership it was about to pass toward yet another century of disruptions.

Smith himself could know little of this at the time. For

his part the catalog was likely satisfying as the realization of an old goal, at last, and as a check on certain impudent upstarts. Humfrey Wanley was unquestionably the foremost object of the latter attitude. George Hickes somehow managed to participate in both Bernard's Catalogue and Wanley's own later projects, without antagonizing Smith. Not so for his friend. Smith never quite barred Wanley from the library entirely but he did his best to discourage him. When Wanley asked to borrow a number of charters in 1697, in response Smith declared himself "extremely amazed at your request," followed by the admonishment that "Mahomet must... go to the mountain." Smith did not really want Wanley to visit the library, either, and attempted to deflect him as best he could.

But Smith's hopes, for example that "this letter Will bee so satisfactory as to put a stop to all further enquireys about these matters," were in vain. Wanley would not take "no" for an answer. At one point, he charmed a maid into providing him access to the library in Smith's absence—much to Smith's subsequent outrage. More often, he simply kept pestering the exasperated librarian. Wanley was brimming with dreams and plans, and as long as potential material for them remained among the Cotton collection, he seemed irrepressible. Smith's bane was posterity's boon as it turned out. Though the older man had bested his rivals with the first published catalog of the library—thanks in part to their having forced the issue—Wanley saw neither Smith's catalog nor Bernard's as a finish line. Between 1697 and '99, Wanley prepared a "book of specimens" of scripts from different ages. As examples, he prepared careful, detailed facsimiles of representative manuscript pages, including seven from the Cotton collection. Within mere decades, calamities made some of these every bit as invaluable as Smith's catalog.

The same could be said of Wanley's *Catalogus Historico-Criticus*, published several years later as part of Hickes's *Thesau-*

rus. Extending the work Wanley and Hickes had performed for Bernard, this landmark compendium cataloged manuscripts in Old English, as well as other archaic languages. Naturally it included a section on Cotton library manuscripts, though in the long run this contributed less to scholarship of the collection than its author must have hoped. Eileen Joy describes it as "strangely misordered," likely owing in part to Wanley's limited access to sources; Smith could claim at least partial victory, after all. The catalog was on the whole an impressive achievement, however, as well as a further irruption by Wanley into the library's affairs in spite of Smith. The Cotton manuscripts' unique Old English text of *The Rune Poem* survived for eventual study and publication only through a transcription that Wanley included in the *Thesaurus*.

Wanley seemed to be shoving his way into the new Cotton library circle whether welcome or no. It may be that in doing so, he was driven by more than boundless enthusiasm, moreover. Despite his fascination with the past Wanley's eye was ever on tomorrow, and by the late 1690s it may have been especially focused on the future of the Cotton library. Sir John would be 80 years old with the beginning of the new century, and had arranged no clear plan of succession. Prospective heirs might have a difficult time dislodging Smith from the library, whatever their intentions, but Smith himself was past 60. Wanley was just 27 in 1699, by contrast. Smith controlled the library for the time being, and partly as a result had claimed priority as author of its first formal catalog. But the race, Wanley may have reflected, does not always go to the swift.

EX LIBRIS
THE PEARL POEMS
Nero A X ff. 41r-130r

Since the mid-19th century, at least, the chief interest of Nero A X has been a series of Middle English poems which share the volume with a codex of theological material and other Latin texts. These poems are also the most mysterious part of the whole. In a recent translation of one of them, *Sir Gawain and the Green Knight*, W.S. Merwin writes "We do not know the poet's name, and cannot say for certain when the poem was composed." For *Gawain*, a misty and mystical work that defies easy interpretation, the enigma of its origin feels oddly appropriate.

Like the Cotton library's other much-celebrated and much-scrutinized poetic manuscript, *Beowulf*, *Gawain* and the other "Pearl poems" only obtained scholarly notice relatively recently. If any literary interest motivated Sir Robert Cotton in acquiring the manuscript from Henry Savile, he left no record of such. The contents of Nero A X suggest that, as usual, religious and historical aspects accounted for most of their significance in the early library.

Only after arriving at the British Museum did anyone make formal note of Nero A X as a volume of poetry. J.P. Gilson may have been the first to bring the poems to any wider attention; some years later, the prolific linguist and Cotton manuscripts promoter Frederic Madden edited an edition of "Sir Gawayne." In 1925 J.R.R. Tolkein and E.V. Gordon collaborated on a new edition, which provided the basis of Merwin's 2002 translation and remains, in his view, "the authoritative text and edition."

After more than a century of study, most scholarship regards a single "Gawain Poet" as the author of all four poems in the manuscript: *Pearl*, *Patience*, *Purity*, and *Sir Gawain*. A common hand obviously wrote all of them down in what eventually became Nero A X. Stylistic similarities, and the absence of any other source for the poems, suggest that scribe and author were one. The Gawain Poet probably wrote around 1400, making him (generally assumed to be male) a contemporary of Chaucer. Compared with *The Canterbury Tales*, however, *Gawain* and the other Pearl Poems are written in an English significantly more difficult for a modern reader to recognize. Most likely, their author lived and wrote some distance outside the London-centered society from which later English primarily evolved. Tolkein and Gordon suggest "an amateur knowledge perhaps, rather than a professional; he had Latin and French and was well enough read in French books, both romantic and instructive; but his home was in the West Midlands of England; so much his language shows, and his metre, and his scenery."

A strong sense of landscape as a part of the narrative pervades *Gawain*, certainly. An author in the west of England, near Wales, may also account for *Gawain*'s slightly odd presence among poems which, in Merwin's description, served "as vehicles of Christian exhortation and piety." Though faith and virtue are important themes, *Gawain* explores them within an overtly Arthurian tale of magic and legend. It seems all the more natural, then, to imagine the Gawain Poet dreaming of Arthur and his knights somewhere near the "Celtic fringe" from which the traditional tales first grew. Beyond this, any attempts to identify the poet have remained controversial. Given the paucity of clues, every suggestion seems at most plausible, but unpersuasive as *the* truth. Curiously, at the end of *Gawain*, the Green Knight's unmasking leaves a similar equivocal feeling… in both cases, doubt seems likely to linger.

CHAPTER 9

The Three Rivals

A DECADE AFTER HE RETURNED a long-lost Greek Genesis to his family's library, Sir John Cotton faced a new dilemma: who would care for the collection after he was gone? His decision would be pivotal to the collection's history, just as much as his father's actions more than six decades earlier. Curiously, although his impact is the more widely appreciated, Sir John himself can seem to disappear into the background of his own library at this crucial moment. His grandfather built the collection and raised its profile to heights never again equaled. Sir Thomas recovered the library, and led its exodus amid war and revolution, while documenting the latter in an extensive if ephemeral collection of his own. Sir John also involved himself with the collection, to which he restored items that had strayed and added new material as well; he took particular interest in the coin collection. Yet it is easy to forget about him as more than a time-server, in comparison with the activity of both his ancestors as well the librarians who handled most of the library business during his tenure. Sir John enjoyed the country as much as his father, but kept the library back in London, and thus often genuinely out of sight.

The Cotton library was never out of mind, all the same, least of all as Sir John contemplated this last problem. In many ways it was the same problem that the library had been fortunate to escape after 1631, thanks to its founder's son and then grandson proving steadfast successors. Several decades later, finding another was not to be that easy.

Sir John's problem was not so much a want of possible heirs as it was the exact opposite. Colin Tite summarizes the Cotton family tree by noting that Sir Thomas and Sir John both married twice, and "all four marriages had been productive of children." This alone suggested a potential for difficulties. One of Sir John's male descendants—women were apparently excluded from consideration—appeared a worthy heir. But too many did not. Worse, the least scholarly of Sir John's progeny were also the youngest. The library might remain safe with his sons and nephews, only for their own children to bring about its ruin. Sir John could foresee this possibility, owing to longevity surpassing his ancestors', and so may have felt more obligation to arrange a lasting settlement for the library.

Such concern was prudent. Though the Cotton family's collection had eluded the fate of so many through two generations of heirs, it had in truth probably reached a natural limit. Studies of family businesses have found that, even among those enterprises that take root with the founders' children, family involvement nearly always fails after the third generation. The conclusion is hardly surprising, either, as common sense recognizes that three generations are generally the limit for shared experience in human families; Sir John had seen, as a boy, something of what the library meant to his grandfather and his peers, but for the Cottons of the approaching 18th century this heritage might count for little.

The library's potential value at sale might, by contrast, count for all too much. Edward Edwards records a story that "Sir John, when conversing, on one occasion, with Thomas Carte, told the historian that he had been offered £60,000 of English money, together with a carte blanche for some honorary mark of royal favor, on the part of Lewis [sic] the Fourteenth, for the Library..." Even if the tale is exaggerated, the collection would certainly have commanded premium prices, and Sir John suspected future inheritors would readily yield to temptation.

For his own part, Sir John had exchanged a considerable sum to reacquire just one piece of the collection. He was hardly going to surrender the whole of a family and national treasure to foreign buyers, no matter their grandeur. He had no wish to sell the library, at all. Its founding intent had always been a *public* resource, and even if Sir John had limited this function he had preserved it, and sought the same in a successor.

He had a few possible models to guide him. As far back as his grandfather's childhood, the Archbishop Matthew Parker had presented his own splendid library to Corpus Christi College, along with an elaborate system of inspectors and contingency bequests to ensure its perennial care; the college guards Parker's books to this day. Sir John might have done something similar, and preserved his library just as effectively. But this too would have violated the spirit of the Cotton library, making the great national archive at the heart of the capital just another resource for the university towns.

Universities were the right kind of institutions, however. They had the resources to support the library's active use, the experience to handle such a project, and the continuity to be reliable custodians long into the future. The main alternative, by contrast, was questionable on all these points. Through the Cotton library's first century of existence the English government had been frequently insolvent, repeatedly unstable, and (even setting aside its decidedly rough handling of libraries under Henry VIII and his son) at best uninterested in taking charge of a library. In the most notable exception, Charles I had seized the library that Sir Robert had offered freely to Elizabeth 30 years earlier—and locked its doors. Two revolutions seemed to have ended the threat of abuse by autocracy, though such must have been far from obvious to Sir John. No option was certain to satisfy his hopes for the library. The only certainty was that Sir John could not protect it forever.

Forced to make a choice from such vexing alternatives, Sir John turned to tradition. His grandfather had always aspired to establish a national library from his collection, officially or otherwise. In his own last will Sir Robert had reaffirmed this wish that the library "continue for the use of Posterity." He had also introduced significant caveats, likely in response to his difficult relationship with the crown in his later years. The same will emphasized his library as a privately owned family heirloom, specifically bequeathed to his son and then grandson, and "not be sold, or otherwise disposed of."

For Sir John, though, strictly honoring the family property directive seemed likely to mean violation of the injunction against selling the library within another generation or two. Therefore he tried to satisfy the spirit of his grandfather's various aims with a compromise of his own. The bequest eventually enacted by Parliament as 12 & 13 William III, chapter 7, is in its way just as paradoxical as Sir Robert's will, and even more complicated than Matthew Parker's. Upon the death of Sir John his collection would become property of the nation, administered by a group of trustees combining Cotton descendants and government officials. These were nonetheless to maintain the library "by the Name of the Cottonian Library for Publick Use & Advantage." In its most thoroughly confusing directive, the act made provision for the library to remain in Cotton House but pledged that both "should continue in [Sir John's] Family and not be sold or otherwise dispersed or imbezled." The trustees would control the library room and "a convenient Way Passage and Resort to the same," while the rest of Cotton House would descend as family property via an extensively described succession plan.

The best that can be said of Sir John's agreement with Parliament is that it transformed a potential ending for the Cotton library into a new beginning. The British Library notes the scheme, today, as the first instance of a British government taking charge of such a collection and "an important step toward the creation of a national public library." The act itself recognized the magnificent gift that it represented, praising all three Cotton baronets and their library, "generally esteemed the best Collection of its kind now anywhere extant." A century later Sir Frederic Madden of the British Museum called it simply "the most valuable present ever given to the Nation;" as shall be seen, Madden had a personal stake in the collection's worth, but subsequent generations have offered little serious argument. England's belated acceptance of the Cotton library represented a grand vindication for the labors of Sir Robert Cotton and his entire generation of antiquarian peers.

The practical reality of 12 & 13 William III, c. 7, was nonetheless a very tentative beginning only, in realizing such visions. By itself it involved little ambition beyond merely continuing the Cotton library as the wondrous but rather ad hoc cabinet of curiosities it had been for decades. The collection would remain in the narrow attic of a private home. The act called for new cataloging and a librarian, but neither of these represented any real innovation. The trustees' librarian was even expected to be, essentially, as much a volunteer as Dugdale or Smith; though the act calls for the trustees to collect £500 from the librarian as security, it says next to nothing about a budget for payments *to* the librarian or any other expense. In fairness to Parliament and its trustees, ample precedent obviously existed for what seems fantastic from a modern viewpoint. The Cotton library in particular already had one librarian working for free; in short order, he would actually face heated competition for his post.

Thomas Smith was anxious about his future with the Cotton library, even before rivals announced themselves openly. As well he might have been. His position had always been both unpaid and unofficial. Nationalization of the library would change only one of these qualities, and for Smith it was to be the wrong one, twice over. The act itself specified the librarian swear a formal oath, though only to promise his "utmost Care and Endeavour for the preserving" of the collection. By itself that was easy enough for Smith. But the act also placed the librarian's selection in the hands of formal government officials, who would be highly unlikely to favor any candidate reluctant to swear fealty to the king as well.

For this reason, Smith's hopes of continuing as the trustees' librarian were realistically doomed from the outset. His hopes and anxieties were nonetheless to persist for several years as fate continually dangled some slender chance for clinging on. At first, Smith could hope that the trustees' takeover might be delayed as long as possible; the month that the relevant statute formally took effect he wrote that "It will now, more than ever, concerne mee, to wish and pray for Sir J^s long life, during wch I know I shall have the same liberty of accesse to his library as formerly." If those prayers failed, Smith could anticipate sympathy from at least one ally among the trustees. By the turn of the century, Sir John had outlived the son of his first marriage, and that shorter-lived John Cotton's own sons were behind much of Sir John's concern for the future. But the son of Sir John's second marriage had become a close friend to Smith, and while outside the direct line for the baronetcy, Robert Cotton of Gedding was named among the four initial family trustees.

DESCENDANTS OF
SIR ROBERT COTTON

Based on the Cotton family tree in Lives of the Founders of the British Museum *by Edward Edwards*

- Thomas (died in infancy)
- Sir Robert Cotton★ Knight = Gertrude Morrice
- Philip Cotton★
- William Cotton

Children of Sir Robert Cotton and Gertrude Morrice:

- Alice = Robert Trefusis
- Sir Robert Cotton of Gedding★, 5th Baronet = Elizabeth Wigston

Robert Cotton Trefusis
Father of Robert George William Trefusis, 17th Baron Clinton, from whose time this title as well as Cornelius Johnson's portrait of Sir Robert Cotton have passed via Trefusis descendants to the present day

Sir John Cotton, 6th and Last Baronet = Jane Burdett

- John (died in infancy)
- Jane

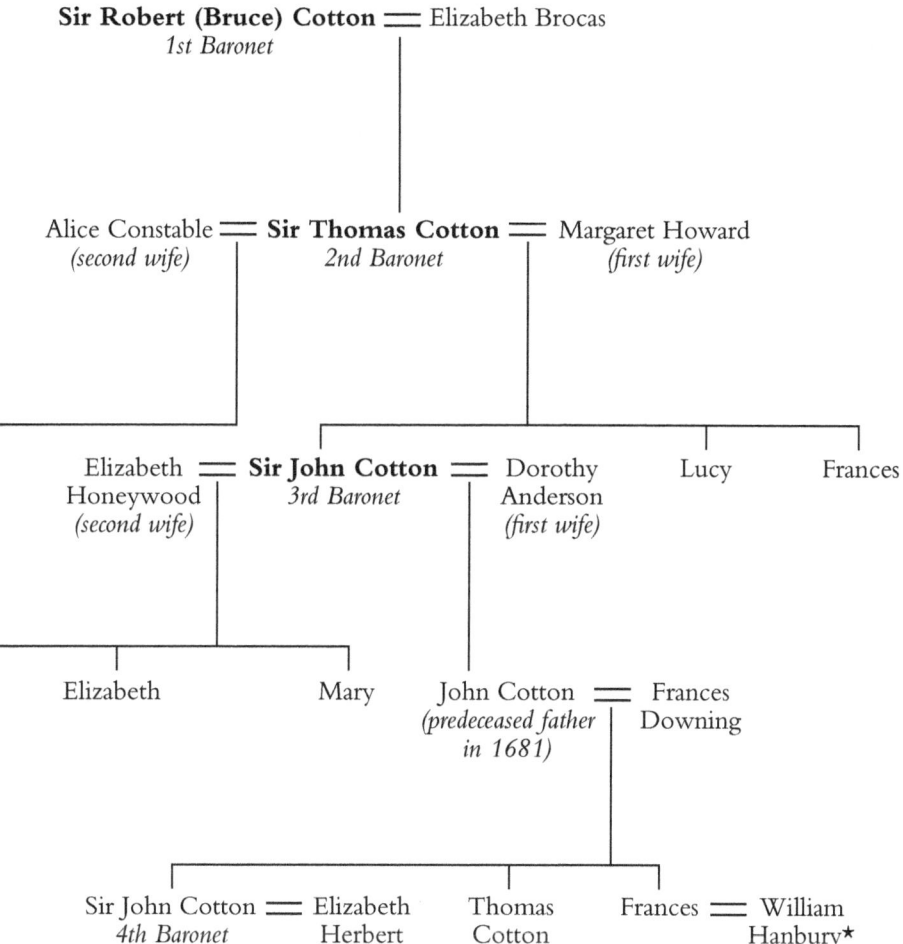

*Library trustee upon its gift to the nation

Unfortunately the other family trustees were not so close. Two were Sir John's half-brothers from his father's own second marriage: Philip Cotton, and another Sir Robert Cotton (knighted on his own account, though never baronet). The fourth family trustee, meanwhile, would prove not only unsympathetic to Smith but outright hostile, at least to Smith's hopes for continued employment. William Hanbury had married one of Sir John's granddaughters, and while the first Sir Robert had other direct descendants living, Hanbury somehow insinuated himself among the trustees' ranks. Though not a blood relation, Hanbury seemed indeed to be the most dedicated courtier in the Cotton dynasty since the early career of its founder. As Smith soon discovered, Hanbury had ambitions for the Cotton library in direct conflict with his own.

As Smith knew already, Hanbury was not alone, either. His attempted end-run around library security aside, Humfrey Wanley had shown Smith respect and courtesy throughout his frustrating years as a rival cataloger. But the prospect of a new management, highly unlikely to retain Smith as library keeper, offered Wanley the hope of a much more complete end-run. Still the dark horse, Wanley had no official role with the trustees, but his energy and résumé as bibliographer might strongly recommend him to them. Wanley had already been an active "shadow librarian," for years, and following the act of 1701 he seemed nearly obsessed with anticipating a place in the Cotton legacy. He purchased Cornelius Johnson's portrait of Sir Robert Cotton around 1703, and some years after that joined in reviving the Society of Antiquaries that Cotton had helped found. Though all three men were outsiders in some way, Smith, Hanbury and Wanley each appeared convinced that the Cotton library could be his charge when everything settled.

The intrigues and skirmishes that surrounded the library as a result of Sir John's "settlement" lasted for years, and might nearly fill a book by themselves. Before attempting to sort them out, it's worth examining what could have motivated so much competition to succeed an unpaid librarian.

Smith's and Wanley's interest is easy enough to understand, up to a point. Despite the friction between them, both men were dedicated scholars. The Cotton collection offered a rich trove of material for scholarship, and the collection's librarian could enjoy the additional benefits of prestige, as well as significant control over those riches. More than prestige was at stake, too. Part of Smith's early antipathy to Wanley rested on their competing ambitions to publish some of the library's unique manuscripts. Although Anglo-Saxon charters and letters of William Camden were unlikely to be bestsellers, publishing choice items from the collection might still provide some modest return. For the nearly unemployable Smith, or a young man like Wanley hungry to make a name for himself, priority access to the Cotton manuscripts was worth some toil even without any official wage.

William Hanbury had negligible interest in scholarship, however. Any records of his career among the Inns of Court remain obscure, but most likely the small potential profits from publishing a few rare manuscripts also meant little to him. The character who emerges from Hanbury's one scene on history's stage is in fact a man on the make. Yet he, too, coveted the Cotton library. The prospect of a salary may have been an enticement, in his case; the trustees eventually acknowledged the wisdom of the idea, at least in theory, and as one of their number Hanbury could have pressed for its execution in practice. Most of his interest appears, nonetheless, to have been financial gain on a scale and by means that his rivals simply would not dare. Hanbury intended by means fair or foul to make the job, and the library, pay.

In Hanbury's defense, the relevant definitions of fair and foul are heavily dependent on context. In Britain as in much of the world, profiting from government office prevailed as customary for a very long time. A professional civil service evolved only slowly from the older informal system of clientage and reward—the early antiquaries had regularly pondered these murky origins—and even into industrial times such indirect spoils were taken for granted much more than today. In still earlier eras, a courtier might frequently not just accept an unsalaried government position but even bid for it aggressively, counting on recouping the investment through a little graft here, a little embezzlement there, etc. One might even resell an office to someone else who would do whatever work could not be avoided, in exchange for a split of the takings.

The Cotton library offered real possibilities along these lines, for the right individual. Even with a catalog, it remained and indeed remains labyrinthine in organization, and a librarian might charge fees for assistance, or simply for access. Loans might also generate revenue, particularly if those "loans" were poorly documented and long-lasting to the point of being more like sales. Sir John had made his arrangements to prevent just such an outcome, and wholesale liquidation would probably be impossible; despite more flexible standards, total corruption on the part of all the trustees was unlikely. But the precise borders of the collection had always been flexible as well, and though the trustees' charter tried to define them more clearly in addition to calling for a complete new catalog, much could go missing without anyone noticing. Anyone, that is, except the broker and buyer, both of whom might "convey away" the Cotton library's greatest treasures again from all too close at hand.

For Thomas Smith, this possibility may have been even more horrifying than the prospect of losing his last chance at scholarly employment. Uncompromising, inflexible non-juror that he was, Smith was not necessarily the best man to transform the

Cotton family's private library into a true public resource. But he was without question the best man to prevent its transformation back into the private property of someone else. Unfortunately he was also long odds to remain its librarian, thanks to that same non-juring inflexibility. All else aside, the fact that the contest for his job began in earnest with the death of Smith's most loyal friend in the whole affair told strongly against him.

Sir John Cotton, third holder of the baronetcy and last private owner of the library that were the family legacies of his grandfather, died September 12, 1702. In his final year he had tried to encourage his successors to keep Smith as the library's guardian. Smith appreciated his late benefactor's kindness, and even amid his anxiety over affairs in London, Smith left the city days later to attend Sir John's interment at Conington.

The incumbent librarian had already begun his active campaign to stay in office, admittedly, and probably concluded that an absence would not reduce his already small chances. Smith learned of Sir John's death immediately thanks to Robert Cotton of Gedding. In a subsequent letter to his friend, Smith described making prompt inquiries after the incoming trustees, only to find that all but one were out of town, themselves. Finally tracking down Lord Chief Justice Holt in London, Smith then received even more discouraging news, that Holt "had empoured by warrant a certain person to secure the [Cotton library]." Smith hastened to Cotton House and found it completely inaccessible, owing to "two fellowes keeping possession of the house, having taken away the key from the Servant." Despite Holt's evasiveness, Smith's real opponent was plain to him: "This is H^s contrivance."

Hanbury had moved quickly to place Smith in check. He tried for an equally rapid checkmate, next; returning to London on September 21, Smith was greeted with a warrant demanding his library keys. The practiced resister was not to be swept from the board quite so easily though. The following morning, he argued his case before Holt. According to Smith, the Lord Chief Justice was far from impartial, asking pointedly "what would the world say, if they should commit the custody of the Library to such an one?" Yet this scarcely constituted a firm legal argument. Later the same day, Smith updated Robert Cotton of Gedding once more, with positive news to share: "I keep the key stil, and am like to keep it, til my Lord Keeper and Mr Harley come to towne."

Yet the other trustees, if less overtly committed to Smith's removal, were for the most part still indisposed to favor his non-conformism. Other than Robert Cotton, Smith's main support was Samuel Pepys, who was not on the board of trustees but might conceivably wield some influence among them. Even Pepys was in talks with another candidate, however. At the same time William Hanbury had begun moving directly against Smith, Humfrey Wanley had attempted to outmaneuver both men behind the scenes, writing to Pepys on September 15. Wanley succeeded in drawing the old courtier into a correspondence, and the end result was promising. Pepys stood by his intent to support his old acquaintance Smith, with one important caveat: he promised to transfer his lobbying efforts to Wanley in the event that Smith's candidacy proved unviable owing to "the matter of the oaths." Given the inevitability that Holt and other trustees would oppose a non-juror, Wanley had won an ally. He would still need the support of the trustees, themselves. But they were about to provide him invaluable assistance simply by default.

Hanbury seemed best poised to benefit from a quick decision, whereas Wanley's erudition and persuasion might win out if only given enough time; the library trustees proceeded to give him just that. Months and then a year passed by, and the trustees moved at a pace so deliberate it bordered on sluggish. Smith, truly concerned for the library, urged them to take greater interest, but the trustees were settling into the habits of the committee at its worst. Their agenda consisted of studies, reports, meetings, memoranda, and more meetings.

Wanley was only too happy to play up to the trustees' preference for bureaucratic pomp. By 1703, he had ingratiated himself sufficiently to lead a subcommittee charged with inspecting the library. Wanley proposed not merely an inspection or survey of its contents but a completely new cataloging; obviously, he still dreamed of supplanting Smith's version with the benefit of total access to the collection. Smith, however, refused to go away. Having admitted the value of his experience to the committee's tasks, the trustees permitted him a place among its number, and there he fought tooth and nail against Wanley's ambitions. Smith claimed poor health to shorten visits to the library; he argued that examination of the loose charters should wait until after the board selected a librarian; he even, so the undoubtedly much-tested committee later recorded, "carried of to his own Lodgings those [charters] which he found to be of the greatest value, for their Security and better Preservation."

In the face of Smith's bewildering tenacity, Wanley's reactions became somewhat more barbed. Upon finally getting his committee's report settled, he provided each trustee with a copy, and even resorted to delivering the Lord Keeper's copy "very neatly bound in Turkey Leather." Within the fine binding, though, he delivered a subtle condemnation of Smith's librarianship. Wanley had been unable to win support for producing an entirely new catalog, rather than updating Smith's, so he took every opportunity to point out the latter's shortcomings: items listed but missing, items noted as missing but present, new items added but unrecorded, "not to mention those which lie upon the Ground, and are not yet placed." Smith's rival did not overlook the minor defeat over the charters, either, noting that "We inspected these Charters, and find some of them to be wanting and others misplaced."

Wanley was growing more and more confident of himself, and more and more determined to secure the trustees' favor. He concentrated his efforts particularly on the Speaker of the House, Robert Harley. Eileen Joy suggests that Harley may actually have played a key role in blocking Wanley's ambitions for a new catalog; she writes in *British Library Journal* that as a voracious collector himself, "it is likely he had a special interest in a less than detailed inventory of antique manuscripts and state papers that he may have been hoping to eventually acquire for his own library." If so, Wanley saw opportunity rather than offense. Soon after turning in his committee report, he was inviting Harley for personally guided visits to the library. A few months later, Wanley proposed that His Majesty's Government might greatly enhance its new library by purchasing that left by its founder's old friend, Sir Simonds D'Ewes. This collection was also much to Harley's interest, and upon the treasury showing little enthusiasm to bankroll its purchase, Wanley helpfully set to work brokering a sale to the speaker. Upon the sale's completion in 1705, the trustees still had not selected a new librarian. But Humfrey Wanley had every reason to anticipate that he would soon take charge of a magnificent bibliophile's treasure.

Wanley was correct. His efforts indeed made him librarian of a collection that, in time, formed a cornerstone of a true British national library. Wanley erred solely in believing it would be the Cotton library. The trustees finally announced their choice in June 1706. Some 256 years later *The Times Literary Supplement* recalled the affair in a lengthy feature by P.L. Heyworth, who concluded with a quote from Edward Edwards: "Hanbury—by a very undesirable plurality—was a Trustee as well as Keeper."

Heyworth found little record of precisely how Hanbury

came from behind to frustrate all Wanley's work. Possibly Wanley's moment had come and gone; delay had allowed Wanley to obtain the support of Samuel Pepys, but further delay had cost whatever value it may have represented, as Pepys died in May 1703. More likely, Wanley simply took on the wrong game in the first place. Heyworth deplores Hanbury's appointment as "the spoils of single-minded self-serving and tireless intrigue," and all these things it may have been. It was also effective. If Wanley was always a dark horse candidate, Hanbury simply rigged the race.

By no means did Wanley go unrewarded. Robert Harley certainly appreciated the young dynamo's energy and ability, and put Wanley to work as his own librarian. It's at least conceivable that Harley was in fact so impressed, he made only token efforts on Wanley's behalf, in order to preserve him for his own library. Such is pure speculation, but whatever its origins, responsibility for the Harley library was a fine second prize. As library keeper for Robert and his son Edward Harley, Wanley helped assemble a matchless collection from the choice pickings of Britain and much of western Europe. The product of his labors eventually entered the British Museum upon its founding, passing in time to the British Library, where it remains honored as "one of the most outstanding collections" of the entire institution.

Thomas Smith enjoyed no such direct consolation. The trustees' decision was effectively the end of his road, with little waiting beyond but disappointment and obscurity, at least for Smith personally. His critical association with one of the great English-language collections eventually revived his memory, to an extent. Many of his papers are not only preserved at the Bodleian Library, but still studied, and if posterity has not always been generous to Smith, his work has not gone unrecognized.

The real loser of the contest was, in the end, the Cotton library itself. During the years of delay by its alleged guardians, the trustees, Sir John's extraordinary gift mostly sat locked away and useless. The modest revival for the library had been snuffed out. Visiting in 1703, the trustees themselves observed many items "which have already suffered great hurt, and will be utterly spoiled if care be not taken of them." They still delayed another three years anyway, and then turned the library's care over to a poorly qualified political appointee. Summarizing the outgoing librarian's view of Hanbury, Colin Tite writes that "The picture [that emerges] from Smith's papers is of a representative of the devil on earth." Smith had ample reason to see his antagonist in the worst light possible, of course, but focusing on Hanbury alone misses something fundamental. Regardless of what threat Hanbury posed in the way of active harm, the library's other trustees had already passively betrayed its charter for years, before his first day. What had survived hostile governments and warring factions might yet perish through dull, ordinary carelessness.

EX LIBRIS
THE JULIUS WORK CALENDAR
Julius A VI

A RELATIVELY MODEST HYMNAL, in most respects, Julius A VI is notable primarily for a 1,000-year-old calendar found at the front. A number of interesting stories about not only this manuscript but the Cotton library, itself, emerge in considering the calendar, how it came to be there, and what makes it significant.

The antiquity of the calendar alone makes it noteworthy. Probably created around 1020 at Canterbury, it is a rare survivor of pre-Norman England; the Cotton library houses a relatively large portion of all the documents remaining from that era, a major component of the collection's own enduring interest to scholars. Even within this context, the Julius calendar is unusual. It is a "perpetual calendar"—a kind of parchment app for calculating the dates of each month's floating holidays in any given year—and medieval scriptoria produced many similar documents. But the Julius calendar is the earliest known Anglo-Saxon example, only two of which now survive.

It is also a "work calendar," so called for two additional features that describe the various seasonal labors of pre-industrial life. Lines of Latin verse, one for each day of the year, accompany the numbers and formulae, while each month sports a lively illustration of a corresponding task. Peasants sow fields in March, while wealthier folk enjoy September hunting, etc. All of these elements, meanwhile, likely reflect models with significance of their own. The calendar probably derives from a late classical work, though its exact source is unknown. An earlier version of the verses is known, however, and might very well have been borrowed by monks of Canterbury. It is recognized today as the Athelstan Psalter, or sometimes, the Galba Psalter—for it, too, eventually found its way to Sir Robert Cotton's collection as Galba A XVIII. The same is true of a French psalter featuring sketches of daily life that offer a very plausible model for the Julius calendar. This book was definitely in Canterbury's library around 1020, and also passed centuries later into Cotton's library as Claudius C VII. In this case, however, it also passed back out. Today, the Utrecht Psalter represents that category of items that stayed out, but happily are at least known and safe.

The Julius Hymnal, meanwhile, still carries marks of Cotton's ownership beyond its emperor pressmark name. In an essay for *Illuminating the Book: Makers & Interpreters*, Michell P. Brown points out that a note on the volume's first folio describes how Cotton himself inserted the calendar in its modern location. Brown suggests that by "restoring a characteristic medieval liturgical program" in this way, Cotton's occasionally criticized cutting and pasting demonstrated sophisticated awareness of medieval calendars' uses and associations.

More recently two other interpreters adapted the calendar, or at least its themes and illustrations, to a different context and a broad new audience. In *The Year 1000: What Life Was Like at the Turn of the First Millennium*, Robert Lacey and Danny Danziger examine the era that produced the Julius calendar, dedicating each chapter to one month of the year. Their book probably could have existed without any reference to the work calendar. But its overt reference to a real, surviving document from that distant past, and the wonderfully human character of the illustrations reproduced, undoubtedly go a long way to making Anglo-Saxon England that much more real and accessible. The result preserves and shares understanding of England's heritage, through new exploration by and for its modern descendants. Sir Robert Cotton assembled his library with just such exchanges in mind, and would no doubt be pleased that it continues to provide a bridge between the two.

CHAPTER 10

The Terrible Calamity

Years after the Cotton library trustees concluded their dubious search for a librarian, disaster struck the collection. Contemporary observers were understandably irate, afterward, and a number of them blamed the library keeper. Robert Harley's son, Edward, wrote in outrage of "the terrible calamity that has befallen the Cottonian Library through the villainy of that monster in nature…" The subject of Harley's thundering denunciation was a rather curious fit for the role of arch-villain, however. The appointed heir to generations of eager plunderers and heavy-handed royal agents was in fact a bookish official of Trinity College, Cambridge, Dr. Richard Bentley.

William Hanbury, seemingly tailor-made for such a part, had long since been and gone from the Cotton library after a remarkably short time in office, given all the years he had spent acquiring it. Treasury archives record Hanbury's resignation in late 1707, barely 18 months after his fellow trustees appointed him librarian. In that time, Hanbury had discharged his duties with some credibility, moreover. The library returned to some kind of life. Hanbury's administration arranged appraisal of Cotton House, repairs, new shelving, and most significantly of all the sale of the house to the nation in 1707. After much haggling by both sides, 6 Anne, chapter 30 rejoined the library's contents and structure under single ownership. Records also confirm fulfillment of a requirement of the original Cotton library act, the enrollment of a new catalog in the High Court of Chancery, although like the previous government catalog this is now elusive. Recent scholarship suggests it may be British Library Additional MS. 8926, a showy vellum document adorned with seals and colored silk.

The "pretentious format" that E.C. Teviotdale ascribes to this catalog calls to mind Humfrey Wanley's leather-bound report of a few years earlier, and Wanley may have aided Hanbury in some capacity. Teviotdale also suggests that MS. 8926 was based on the classified catalogs of decades earlier, though, which would point away from Wanley. Another man named John Elphinstone is more readily confirmed as occupying a deputy librarian's role from early on. In any event, Hanbury may have done relatively little on his own—a caveat that applies to activities both appropriate and otherwise.

A number of items left the Cotton library following its nationalization. Edward Edwards blames Hanbury for selling many of these, allowing at most that they may not have been formally "part of the Cottonian library, though it is plain as sunlight that a really faithful trustee would have made them part of it." Yet Hanbury acted neither independently nor uniquely. Edwards asserts that Wanley assisted in selling manuscripts from Cotton House, and as before their end buyer was Wanley's patron Robert Harley, a sitting Cotton library trustee.

William Hanbury cannot be absolved of blame, entirely. One suspects that Thomas Smith, by contrast, would have defended every last scrap of paper in Cotton House, no matter who sought to purchase them. But Hanbury, whether beckoned by new schemes or simply unenthusiastic about prospects for further self-enrichment in the library, bowed out by his second winter. The system that appointed him—and at least one individual who conspired with him—remained. When, years later, Edward Harley sought someone to blame for the Cotton library's diminution, he should have looked considerably closer to home.

Even by modern standards, the Cotton library trustees were not notably corrupt, per se. Edwards pulls few punches in *Lives of the Founders of the British Museum*, and still charges them with nothing worse than sale of some ancillary material, extraneous to the core collection. Given Sir Robert's methods in assembling the library originally, this is a lapse but not of itself a calamitous failing.

A lack of vision among the trustees was a more substantive shortcoming. The Cotton library was officially *the* national library, not only of England but, after 1707, of Great Britain. (One hundred four years after King James attempted to sell the idea of a truly United Kingdom, an economic carrot-and-stick approach had achieved what antiquarian arguments could not.) For decades the putative British library functioned, nonetheless, more like an obscure sinecure. The trustees' want of greater ambition is all the more dispiriting given the many better examples before them. The dream of a true national library had not died out with the first Society of Antiquaries. In the mid-17th century, the intellectual John Dury argued eloquently for the utility of a national library. In 1697, future "monster in nature" Richard Bentley published a *Proposal for Building a Royal Library* for public use. A decade later a doctor named Hans Sloane wrote of "great designs on foot for uniting the Queen's Library, the Cotton, and the Royal Society's together." Significantly, Sloane tempered his letter's enthusiasm, however: "How soon they may be put in practice time must discover." The instinct toward patience was not to prove misplaced.

Leading figures in government, Cotton trustees included, were in truth neither unaware of nor entirely unresponsive to such lofty goals. The great source of their failing was more mundane. For half a century and more after pledging a stewardship worthy of "the best Collection of its kind now anywhere extant" they never, ever, followed through.

They prepared a new library catalog—but it was likely just one more piece of paperwork filed away and forgotten. Despite genuine need for a new catalog even after Smith's work, and despite having Wanley champing at the bit, they did not advance the project of library cataloging at all; if Teviotdale is correct, they actually set it back by referring to much older lists.

The trustees' administration eventually joined additional collections to Cotton's, as Sloane and others hoped—but in doing so they only exacerbated other problems much more fundamental. Around 1707, the newly purchased Cotton House took receipt of the "Queen's Library" or Old Royal Library, the greatest part of those books and manuscripts assembled by successive monarchs going back to the Middle Ages. Yet the move seemed no more than an extension of another hoary crown tradition, that of stuffing documents into any government property that had space. Treasury papers also record "Gresham College, library, removal to Cotton House" for the same period, and according to Kevin Sharpe, Simonds D'Ewes's library shared space with the Cotton manuscripts for a time as well. Both reinforce an impression of Cotton House as more warehouse than library, particularly as housing D'Ewes's collection was presumably no more than a temporary convenience for the Cotton trustee who actually purchased it. The 1715 acceptance of 44 volumes of manuscripts from a Thomas Rymer was probably more of a legitimate accession to the Cotton library, but given the conditions that prevailed, it probably increased disorder and clutter as well.

The only constants of the trustees' management seemed to involve leaving no corner uncut, baking nothing more than halfway, and delaying every priority task. The best excuse one can make for them is budgetary—Queen Anne's treasury was no readier to fund a great academy than Queen Elizabeth's had been—and this merely passes blame from the trustees to the larger government. Given the prominent roles that half the trustees occupied in that government, its parsimony is a very limited excuse. It was also dubious as a financial calculation, particularly when it came to the Cotton library's home. In housing their collection, the trustees' approach might provide a perfect illustration of the adage "penny-wise, pound-foolish."

The initial plan of keeping the library within an otherwise privately occupied home never had much to recommend it. From that perspective, the trustees' purchase of Cotton House was one of their wiser moments as well as an unusually liberal one, financially. Yet the central need of the library was a secure, functional space for research and scholarship. By 1707 Cotton House no longer met these criteria, even to the extent that it ever had in the first place. The trustees knew as much, moreover. Treasury Papers from 1706 report that "The place wherein the library was contained was a narrow little room, damp, and improper for preserving the books and papers. There was only one window at each end, and the arch over one of them in a ruinous condition was ready to fall, as was also the arch upon which the room was built." The great architect Christopher Wren's own office surveyed Cotton House, and warned that proper repairs would require pulling down much of the building. His report proposed moving the library to a space in the House of Lords.

Despite Wren's alternative site being both larger and cheaper, the trustees rejected it. Instead, they sank £4,500 into the decayed Cotton House. One cannot help suspecting some degree of corrupt dealing, or at the very least conflict of interest, here, and not solely on Hanbury's part; multiple of the trustees were also members of the Cotton family from whom they were purchasing the property. One may also wonder how honestly some of the subsequent funds for repairs were disbursed, particularly as even the indolent trustees evacuated the library for safety reasons 15 years later. By then John Elphinstone, a de facto librarian as deputy to frequently absent superiors, had spent years protesting both the state of Cotton House and his own paucity of any money to meet its needs, or his own. (Once the librarian was no longer one of the trustees, the latter seem to have neglected their vague pledges of a salary for the former.) Despite its impersonal shorthand, one item in the Calendar of Treasury Papers is eye-opening for the pathetic plea it records from Elphinstone. The caretaker warned that

> the best collection of its kind now anywhere extant… of great use and service for the knowledge and preservation of our Constitution… is now contained in rooms near adjoining the river, and will perish by dampness if provision is not made for firing. Has been at charge of 35/. for firing and for cleaning the rooms, and has received no salary. 30/. a year will be but sufficient for the necessary expenses. Prays for the 35/. mentioned…

The treasury grudgingly scraped together a few bits "for defraying the charges of firing, candle, &c.," but otherwise left library and librarian to make do until 1722. By then, Dr. Richard Bentley was officially managing the library, possibly with Elphinstone's help at first; later another deputy, David Casley, began a long tenure as the manuscripts' day-to-day custodian. Bentley had his own duties as Master of Trinity College, Cambridge, though no one seems to have considered this an obstacle to his managing a library in London. He was already keeper of the Old

Royal Library when it moved into Cotton House, and the trustees seemed satisfied with entrusting all of their collections to the academically qualified and administratively convenient doctor.

Bentley did agree with the long-established consensus that Cotton House was impractical to maintain. Records from his first years as librarian noted that the doctor "refuses to be at the expense of keeping Cotton Gardens in order." Finally, the trustees stirred themselves to respond, and in 1722 the Cotton library resumed the peripatetic existence of its earliest years. It briefly returned to The Strand, which it had left a century before. Along with recently appended companions, most of the same volumes now moved into Essex House, leased by the trustees for seven years.

At the end of the lease the library was off once more. Pointed concerns about a risk of fire may have spurred what amounted to remarkable haste, compared with the 20 years the trustees had taken to seek better accommodations than Cotton House. Simon Keynes, writing in *British Library Journal*, proposes that "latterly the landlord at Essex House had begun to agitate for payment of his rent;" this may also have played a role. At all events, late in 1729 the Board of Works brought to the library's weary administrators and long-suffering paymasters the momentous news "that we have heard of a House in Westminster by its situation much more safe from fire & more commodious in all other respects belonging to Lord Ashburnham…"

The Westminster mansion called Ashburnham House had multiple advantages as a home for the Cotton library. Many of these were mainly symbolic, it must be acknowledged, but their combined symbolism makes a compelling impression. The home incorporated part of a prior's residence, from a medieval monastery, closed by the Dissolution to which the library owed much of its own origin. The newer building that greeted the Cotton library was designed by a disciple of Inigo Jones, an early library patron. The site itself, in Little Dean's Yard, had once been well known to Sir Robert himself; as a student at nearby Westminster School, the young Cotton had first discovered history's fascination at the feet of his mentor William Camden.

If library trustees perceived an encouraging sign in such resonant links to the collection's past, Ashburnham House offered little obvious reason to dismiss it. The house was indeed capacious, a valuable trait given all the material that had already joined the Cotton library in just a few decades. Symbolism aside, Westminster was probably a better location than the Strand for the archive of state papers that Sir Robert had amassed. Little Dean's Yard is, on the other hand, something of a cloistered space, but as the trustees had never shown great concern with an inviting reception for the general public, this was not necessarily a deficiency particular to Ashburnham House. In general, the property secured in early 1730 was no worse than those sites preceding it, and may have been at least marginally better judging from the reports on Cotton and Essex Houses. The Board of Works had actually recommended Ashburnham House, by contrast.

More than one retrospective account has commented on the unfortunate coincidence of the house's name. If Ashburnham House foreshadowed any threat from fire, though, it was realistically no greater threat than most of London. Justin Pollard's description of the house as "an ancient pile of tinder-dry wood" could have applied to the greater part of the city in 1731, and as Pollard notes later in *Alfred the Great*, keeping open flames amid that pile was simply a fact of life. Cool, damp and frequently gray London required a source of light and heat to function. Without ready alternatives, people made do with fire and accepted its attendant risks even after much of the city was incinerated in 1666. Modest reforms had followed the Great Fire, but no more than that.

The Cotton Library, if it was in the city at all that fateful September decades earlier, had remained safe in Westminster and untouched by the conflagration. At most, an item or two on loan had been lost, and decades later John Elphinstone's urgent pleas for his charge's safety concerned threat from damp, in the *absence* of flame. Responsible custodianship of the library *needed* a fire burning, at least somewhere in the same building. As a policy, this was mere practicality, and no reasonable observer would have suggested otherwise. The subsequent administration of Dr. Richard Bentley certainly did not.

For the Cotton library, Friday, October 22, 1731 began as an unremarkable day. To most appearances it also ended that way, with same the slow, even dozy character that had typified the years since the rival librarians' intrigues ended. As the occupants of Ashburnham House settled in for the night the only obvious anomaly was the presence of the current librarian on-site. Dr. Bentley's duties at Trinity College required his presence in Cambridge most of the time. As a practical matter, he had turned the role of librarian over to his son years before. Whether or not the senior Bentley's "resignation" was official is questionable—contemporaries still considered him responsible for the collection—but most of the time his son and a deputy were the only library staff, excepting a few household servants.

Dr. Bentley and his wife happened to be visiting London that weekend, however. Their son having charge of a commodious mansion, they naturally availed themselves of a chance to spend some time together and avoid the trouble of an inn. Ashburnham House was entirely comfortable; the weather had turned a bit cool for Dr. Bentley, but a crackling fire had warmed the evening splendidly. As the Bentleys turned in, everything seemed in order for a restful night.

Awareness that something had gone wrong must have dawned gradually and hazily. A figurative haze may be assumed, given the time; it was near 2 a.m. and everyone had been asleep for hours. A further, literal haze must have added to the Bentleys' disorientation even as it provided a clue to the reports of other sleep-dulled senses. Eventually, Dr. Bentley awoke fully to awareness of "a great Smoak." Compared with modern counterparts, the nose of an 18th-century Londoner must have been relatively inured to indoor fires, but something was clearly amiss now. Some part of the house was apparently on fire.

This by itself was a situation amiss, but not unknown, and no cause for instant panic. The mayor of London, roused in the night by report of fire in 1666, had responded dismissively: "Pish! A woman might piss it out!" The subsequent catastrophe argued against so entirely casual an attitude, but the Bentleys and their staff took much more prompt interest. They readily found the source of the smoke. The fire banked up earlier for Dr. Bentley had spread to a wooden mantle-tree running atop the fireplace. Afterward the doctor was uncertain "whether he did not leave the Blower on the Stove when he went to Bed," but at the moment it did not matter. The flames had already spread to the various wooden structures around the fireplace—the frame, the wainscott, the wall studs—and reached the floorboards of the room above. A first note of real concern may have sounded as someone voiced the implication: that room contained the Cotton manuscripts.

The occupants of Ashburnham House attempted to extinguish the fire. Unfortunately, the tools on hand were simply too limited. The flames had spread beyond them. Finally Dr. Bentley acknowledged that the situation had become an emergency. The Bentleys roused neighbors; someone sent a boy to alert the nearest fire company. Meanwhile, Dr. Bentley began the most important work. With Casley and whoever else was brave enough to join them the nearly 70-year-old doctor headed upstairs, away from safety, to start moving books and papers outside. The time had arrived to evacuate the library.

Even now Dr. Bentley remained unhurried. A fire was spreading through Ashburnham House and it was beyond his control; someone was calling out a fire company, but their response time was anyone's guess, and of course their aqueous intervention could also prove damaging to a document archive; meanwhile, flames were steadily burning through the library floor from below. But the library room itself was not on fire, per se, so Dr. Bentley decided to rescue the furniture.

The treasury had spent good money on bookcases—whereas the manuscripts in them had cost the exchequer nothing—and the doctor's concern for their investment was exemplary. All the same, those fine, solid cases were also large, heavy and replaceable. Dragging them down a flight of stairs and out of the house took considerable effort and time, both of which might seemingly have been better dedicated to the countless irreplaceable documents the bookcases contained. The floor was growing warm and emitting smoke, yet priceless volumes like the Cotton Genesis sat unmoved as people struggled to save wooden cases. At best, one may allow that no one was thinking clearly, and perhaps in the confusion Dr. Bentley hoped to evacuate the library more efficiently by carrying out the shelves whole rather than emptying them. Calmer reflection probably would have recognized such a calculation as misguided, and for that reason are fire drills planned and conducted in advance. But in 1731, such basic precautions were unknown, at any rate to those meant to safeguard the Cotton library.

The library's first disaster plan emerged on the fly, instead.

Leading an impromptu committee in a genuine smoke-filled room, Dr. Bentley introduced new policies as events warranted. As he and other rescuers sweated, and strained, and probably cursed with increasing frequency, circumstances at last forced him to concede his save-the-shelves policy as unviable. As summarized later, "the Fire increasing still, and the Engines sent for not coming so soon as could be wished, and Several of the Backs of the Presses being already on fire," Dr. Bentley resolved a new policy: Get the library collection outside. Immediately.

Rescuers dispensed with carrying material down the stairs entirely at this point. Grabbing armfuls from the more accessible shelves they hurled ancient charters and illuminated bibles and medieval chronicles out the window. In the courtyard below, the fire company finally joined the commotion. Above, however, the choking and coughing men still within the burning library understood that whatever they left behind them was unlikely to escape at all. Most of what remained had caught fire, by then. The fronts of some shelves were covered in flame. Dr. Bentley and his son took up hatchets and smashed open the backs; they pried away splintered boards and grabbed whatever they could reach. The volumes themselves were undoubtedly smoldering in many cases, and possibly beginning to drip as the heat melted fat of a long-dead cow or sheep from vellum pages.

Whether Bentley realized it or not, the fire company had their engine set up and a stream of water targeted Ashburnham House. They would contain the blaze to that building and extinguish it in time—yet they were not going to extinguish it quickly. The "House in Westminster by its situation much more safe from fire" *was* one enormous fire. If any voices carried above the noise, they had probably cried for some time for Dr. Bentley and son to save themselves and get *out*. Heeding either these or else internal voices of self-preservation, the last men in Ashburnham House took the advice and fled. Leaping from a window by one account, they reached the courtyard and safety; all that was most important was safe from the fire. No one lost his or her life.

As for the many inanimate if irreplaceable items in the house, certainty was impossible for the time being. Most of two large collections and pieces of others lay scattered around Little Dean's Yard in chaotic heaps. From a cataloging perspective, it was an entire additional catastrophe. But at least the bulk of material would survive. Though disaster found the Bentley administration poorly prepared, they had made a heroic effort to redeem the failing.

As he looked around at the results, Dr. Bentley clutched one last book saved from the Royal Library, an important early bible known as the Codex Alexandrinus. Whatever remained behind of that collection, and the Cottons', was beyond rescuing. Determining just what had perished and what survived would not be easy. Extensive study would be necessary, beginning as soon as possible, and even then precise answers might not emerge for years. In some cases, the exact losses of that smoky, confused night in October might never be known.

CHAPTER 11

Sifting the Ash

THE COTTON LIBRARY FIRE significantly damaged the world of English letters. Andrew Prescott, who has written extensively on the fire and its consequences in *Sir Robert Cotton as Collector*, calls it "perhaps the greatest bibliographic disaster of modern times in Britain." Yet the fire gave, also. There can be no comparison with what it took away, but so dramatic an event has inspired new and occasionally wonderful writing in circles that may seem otherwise dry and dull.

A Reverend Thomas Fitzgerald, affiliated with Westminster School at the time of the fire, was moved to verse. *Upon the Burning of the Cottonian Manuscripts at Ashburnham House* reflects on the documents' survival through invasions and religious purges only to perish by domestic accident. Justin Pollard's detailed account of the fire in *Alfred the Great* offers many trenchant remarks; in the library policy leading up to the fire, he sees "the usual political solution: ignore it and hope that it went away. And some of it was about to do just that." Describing the scene immediately following the fire, by contrast, he poignantly writes of Dr. Bentley and others standing helplessly as "blistered and burnt fragments of paper and parchment" gradually fell around them "like black snow." Prescott notes a tiny element of humor in his findings, however bleak; as a rule, the Caesars did not die comfortably and "it is almost as if the books in the affected presses were doomed to suffer ends as unfortunate as those suffered by the emperors after whom the presses were named."

After nearly three centuries, however, the most remarkable writing on the Cotton library fire may still be some of the earliest. In 1732 the House of Commons published *A Report from the Committee Appointed to View the Cottonian Library, and such of the Publick Records of this Kingdom, as they think proper, and to Report to the House the Condition thereof, together with what they shall judge fit to be done for the better Reception, Preservation, and more convenient use of the same.* At more than 200 pages, it arguably delivers on the ambition of its title. The report presents a detailed account of the fire itself, invaluable to every study that has followed including the present work. Salvage efforts also receive attention, as do the first attempts at accounting for every item damaged, destroyed and spared by the fire. The committee even makes a brave attempt at going beyond a purely reactionary approach for once, studying at some length how other "Publick Records" might be shielded from similar disasters, to which most of them were easily as vulnerable as the libraries at Ashburnham House.

For all that the parliamentary report includes, though, its most commendable aspect may be its one notable omission—finger-pointing. Bentley, "that monster in nature," did not escape criticism entirely, of course. For his own part, Dr. Bentley perceived in the fire "the Nemesis of Cotton's Ghost to punish the Neglect in taking due Care of his noble Gift to the Publick," a curiously ambiguous assignment of blame given the doctor's own relationship to the library. In general, however, a spirit of cooperative rebuilding seems to have characterized both the report and the events it describes. Rather than becoming scapegoats, Bentley and his son played active roles in the initial salvage, and remained involved with the library afterward; the library's various custodians seemed united in a preference for useful activity and setting the past aside. Whether this represented noble intentions, or naïve overoptimism, time would reveal.

In the immediate aftermath of the fire, at least, the British government responded with ardor. Much credit for this new resolve belongs to the fine leadership by example of Arthur Onslow. First elected Speaker of the House in 1728, Onslow's eventual three-decade career as speaker earned praise for responsible and meticulous management. The *Oxford Dictionary of National Biography* describes him as "a man of rare integrity in an age of corruption." It also notes his deep interest in precedent and procedural detail, both of which would have pleased Sir Robert Cotton, as would a campaign for the House of Commons to begin printing its journals.

In the days and weeks after fire crispy-fried some of Cotton's own state papers and other volumes, Arthur Onslow took up the work of salvaging what remained with Cottonian enthusiasm. He arrived quickly at the scene of disaster. Living nearby, he could hardly have avoided making an appearance for form's sake. But Onslow just as quickly went to work organizing a recovery effort, establishing early the tone of taking responsibility rather than casting blame. The speaker supplied practical tasks to Bentley and others likely grateful for something to do, besides dwelling on the catastrophe they had failed to prevent. There was much to do.

The most urgent priority was shelter for the shelves and loose heaps of documents left homeless. During the initial evacuation, those present had moved some of these into the nearby apartment of the Captain of Westminster School, and others to the Little Cloisters. Once all that would be rescued had been, search commenced for better temporary quarters. By Sunday's end, the remnant collections were "convey'd into the great Boarding House opposite to Ashburnham-House." Finally, on Monday the government men arranged to move everything once more into a new Westminster School dormitory. Some of those doing the moving must have felt hard-used by that point, particularly those who had already carried the same items two or three times in 48 hours. The new dormitory, too, could only be yet another temporary stop. But it would do for a while, and provide a space for other priorities. Having addressed the immediate source of harm and found at least short-term shelter, the rescuers turned to treating the wounded.

Most if not all of the documents left behind in Ashburnham House were lost, while those that had escaped completely unscathed would keep. Coins and various other artifacts were also for the most part undamaged by intense, but relatively brief, exposure to heat and water. The third category, in between intact items and total losses, was a more complicated story.

In some cases the distinction between damaged and destroyed seemed irrelevant. The greater part of the printed books, mainly from the Royal Library, were unreadable; paper pages scorch easily, and have little chance in a large fire unless removed quickly. Documents on vellum or parchment, including most of the Cotton collection, responded somewhat differently though. Many had also suffered extended exposure to the fire. The pages of *Beowulf* offer a famous example of the singed edges that resulted. But the dense hardwood bookcases for which Dr. Bentley had shown such concern had slowed the fire's advance, as had the volumes' tight fit within the purpose-built shelves, which limited fire's access to its oxygen fuel. Instead, the heat of the surrounding fire went where the fire itself could not, and its effects proved the real challenge for conservators.

Most fat should be scraped away during parchment-making, but where fat had remained it seeped out and then congealed, sometimes forming a brittle crust. The collagen that made up most of the manuscripts' substance responds more slowly to heat but it, too, has a threshold, and volumes that reached it suffered lasting and sometimes bizarre effects. The British Library's Medieval Manuscripts blog has examined some of these, still evident centuries later. As conservator Ann Tomalak explains, the key to parchment's fate in such conditions is the rapid contraction of collagen fibers upon reaching a crucial threshold, the shrinkage temperature. So sudden is the fibers' irreversible tightening that parts of a page shrink at different times, as heat gradually spreads inward from the outer edges. The staggered pulling produces a wavy appearance at the same time as it leaves the once-flexible skin hard and brittle, particularly at the edges. In some cases, the 1731 fire's combined effects on collagen and fat effectively sealed volumes shut. In others, including a Royal Library manuscript preserved at the British Library today, the result was stranger still. When opened the scorched and warped pages spread like a fan; Prescott offers a memorable comparison to "an irradiated armadillo."

The first people to consider these pitiful objects knew little of the intricate chemistry involved, much less of irradiated *Dasypodidae*. They turned to the expertise they had, and did what they could. Onslow formed a semi-official triage committee, including Dr. Bentley, David Casley, and keepers of various government archives. Documents damaged by fire were by no means unprecedented, and these men probably brought together a credible body of expertise, such as it existed in 1731. If their efforts appear rudimentary, it was mostly as a result of how little could actually be done.

The scale of the task before Onslow's committee seemed massive. Very reasonably, they broke it down into sections. They sorted out the intact volumes from the damaged, then sorted these into fire-damaged and water-damaged. Their first efforts focused on the latter category, and, ironically, involved exposing documents to the heat of a fire once more. Many of the last volumes out of Ashburnham House, and possibly a fortunate few that survived inside, had been doused as firefighters set to work. Mold might set in if these weren't dried quickly. The parchments, painstakingly stretched flat in earlier ages, could also begin reverting to the shape of their animal origin. Onslow's committee needed to dry all of these items out. Some volumes, only slightly damp, they unbound and then hung up as individual leaves to dry like clothing. Others had already soaked too thoroughly for too long; air-drying might be too slow, so conservators turned to the only tool that could drive out moisture more rapidly. They placed them near a fire—presumably under careful supervision.

After containing the threat from damp, the remaining damaged items appeared more or less stable. The committee prioritized, next, those problems that seemed within their power to solve. Paper books with only mild damage, mainly stains from ash and smoke, they also treated somewhat like laundry. They unbound these and soaked the pages in water, followed by an alum solution "to strengthen and fortify them," then line-drying. Some of the parchment manuscripts, "so hardened, and shriveled up, as not to be legible in their present Condition," also received a gentle soaking in hopes of loosening up the cockled pages once more. Onslow's committee hired a bookbinder to assist with all of the unbinding and washing, and, as much as possible, to rebind volumes afterward.

For parchment volumes left heat-sealed by the fire, the conservators ultimately resorted to even less sophisticated means. The experts resolved that "the glewy Substance which has been fired out upon the Edges, be taken off by the fingers carefully," and then the leaves separated one by one; "an Ivory folder" emerged as the most useful aid.

Viewed with the benefit of considerable hindsight, the committee work of late 1731 had its blind spots, as will be considered in due course. Yet the actions that they did perform hold up remarkably well. In many ways the primitive simplicity of their efforts was a virtue. Many of the "advanced" techniques applied to the same problems in subsequent eras eventually did more harm than good. As of the early 21st century, conservators have generally settled on simple methods recognizably similar to Onslow's experts'. Per Tomalak, current best practices consist mainly of moistening cockled parchment to restore flexibility and then flattening it as effectively as possible. Modern conservators employ controlled humidity rather than immersion in water, but like Onslow's team they attempt little active restoration beyond this. They, too, do what they can and then move on to caring for documents in the condition they are in, and preserving them for the future.

Onslow's committee gradually shifted from responding to disaster, to understanding it. They had performed triage on the survivors, sorting and caring for their injuries, and their bookbinder was slowly sewing up wounds. The rest of the committee could begin counting the dead.

A perfect inventory of losses to the fire was all but impossible, owing mainly to the lack of a perfect inventory of holdings before it. In the decades since Smith's *Catalogus* of 1696, official and would-be custodians had produced multiple updates, lists and alternate guides to the Cotton manuscripts. None of these was perfect even when new, and unsurprisingly the profusion of sources only added to confusion, as did the presence of multiple other collections among the trustees' holdings. By 1731, most of them were probably mingled to some degree with Cotton items and none of them were cataloged any more completely. Thomas Smith received a minor vindication as Dr. Bentley and his colleagues turned to the *Catalogus* as their primary reference, probably because it was the one inventory both completed by an intimate of the collection and formally published. It was, nonetheless, also 35 eventful years out of date.

As a result, the committee's conclusions were inevitably an estimate. Officially, they recognized 958 volumes in the Cotton library before the great fire. Of these, they reported 114 "totally destroyed," and described a further 98 as "considerably damaged." As raw numbers, these seem mercifully limited compared with the possibility of utter catastrophe, and those who had seen the fire or the remains of Ashburnham House understandably saw cause for relief. In their report to Parliament the committee expressed themselves "surprized, that so few of the Manuscripts and Curiosities belonging to the said Library were consumed or defaced." Subsequent scholarship has revealed errors in their assessment, but the net result of these and later restoration work has been an even greater survival rate. As of 1997, Prescott found that at least some fragment of nearly every volume from the Cotton library is "available for consultation today." Of complete victims, the fire may now claim but 13, mostly from the miserable Emperor Otho's press. (Supporting Prescott's suggestion of a historical sympathy; following a defeat in battle the luckless Otho stabbed himself after lasting just three months as emperor.)

A list of bound volumes does not begin to convey the depth of the Cotton library, however, and such accounting is equally incapable of conveying the depth of its losses. Most of Sir Robert's volumes, as well as those possibly assembled by Dugdale or another successor, are massive compendiums of individual manuscripts. Many more documents, including some of the collection's most valuable, never formed part of a bound volume at all. Viewed at this level the losses at Ashburnham House were truly heartbreaking. An appendix to the committee's report describes individual items' damage, and even though it considers bound volumes as a unit it makes depressing reading. Here and there, the committee suggested some prospect of future use. Much more often, their notes are similar and blunt: "A Bundle of loose Leaves, burnt at the Ends and Sides; not of much use" ... "This Book is so shrivell'd up, as to be quite useless" ... "This Book is a burnt Lump."

The centuries since have permitted partial repair of many such lumps and fragments. Time has also permitted a greater appreciation of them as unique pieces of history, however, rather than simply bundles. Pollard suggests that "The list of [lost] contents reads like a roll call of the dead." Many of the entries are Anglo-Saxon items, including a biography of Alfred the Great written by a priest named Asser, who lived during Alfred's reign and knew him personally; Pollard and other scholars of the great king are left with only a much later and heavily edited copy. Asser's biography is joined by multiple medieval chronicles, each one an irreplaceable record. Of an even earlier illuminated Northumbrian gospel book, produced in the 8th century, only bare fragments remain. The *Beowulf* manuscript survives with burnt, brittle edges, yet this places it among the fortunate, compared with other pre-Norman items.

Losses from other categories are equally striking, even if they are fewer. The papal bull awarding Henry VIII the title "Fidei Defensor"—a title still cherished by his successors despite many ironies—survives only as a charred relic. The Book of Genesis equally cherished by the Cotton family is now but a handful of scorched pieces. Fire also damaged one of Sir Robert's two copies of Magna Carta; the harm is particularly regrettable to one of just four that survive anywhere, as well as the only one retaining its great seal. The seal remains, but only as a featureless blob.

One of the best things Onslow's committee did was to keep

nearly everything, even when "not of much use" seemed all that could be said. Loose leaves that no one could identify, "burnt lumps," and even scraps; even if the experts could not see any hope of recovery, they had seen more than enough wastage. Their methods remained makeshift by the standards of modern curation, reflecting the old archival policy of bulk storage in any convenient space. One of the committee archivists, Reverend William Whiston, suggested greater care to preserve what organization might yet remain, but his colleagues found this an ambition too far. Ruined books and leftover fragments went into bibliographic junk drawers. But they did not go to junk yards, at least. They remained part of the library, where someone might yet learn something from them. Future conservators could perhaps restore what Whiston, etc., could not; future scholars could study them as artifacts of a historic event. If nothing else the fragments could also offer a reminder, from that moment on, of the price of carelessness.

Toward the end of his committee's work, Arthur Onslow prepared two new documents that would, like the blackened leftovers, memorialize the terrible fire, but would also look ahead to recovery and better stewardship. One was the committee report itself. After recounting what went wrong at Ashburnham House the report invited Parliament to consider the vulnerability of all "the Repositories of the publick Records of this Kingdom." Inspection found most of them worse fire-traps than any of the Cotton library's various homes. The Court of Common Pleas' records office seemed "almost too ruinous to be repaired;" the archives in Westminster Chapter House stood over vaults "said to be filled with spirituous Liquors," while below those in the White Tower were "Stores of Gunpowder belonging to the Office of Ordnance." Perhaps most ominous of all, within the

King's Bench Treasury records, "Communication between the Rooms is interrupted by a Painter's Shop, wherein is a Stove-Chimney." Meanwhile, the Cotton library and its associated collections remained camped in a dormitory.

The committee proposed sensible and obvious reforms to all of these circumstances. Their suggestions for the nascent national library were, in particular, all long overdue. To replace Ashburnham House they recommended returning the collection to its home of so many decades, and finally funding a new Cotton House rather than migrating in search of bargain space in one older building after another. Reinforcing the call for a proper, active library rather than a warehouse with absentee management, they urged that "a proper Stipend ought to be granted to the Keeper of the said Library, to engage him to… greater Care and Diligence, for which there is at present little or no Allowance." As throughout his efforts since the fire, Onslow was ready to look past Dr. Bentley's individual faults in favor of addressing a larger picture, in much greater need of correction.

Onslow's second new document pursued a much more modest rehabilitation, as well as one largely symbolic. The symbolism of the third Cotton Magna Carta was, all the same, considerable. Cotton Charter XIII 31a, dispatched by Sir Edward Dering to his troubled friend a century earlier, appeared to be in poor condition itself after the fire. In addition to its melted great seal, the committee experts worried that the text itself could deteriorate further and might "not much longer continue legible." The Speaker of the House therefore directed its transcription while most of the original's text remained. A copyist transcribed the damaged charter onto new parchment, consulting the library's other copy where words were in doubt. Keepers of records checked the work carefully, then formally endorsed the new copy on its reverse. Alongside their testimonial, the new Magna Carta briefly recorded the circumstances of its own creation 517 years after King John's reluctant acknowledgement of voices other than his own.

The new Magna Carta could not replace the original, and in a sense was entirely unnecessary. While many Cotton documents remained unique exemplars, by 1732 transcripts of Magna Carta were plentiful, and its text was in no danger. Yet the damaged original itself was in some sense no more than symbolic, just like all of the 1215 charters. People had (belatedly) kept and cared for them for that very reason. Magna Carta arguably never had any significance, by itself, except as reminder of a promise worth the perpetual effort necessary to enforce it. Onslow's commission of a new copy very consciously symbolized much the same commitment. The report underscored this, majestically directing that the new charter "remain in the Library *ad perpetuum Rei Memoriam.*"

The library's custodians observed the letter of that promise. The transcript has, in fact, remained with the Cotton library ever since. In the near term, however, that meant remaining in makeshift storage at Westminster School with no clear plan for proper accommodation. In this and nearly every other way the government trustees betrayed the spirit of the new Magna Carta, and all of Onslow's work. Despite all that had happened the pull of old habits reasserted itself once again. Colin Tite writes that Onslow's report met the same fate as so many other road maps to a worthy national library: "Its proposals and good intentions— the erection of a library building, the proper payment of a library keeper—were, naturally enough, ignored…" Parliament and its trustees went back to ignoring their collections. If the fire had any deeper impact on Dr. Bentley it mattered little, as he soon left the library entirely. His replacements evinced no more interest in caring for their charge than Parliament did in funding it.

Onslow's own interest in the Cotton library remained sincere, as events would reveal in time. But he was Speaker of the House of Commons, with many other responsibilities that he also took seriously, and only limited power to accomplish them all. He had brought the collection back from the brink of disaster and tried to point the way to genuine renewal, but could do no more than that, without help. History's continuity was approaching obstinacy; for generations, ambitious plans for a national library had been plentiful, and now at last they had an interested and effective potential foreman in government. Yet the old inertia continued all the same. Some crucial x-factor capable of changing the equation was still missing. Until someone stepped forward to supply it, both the dream and the substance that were Sir Robert Cotton's legacies would continue to languish, forlorn and neglected.

PART THREE
RESTORATION

CHAPTER 12

Dr. Sloane's Museum

OF ALL THE BEQUESTS to Britain's national collections, Sir Hans Sloane's may be the most extraordinary. Its riches are considerable, certainly. Over his lifetime Sloane amassed 50,000 documents, in addition to medals, coins, and botanical specimens. Its influence on the destiny of the greater collection it joined is even more significant, for the long-overdue transformation of the Cotton and other national archives into a true institution owes more to the last will of Hans Sloane than to any other single factor. That will stands out among the other founding contributions most of all, however, for one remarkable peculiarity: Sloane made his great "bequest" contingent upon payment, to his heirs, of £22,000.

This is an unusual sort of bequest, to say the least. Stranger still is the fact that Britain's government accepted it, and followed through on the ambitious hopes of its "donor," after decades of indifference to genuine gifts made toward the same end. Against that background, the wonder is not that Sloane sought payment for his own contribution to a national library, but that he did not give up on the concept entirely. The Sloane who wrote in 1707 of "great designs on foot for uniting the Queen's Library, the Cotton, and the Royal Society's," and mused on "How soon they may be put in practice" might well have been aghast had he foreseen that the answer was "nearly 50 years."

In the decades in between, as Sloane built up his own collection into a grand but unofficial museum, Parliament and its trustees seemed determined to prevent Britain's official collections from amounting to anything at all. In 1707, the crown entrusted them with major parts of its own library to join the irreplaceable treasure donated by Sir John Cotton. The trustees then pushed these and other smaller gifts around London like a stateless exile, before nearly presiding over their immolation in 1731.

Despite this mismanagement, and abject failure to keep promises made to previous donors, more came forward. Historian Thomas Madox left his collections to the nation's pseudo-library, as did an obscure figure named Arthur Edwards. The *Dictionary of National Biography* finds little trace of Edwards as an individual beyond service in the Horse Guards and membership in the revived Society of Antiquaries, but it awards him an entry for his generous gift to the Cotton library. In addition to a collection, by volume at least, much larger than Cotton's own, Edwards pledged shelves, portraits of various dignitaries, and £7,000 "to erect and build such a house as may be most likely to preserve that library as much as can be from all accidents." Given the recent fire that undoubtedly motivated Edwards, even the Cotton library trustees might have found this offer impossible to ignore. Their collections still needed a new home when Edwards died in 1743. Yet Edwards' will reserved the money as a life-interest, and in the event, the beneficiary's longevity prevented any use by the trustees for decades. As before, fate seemed set on thwarting such good intentions.

Hans Sloane turned 83 the year that Arthur Edwards' bequest became the latest such plan to go awry. Since his birth in Ireland, the same year that Britain abandoned its republican experiment and recalled the Stuarts, he had enjoyed almost unbroken prosperity. He had studied medicine as a young man, eventually establishing a prestigious and lucrative clientele in London. He chose to embrace fruitful advances such as inoculation and quinine, and in 1716 became one of the first physicians honored with a baronetcy. He attained not only membership but considerable prestige in the Royal Society, succeeding Isaac Newton as its president in 1727.

All the while, Sloane steadily built up a grand library and cabinet of curiosities that Sir Robert Cotton would have commended. Likewise Sloane's eventual creation of a museum, patronized by notables of the day—Handel allegedly "outraged his host by placing a buttered muffin on one of his rare books"—at his home in Bloomsbury. In time, Sloane even expanded into an adjoining property, then in 1742 moved the entire collection to a mansion in Chelsea. The prosperity of Sloane's private museum contrasts dramatically with Britain's national collections during the same period. Thus does the ultimately successful transfer of the one to the other seem, again, so incredible.

In the end, however, Sloane faced much the same dilemma as Sir John Cotton and every great collector. Like Sir John, Sloane enjoyed considerable longevity but he was not going to live forever, and could not take it all with him. Family interest in maintaining such collections almost invariably failed. In addition to the Cottons' experience, much of Sir Robert Harley's vast library went onto the market in the 1740s, after his son's death. Sloane concluded that his own life's work deserved some more durable arrangement. Presumably he also, like so many before, found the idea of leaving a legacy to the nation appealing despite how poorly it had thus far worked in reality.

His decision to place a price on his collection therefore seems all the more strange. Perhaps he simply accepted that entrusting his life's work to the nation would mean risking it, no matter what, and that he or his heirs ought at least to receive some sort of compensation. As a principle, this was eminently reasonable; as an expectation, it might have bordered on derangement. Britain was, in some sense, every bit as prosperous as Sloane himself by the mid-18th century. The "Seven Years War" that began in 1756 was to end in effective global hegemony for its empire. Yet that empire was not only acquired in "absentmindedness" but perennially governed on a shoestring budget. The reaction of King George II, when informed of Sloane's will and its price tag, was reportedly—and correctly—"I don't think there are twenty thousand pounds in The Treasury."

Edward Edwards among others writes eloquently of the generosity of Sloane's offer, and acidly about the British government's response. As he points out in *Lives of the Founders of the British Museum*,

> A private citizen, of moderate means, had been willing to expend seventy or eighty thousand pounds—besides an inestimable amount of labour and research—upon an object essentially and largely public. Yet a British Parliament could not summon up enough public spirit to tax its own members, in common with their fellow taxpaying subjects throughout the realm, to the extent of a hundred thousand pounds, in order to meet an obvious public want, to redeem an actual parliamentary pledge, and to secure a conspicuous national honour for all time to come.

Despite which the money was not there, and in half a century of pledged responsibility for the Cotton library, national honor had signally failed to precipitate it. Yet somehow it all worked. In some way, finally, this time really was different. How?

Part of the answer, and an important part, is that Sloane had a partner that the Harleys, the Cottons, Dr. Dee and all of the others did not. Sloane had Arthur Onslow, just as Onslow finally had in Hans Sloane the x-factor he had been missing for 20 years. After the Ashburnham House fire, Onslow had urged Parliament to live up to its commitments as a national librarian—and met with indifference. A decade later he had witnessed the same indifference lead to dispersal of the Harleys' printed book collection—a potential national treasure that would never be reassembled. By 1753 the Harleian manuscripts were in danger of going the same way, as was Sloane's entire collection. The cost of acquiring both, as well as then creating a home worth filling with such riches, would be more than twice the nonexistent £22,000 just for Sloane's estate. Yet Onslow was determined not to miss this third chance, and determination—perhaps a measure of desperation—finally sparked inspiration. In an age of speculative enthusiasm no less avid than today's, the one reliable way to attract money was to promise a chance at more, and Onslow resolved to make up his need of capital by giving it away. He organized a lottery.

Parliamentary lotteries were not new, but they remained controversial, as past experience had left many of Onslow's colleagues skeptical. The contracted lottery operators were consistently corrupt, and in the event, the museum lottery proved no different. It did not need to be, though. Every lottery, no matter how honest, depends after all on popular enthusiasm overwhelming skeptical restraint. The general public readily played its part in the museum lottery, and Parliament, if occasionally more scrupulous, eventually gave its consent in the face of an experienced Speaker of the House and a compelling cause.

When Parliament passed 26 George II, chapter 22, few of its general objectives were new, but at last they were actually going to happen. Intentions for "providing one General Repository for the better reception and more convenient use of the [Harley and Sloane] Collections, and of the Cottonian Library, and of the additions thereto" were accompanied by money, and money made the difference, possibly in more ways than one. In one sense, the long-dreamed national library became real thanks to Arthur Onslow and the funds he raised, through creativity and political expediency. In another sense, however, the turnaround may also owe much to Sir Hans Sloane and the funds he demanded. Before Sloane, many collectors had offered British governments invaluable libraries and other treasures, and asked nothing in return; perhaps it should be little surprise that those governments set a corresponding value on such gifts, until someone finally raised the bar.

In the story of the Cotton library, the 1750s mark a time of both new beginnings, and of endings. By some strange synchronicity many of the traditions founded nearly a century and a half earlier by Sir Robert Cotton ended, at least as family traditions, within the space of a single decade.

The Cotton family had already been drifting away from Sir Robert's legacies for some time. The same year that their neglected namesake library burned in London, scholar and collector James West visited the old family seat at Conington. He found that descendants had largely abandoned the property, including Sir Robert's stone inscriptions, which were exposed to the elements and gradually undoing their excavation. Eventually a grandson and namesake of Sir John Cotton followed his example, and gave the stones away. Thus in 1750 the last piece of the larger Cotton library left the family.

The 18th-century Sir John chose Cambridge's Trinity College, rather than the national government, and his decision is replete with significances for the period. In an article about the stones for *Sir Robert Cotton as Collector*, David McKitterick notes the irony of the timing, three short years before the foundation of the British Museum, which might otherwise have united the entire Cotton collection under one roof for the first time. Lacking the benefit of hindsight, Sir John's reluctance to surrender even more family heirlooms to Parliament's trustees was nonetheless entirely understandable. Yet it appears that the stones' dispatch to Cambridge reflected alienation from Sir Robert's legacy as much as interest in it. Per McKitterick, Sir John meant to honor his great-great-grandfather's alma mater—erroneously, as Sir Robert never attended Trinity College.

Sir John's well-meaning but confused farewell, to the last material heirlooms of his dynasty's founder, is all the more poignant as it preceded the dynasty's own swan song by just two years. The Cotton baronetcy failed with the death of Sir John, sixth and last to hold the title. Other branches of the family tree continued, and distant descendants still honor their relationship to the baronetcy's founder to this day. But none of them qualified for his title, per formulae that Sir Robert might once have whiled away an evening studying with his antiquary friends. One can only guess what he would have thought about their application to his family, or about his other legacies' nearly simultaneous disappearance, at least into larger collections. For 150 years his library had stood as an institution itself, and even as the trustees joined it to other archives, people still referred to all of them as the Cotton library. In the British Museum it would be just one collection among many, and for all anyone knew, even that special status might eventually melt away.

The end of the independent Cotton library was, however, at least twinned with the hope of a new beginning. This would certainly have compensated for much, even with the library's creator. For by 1753 the state of Sir Robert Cotton's library was nearly as sad as that of his derelict estate or his extinct baronetcy.

Since the partial restoration by Arthur Onslow's committee 20 years before, next to nothing had happened to the collection. Many damaged charters, manuscripts and scraps remained hidden in drawers. The whole library, meanwhile, had remained piled in "temporary" storage long enough for the new dormitory of 1731 to become "the Old Dormitory." What few changes took place were almost entirely bad. The librarianship passed repeatedly from one substitute to another. Dr. Bentley's son sold the office to a surgeon named Claudius Amyand, who in turn left the job's responsibilities to the deputy David Casley; age and infirmity eventually impaired Casley so much that by the late 1740s the library's operation depended almost entirely upon his wife.

Very likely, all of these people contributed to further losses from the collection, either actively or passively. In 1760 a Joseph Ames sold several damaged Cotton manuscripts that he had acquired from Mrs. Casley, as souvenirs of a visit. No direct evidence implicates Claudius Amyand in losses, but scholarship does not seem to have motivated his purchase of the librarian's job, and as a result one suspects a more mercenary interest. The Cotton collection certainly lost a great number of antique coins, by one means or another. In 1748 the reverend Samuel Pegge found fewer than half remaining of the 34 Cotton coins pictured in John Speed's *Historie of Great Britaine*. Their loss was but small change, moreover; in 2000, Marion M. Archibald observed in *British Numismatic Journal* that as many as one-third of Sir Robert Cotton's coins have ended up someplace other than the British Museum. Though many are in other museums, today, Archibald found that they often passed through private collectors' hands in the interim. The same James West who noted the decay of Cotton's stone collection, at Conington, seems to have profited from the decay of his coin collection; by comparing records Archibald found that West acquired as many as 15 coins that previously belonged to the Cotton library.

Condemning West and others is all the same difficult, whether they acquired pieces of the Cotton library through Mrs. Casley's liberality, through secondhand purchase, or through outright theft. Sir Robert acquired many of the same items via similar means, and by the early to mid-1700s the arguments in his defense were at least as applicable to the day's own relic-hunters. The Cotton library had become exactly the sort of shabby, disordered and maladministered government archive from which Sir Robert had poached—or rescued—so much of it in the first place. In 1753 and again in 1756, the trustees of the nascent British Museum sent examiners around to report on the library's condition, and their conclusions are damning. The collection as a whole was disorganized, and suffering from damp. "The medals or coins," they wrote, "have been found by us in a most confused state." Their remarks upon the Vitellius press come close to being an indictment:

> Besides the damage done by the Fire to the MSS. of this Press, it hath suffered no less by the Carelessness of those that have been the first employed in preserving them, as well as by the extraordinary Dampness of the Place [and it has for some time] afforded both Lodging and Food to numberless Shoals of Worms and other Insects…

Such were the riches of the Cotton library, however, that even after the ravages of fire, carelessness, and hungry bugs, what remained could inspire awe. For the 1756 report, Matthew Maty and Henry Rimius examined the library at length, and their comments have an element of Egyptologists finding an entire new tomb complex: thieves or decay had removed some artifacts, undoubtedly valuable, and yet "wonderful things" almost beyond count remained. The same disorder that they described no doubt contributed to the sense of discovery. Pulling open one unmarked drawer, they lifted out a copy of Magna Carta, "still very legible" despite its damage. Their eventual report swings between dismay at the state of the library and near giddiness at the riches falling into their hands. "We beg leave to mention various highlights," they write, before describing one after another. In addition to Magna Carta, they wonder at the survival of "Robert de Bruce's claim to the crown of Scotland," archbishops' message to Henry VIII of "compliance with his desires in the affair of the divorce with Ann of Cleves," and an array of items of age "sufficient [alone] to render them venerable."

The choice pickings of dissolved monasteries and leaky archives had, in a sense, been lost and found all over again. The Cotton library was back where it began, except that in reliving its history it was about to experience a new and better version. This time the petition did not fail. The new British Museum was not a perfect institution, nor was it exactly "The Academye for the Studye of Antiquity and History Founded by Queen Elizabeth." But it was very much a realization of the Tudor antiquaries' grand vision in every way that mattered, including the most important: it finally, truly existed.

One hundred fifty years after antiquaries' petition for a national history academy—and 50 since Parliament's vow that the Cotton library "be kept and preserved... for Publick Use and Advantage"—the development of the British Museum could hardly be called sudden. Nonetheless, once begun in earnest the progress of the museum was astonishing compared with all that preceded it. Parliament raised funds, purchased Sloane's and what remained of Harley's collections, and organized a new board of trustees. Despite including many of the old Cotton library trustees, the new board then purchased, staffed, fit out and opened the museum scarcely two weeks into 1759. The Cotton trustees had spent more time dithering over the appointment of a single librarian.

The museum trustees' efficiency is all the more impressive given their membership of 41. The size of the board may, counterintuitively, have worked to aid decision-making. Even after reserving 20 seats for high officials of state, and six more for relations of the Cottons, Sloanes and Harleys, space remained for electing 15 people with the interest and qualifications to perform some actual work. Moreover, the legislation of 1753 wisely specified a select committee of just three principal trustees. Though all of these were officials, for the first several years at least their number included Arthur Onslow, in his capacity as Speaker of the House. Onslow's reputation as a statesman and his enduring advocacy of the nation's library were undoubtedly considerable aids to getting things done, even after he retired as speaker and as a principal trustee, to return as an elected member.

Plenty of work needed doing. The raw shelving necessary, alone, suggests the scale of the task. The Harleian manuscripts required 1,700′ of shelves, and Sloane's collection a princely 4,600′; the Cotton volumes claimed just 384′, although a good deal of material remained yet in boxes. These were just the three "headline" collections, meanwhile. The Cotton library arrived with its various companions of recent decades, such as Major Edwards' collection, and the entire Old Royal library, which King George II formally donated to the museum upon its foundation. The collective cabinets of curiosities, if small by comparison, meanwhile constituted an entire further category alongside printed documents and manuscripts. All of this material needed space, not only for storage but for display and study.

The museum trustees found their space in a Bloomsbury mansion called Montagu House. The choice was another expedient, as they were once more fitting the libraries into a "fixer-upper," rather than a new purpose-built site. Montagu House had genuine drawbacks, too; in the 1750s, Bloomsbury was the remote fringe of the city. Perhaps more disconcertingly, the house occupied the site of a previous Montagu House that had burned to the ground. But the proceeds of the lottery would only stretch so far. Even with more funding, building from the ground up might by contrast have stretched on all too long, and risked precious momentum by delay. Arthur Onslow likely weighed the alternatives and chose to get the museum opened, and to trust in a better staff to prevent a repetition of Ashburnham House. Montagu House would, at least, have qualified paid professionals minding its contents.

The British Museum that opened its doors January 15, 1759, nonetheless long remained a work in progress. Though promising free entry to "all studious and curious Persons," museum visits were largely restricted to guided tours at specific times, and a maximum of 60 people per day. Formal restrictions may have been less of a deterrent than the arduous process required to obtain a ticket; most applicants had to make at least two trips to the museum before they could see a single display.

The museum staff was an immeasurable improvement over the days of absentee librarians and unvetted surrogates. Yet the budget for salaries, and almost everything, still frustrated employees for ages. Further purchasing had to wait many years, and while curators arguably had their hands full with the founding collections, those collections continued to dwindle and budgetary pressure played a part. The early museum made repeated sales of "duplicate" items that subsequent generations have sorely regretted.

The Cotton library, long shorn of its printed material, was generally exempt from this program. But items continued to go missing from it, in part because as always its owners had only a limited knowledge of its contents. The museum renumbered the Cotton charters upon receiving them, without materially reducing confusion or complexity. The rest of the Cotton manuscripts kept their emperor pressmarks—in spite of grumbling—but they needed a new catalog as badly as ever. Many items still needed conservation. The museum had judged some legible enough to go back onto shelves, but a great number remained in boxes, awaiting someone to take notice. Arthur Onslow had performed what salvage he could, three decades before, and more recently helped provide the manuscripts their first real home since Cotton House. As a result, studious and curious persons were once more congregating around the Cotton library. Sooner or later, with some luck, it would cast its spell on some new champion.

EX LIBRIS
ANGLO-SAXON PENNIES
BMC I, p 88, 29; BMC I, p 138, 698;
BMC II, p 98, 102; BMC II, p 106, 6

Compared with an illuminated gospel book or great charter, the Cotton coins are easy to overlook. As much as one-fifth of the original collection has vanished since Sir Robert's time, and the great majority of what remains at the British Museum today is stored behind the scenes. Half a dozen thin, dull and somewhat crude pennies constitute the ongoing public display of Cotton coins. Yet even this peek reveals much about why contemporaries praised Cotton's "famous cabinet." These tiny discs, which the museum itself once classified "metal manuscripts," have remarkable stories to tell.

A penny of King Aethelward may have both the most tantalizing story to relate, and the least to say about it. Although the term Dark Ages is out of fashion with scholars, certain corners of post-Roman Britain remain very dimly lit, and Aethelward's kingdom is one of them. In *English Hammered Coinage*, Jeffrey J. North relates that "Practically nothing is known about the history of East Anglia between 793 and 870;" the approximate dates for Aethelward's reign are 840 to 865. Evidence from coins provides the source of that rough timeline, as well as the greatest part of scholars' information about Aethelward and his dynasty. Despite the bare simplicity of its design, the Aethelward penny also hints at the distinct cultural traditions still sorting themselves out in early Anglo-Saxon England. Though the glyph encircled by Aethelward's name represents its first letter, it is an "A" with a decidedly runic character. On other coins from the era, numismatists recognize occasional true runes mingled with the Latin alphabet, a reminder of how much the "English" were but recently a foreign element in England.

Eventually, of course, Saxon society settled in only for new invasions to leave their own marks. The battles between Anglo-Saxon kingdoms and Vikings colored the history of England for more than a century, and the Cotton pennies record this back-and-forth in occasionally surprising ways. Alfred the Great rallied an England that might otherwise have fallen entirely to the new arrivals, and his descendants consolidated and continued his work. Coins of Edward and Athelstan, the great king's son and grandson, record the dynasty's continuity. Edward, in partnership with his remarkable sister Aethelflaed, took to the offensive and gradually brought more and more of the "Danelaw" under English control. But reconquest remained incomplete until Athelstan's capture of York in 927. The Athelstan penny displayed at the British Museum claims, like Edward's, only the title of "king," but Athelstan later made two significant modifications to the coinage.

One of these was displaying the title *Rex Totius Britanniae* (in abbreviated form) after 927. Athelstan's other change to England's coins was considerably more far-reaching. His decrees at Grately represented a major reform of the coun-

Pennies of Anglo-Saxon Britain

try's minting, assigning a fixed quota of moneyers for every borough; what was more, shoddy work would not cut it. Translated into modern English by North, Athelstan's decree established "that there shall be one coinage throughout the king's dominion... And if a minter be convicted of striking bad money, the hand with which he was guilty shall be cut off and set up on the mint smithy..." The introduction of mint identification on most coins complemented this new accountability, while the entire program suggests the power and confidence of the resurgent English state.

As one other Cotton penny illustrates, however, that power remained fragile. During their periods of ascendancy the Vikings also minted coins, sometimes in the name of kings, but often in the name of a saint. The Cotton coins include one of their pennies, minted in Lincoln in the name of St. Martin. Notably, though one face features the saint's name and the reverse features a cross, the name of St. Martin shares space with a very prominent sword. Numismatists have speculated on what the sword represents; North suggests it is "the celebrated sword of Carlus which was regarded as a symbol of sovereignty by the Scandinavian kings of Dublin." Whatever its intended meaning, the combination of sword and coin may offer a simpler and deeper significance. To whatever extent it had ever been true, the Viking presence in England was obviously no longer barbarian raiders. They were a rival, organized power that was nonetheless more than ready to fight.

Alfred's dynasty had subdued that power but by no means broken it, a fact reflected in arguments over the St. Martin penny's date. Officially, the English controlled Lincoln from 918, implying that the coin was minted in that year or earlier. Some scholars, however, suspect a mint date as late as 925. As the authors of *Coinage in Tenth Century England* note, if true, this would "point to a period of Viking authority in this area that is not recorded in the historical sources." It would not be the first or last time that a government overstated its reduction of an enemy. Whatever the penny's date, the Vikings in England were far from finished as warriors, moneyers, or rulers. Athelstan died in October 939. Before the year was out, Anlaf Guthfrithsson reoccupied York.

CHAPTER 13

The Turning Point

CERTAIN THEMES AND CIRCUMSTANCES appear again and again in the story of the Cotton library. Lost manuscripts, inadequate catalogs, grand plans undone by inertia and neglect; such dismal patterns are all too persistent. So, too, is a larger motif of repetition itself. The collection's arrival at the British Museum did not break any of these patterns.

It did, at least, mark the beginning of a shift in their details. Under the pre-museum, parliamentary trustees, the Cotton library reached its nadir. Its history since has continued to feature episodes of injury and indignity. But these became fewer, in number and in severity. Having survived much worse already, the Cotton library could safely move off the "endangered" list. Under the protection of the British Museum the collection was at least stable, even during periods of neglect; losses to and of individual manuscripts did not cease immediately, but they were balanced by instances of recovery. Slowly, the balance trended more and more in favor of the latter.

Recognizing that gradual trend depends upon a very large time scale, however. For at least half of the collection's long history at the British Museum, progress in fits and starts remained the rule. Andrew Prescott has chronicled the intermittent bursts of interest, and their frequent failure, in "'Their Present Miserable State of Cremation': The Restoration of the Cotton Library." In his telling, over and over museum personnel flirt with reviving more manuscripts from the damages of 1731, only to get cold feet and withdraw.

The museum's first decade saw two such overtures, just months apart. In July 1757 the museum authorized a Mr. Mores to examine the "burnt lumps" and other stored casualties, which he believed might be saved. Unfortunately his optimism went untested, as did that of a French bookbinder who offered his own services the following February. Mr. Padeloup got as far as demonstrating his technique on a damaged leaf from another collection, and then on a Cotton manuscript that March, in both cases impressing museum officials. The projected cost, however, quickly cooled off their ardor. One of the keepers may have pictured bins full of loose pages, multiplied them by Padeloup's rate of four sheets for a shilling, then thanked him very much for his time and bid him good-day. "Thus," Prescott writes, "matters were left for another forty years."

In the interim, relatively little disturbed either manuscripts or museum. The habits of the old trustees had not disappeared entirely from the new British Museum board, and for half a century the BM remained a relatively sleepy place. Most of the Cotton library sat quietly amid the museum's other manuscripts. The surviving Cotton coins remained near them, sharing a "medal room" with similar objects from the Harleys' collection. The worst damaged of the parchment manuscripts, by contrast, effectively remained in limbo. By 1775, these had a space of their own as well—but removal to a garret is typically a means to put something out of the way and forget it. The "charter garret" accomplished this dubious end readily.

The museum's custodianship could claim some small accomplishments for itself, even amid its early plodding. In 1781 some sharp-eyed person made a wonderful discovery in a bookseller's list: an English chronicle, updated through Henry VIII, which upon investigation proved a stray from the Cotton manuscripts. This particular chronicle appeared to have been missing for several decades, at least; the British Museum nonetheless purchased it back and restored Otho B XIV to its rightful place. For the inheritors of Sir John Cotton's bequest it was a commendable gesture.

Unfortunately, the most prominent of Sir John's own recoveries was not only badly damaged, but still deteriorating at the British Museum. After the great fire, David Casley identified approximately 60 recognizable pieces of the Cotton Genesis. Some of these vanished in the 1740s, before the museum's time, when the artist George Vertue borrowed them to prepare reproductions. Yet 40 years later the remains of the Genesis continued dwindling away, and the person most responsible was not only a British Museum employee but the assistant keeper of the department of manuscripts. In 1784, Andrew Gifford borrowed an unknown number of the Genesis fragments. Upon Gifford's death many of these went by mistake to Bristol Baptist College, along with the personal collections Gifford had willed them; others may simply have been thrown away. Meanwhile, years passed by without anyone even noticing. Near the turn of the century a newly appointed principal librarian finally took stock of the Cotton Genesis. He counted no more than 18 pieces.

At the time that Joseph Planta became principal librarian of the British Museum, that modestly titled officer was responsible for much more than books and manuscripts. After the board of trustees, the principal librarian was the topmost official in Bloomsbury, and the entire museum came under his purview. The title was nonetheless appropriate, in those days when the BM was more library than anything else. In Planta's case it may be even more appropriate, for his inventory of the Cotton Genesis, around the time of his 1799 promotion, touches on his three major achievements.

That Planta recognized the erosion of the Genesis fragments, until then completely unnoticed, points to his greatest impact on the museum during his own era. Under Planta's encouragement the drowsy, insular British Museum of the 18th century began to perk up at last. His background is somewhat curious as a candidate for reformer; in 1773 he effectively inherited his first job at the museum from his father, who had served as an assistant librarian since the museum opened. Occasionally, though, an insider may see the failings of an institution better than anyone. Such was surely the case with Planta, who spent years as curator of a department of manuscripts with almost no wherewithal for acquisitions.

Upon rising to principal librarian, Planta pushed for new activity throughout the museum. His leadership saw major acquisitions, including the Rosetta Stone and the Parthenon marbles acquired from the Ottoman government by Lord Elgin. Planta also supported greater efforts to share the museum's collections, with larger reading rooms, expanded public accessibility, and more staff assigned to visitors. All of these things cost money, and credit must be shared with the museum's trustees and the government that ultimately funded them. Yet what has proved Planta's most enduring legacy was actually a largely personal effort; moreover, to the extent that the museum trustees played a part, it was primarily by turning down one of his requests.

Writing at the end of the 20th century, Colin Tite declared that although "deficient in many respects," Joseph Planta's catalog remains the best option for consulting the Cotton manuscripts. Tite's qualified tribute is all the more impressive given the long history of catalogs that came and went before it. Beginning with Maty and Rimius reporting on the Cotton library while it sat in the Old Dormitory of Westminster School, the British Museum continued to struggle with updating Smith's catalog and the rough inventories prepared after the fire. In 1777 they purchased a private catalog, prepared by Samuel Hooper with help from collector Thomas Astle. In the catalog's preface Hooper proposed that "The many defects in the Catalogue of the COTTONIAN Library published by Dr. Smith in the year 1696... will sufficiently evince the necessity of the present publication," which he promised "will be found, as to arrangement and contents, so far superior to Dr. Smith's, as to leave no room for similar complaints." Fifteen years later, Joseph Planta thoroughly endorsed the criticism of Smith, but found Hooper's other assertions less persuasive.

Planta had likely spent considerable time dwelling on the museum's founding collections, given the long proscription against new purchases. He could hardly have failed to note the generally poor state of their cataloging, a defect the Cotton manuscripts shared with most of the museum library. In time, Planta's administration assaulted this problem on nearly every front: new manuscript catalogs, a catalog of printed books, and the first-ever synopsis of the entire museum. When it came to the Cotton library, though, Planta's thinking was more holistic still. Reporting on the collection's perennial organizational muddle in 1792, while still assistant keeper, he advocated sweeping away all of the accumulated idiosyncrasies going back to Sir Robert Cotton himself. The museum should start over, he told the trustees, and rearrange everything "in a classical order, which no doubt ought always to have been the preference."

The trustees vetoed the idea, and for once students of the Cotton library have reason to be grateful for do-nothingism. Around the same time most of Sir Hans Sloane's book collection virtually disappeared into the museum's larger holdings, as the result of a general reshelving. Whatever their reasons, the trustees declined a similar dispersal of the Cotton manuscripts. The "Galba psalter" would remain Galba A XVIII, and the "Julius work calendar" would stay within Julius A VI.

Planta gave way with good grace. The trustees, by then including Astle, supported the object of a new catalog otherwise. With their approval, Planta proceeded to invest considerable energy and no small amount of pride indexing the collection using the traditional emperor system, instead. For the next decade, he labored on a Cotton manuscript catalog to stand the test of time; his result, first published in 1802, has done precisely that. Scholars have questioned it, criticized it and amended it, but for 200 years and counting, they have been unable to disregard it.

For the nonspecialist, though, the Planta catalog's most interesting feature may be the ironies in which it abounds. Planta's most long-lasting legacy began, as noted, as a second choice. After its completion he nonetheless boasted of its superiority to every attempt that preceded it, particularly Smith's. In his own catalog's preface, Planta flourished his improvements upon Smith, which were substantial; Planta describes 26,000 separate articles compared with the 6,200 of Smith, mostly the result of more detailed examination of state papers. Planta also attempted to identify, or at least suggest, authors and dates for many of those papers and other manuscripts lacking this information. Yet this interest in identifying sources had one notable exception. Tite, who has studied the various Cotton catalogs for many years, writes that while Planta produced much original work, a good deal of his 1802 catalog was nonetheless a "reprinting of work done in the seventeenth century." The work of none other than Thomas Smith, whom Planta never names except to denigrate, is foremost among this.

Irony also connects Planta's catalog, in unfortunate fashion, with his other notable impact on the Cotton library. In addition to poring through the shelves of more or less intact Cotton manuscript volumes, Planta attempted to complete once and for all the restoration of damaged items in storage. In this he fell considerably short of his goal. To all appearances he never even set foot inside the charter garret despite its being a few steps from his office, and much of the work he did perform consisted of simply sifting and sorting. Nonetheless, he did contribute to the process, even if he did not complete it. Planta examined 105 damaged "bundles," from which he reconstituted 44 volumes. Even if these were less than perfect restorations, in combination with his catalog a good deal of material was once more available for consultation—a blessing that proved in some cases a curse. As Prescott observes, "the provision of the catalogue encouraged the use of brittle manuscripts... Every time one of these... was issued in the Reading Room, fragments of text were probably left all over the Museum." The Cotton library had made progress, but it remained two steps forward, one step back.

The fanfare of this restoration's "completion" likely had an opposite effect on the remaining damaged items, meanwhile. Planta declared that after his work, everything that might be restored to the Cotton library had been restored, and that whatever remained was both beyond hope and primarily "obscure tracts and fragments of little importance," anyway. Later scholarship resolved otherwise, but Planta's contemporaries mostly accepted his verdict. Most of the items Planta had overlooked remained overlooked for another generation—a curse that may have been a blessing in disguise.

A library's users are always a potential hazard to its collections, yet, in general, their threat is limited. They may commit accidental harm—as was the case with fragile Cotton manuscripts—but few library patrons intentionally make significant physical alterations to an item. The same cannot always be said of library *keepers*, and it may be their number that did the most harm in the decades after Planta's restorations.

In 1825, at last recalling the charter garret, museum staff removed a few items that in the event would have been better off remaining forgotten. Keeper of manuscripts Henry Ellis had hopes of opening a new round of restoration, and provided sample damaged charters to the experimenter William Wollaston. Still esteemed as a scientist today, Wollaston proved rather less capable as a conservator. Decades afterward, another keeper of manuscripts wrote that as a result of Wollaston's unknown method, his test subjects' "leaves are almost like *biscuit*, and contracted to one third of their original size!"

Ellis permitted a second attempt, but it produced much the same unfortunate effect. Still more unfortunately, Ellis and others at the museum seemed determined to plow ahead even after cashiering Wollaston. Assistant keeper of manuscripts Josiah Forshall was keen to have a go of his own, and with approval from the board of trustees he began another restoration campaign in 1826.

Forshall's methods were probably simpler than his recent predecessor's, and did not produce nearly such intense harm. As a result, however, Forshall made a much wider impact, and like Wollaston's it was less than admirable. Forshall repeated some of the actions of the earliest restorers—scorched manuscripts were immersed in water, or possibly a solution with zinc, and then carefully dried—but he was mostly confronting items already set aside as too damaged for these methods to do much good. Wollaston's chemical therapy having failed, Forshall turned, instead, to surgery. He sliced into damaged works, not only to disassemble them for laundering but to carve up individual pages. He hoped thereby to reopen some of the most stubbornly fused "lumps" and flatten out the shrunken, warped leaves. In a sense he succeeded. But the work's merits came at a high, and possibly needless, cost. Later eras, in Prescott's words, found Forshall's cuts "to be unnecessary and indeed to be a considerable hindrance to further repair of the leaves."

In fairness to Forshall, contemporaries seem to have judged his efforts more favorably. From their perspective the fragments, "lumps" and "crusts" of the Cotton library were so far gone that any method of prying meaning out of them was worth trying. Sir Robert Cotton, himself, had managed the library as a utilitarian resource more than a collection of preserved artifacts. Cotton also made exceptions, however. His beloved Greek Genesis was among them, and in identifying dozens of fragments that had escaped Planta's inventory Forshall showed it a similar appreciation. By contrast, Forshall's treatment of the damaged Magna Carta was rather less careful.

If anything in the Cotton library deserved to be handled like a delicate relic, it was Magna Carta; though Sir Robert had two copies, both were priceless mementos of national history. No one needed to handle them to study their well-known text. Forshall had absolutely no reason to take any risks with them. Nonetheless he entrusted the damaged charter to a Mr. Hogarth, a "restorer" who seemingly accomplished the opposite effect. Since the 1731 fire, witnesses had left reports that the text remained quite legible, but these seem to cease with Forshall's tenure. Today the damaged Magna Carta is all but unreadable even with the modern lighting that has brought back other texts. Forshall's other tampering, misguided though it may have been, is forgivable. His needless gambling with Magna Carta is not, and while the hand of Hogarth may be directly responsible, Prescott's judgment of "the greatest blot on Forshall's [entire] record" invites little argument.

The damage to Magna Carta may not have been immediately evident, and this may have sheltered Forshall from criticism by contemporaries. What questions he did confront had more to do with material that he hadn't touched than with material that he had. A parliamentary committee, while reviewing his efforts, asked about reports of a "great quantity of crusts of fragments of manuscripts remaining unopened." Forshall's answer was the same that Joseph Planta had given two decades before, and despite the obvious implications for such assurances they met with the same response. The Cotton library had been restored; a few bits of rubbish remained, possibly worth keeping as curiosities but nothing more.

The door to the charter garret closed again. Given the consequences of Planta's and then Forshall's campaigns, it would have been fair to hope that it might remain closed, too. But the British Museum had invited in the curious, and they had answered. For good and for ill the Cotton library was no longer in the hands of indifferent caretakers, but of active men with the same enthusiasm for rearranging and sharing as its founder. Posterity could only hope, therefore, that the next to tackle Sir Robert's manuscripts would also share his tempering instinct for preservation.

EX LIBRIS
MAGNA CARTA
Cotton Charter XIII 31a and Augustus II 106

In 2015, MAGNA CARTA TURNS 800 years old, and many are celebrating its enduring significance. Yet if one surveys the entire eight centuries of its existence, the real great tradition of Magna Carta might be one of arguing over what that significance is or should be.

In reviewing those arguments, one could scarcely want a more appropriate context than the Cotton library. The collection not only includes two of the four copies to survive from 1215, but has been their home for nearly half of their existence. With his acquisition of them in the early 17th century, Sir Robert Cotton stands Janus-like in the middle of Magna Carta's story, equidistant from modern societies and King John. His era was genuinely pivotal in that story, moreover. Cotton's life and activities as a collector bridge the late Tudor period and the fractious politics of the early Stuart dynasty—precisely the years in which scholars now perceive Magna Carta transforming from dusty parchment to totem of justice and liberty. Whether or not Cotton actually saved either copy from a tailor's scrap bin as tradition alleges, it's no coincidence that he ended up with half the surviving manuscripts, for the great charter's significance was indeed sunk low before its mid-life resurgence.

But, then, the power of Magna Carta had been precarious

from its very beginning. King John only agreed to its terms grudgingly in the face of a threatened revolt by England's barons, and the moment they dispersed he not only retracted his consent but cajoled the pope into issuing a formal denunciation—a copy of which is also in the Cotton library. It, too, may have represented more than just historical interest for Cotton. By his time, England had denounced the papacy itself, and for Cotton's circle the appeal of holding up Magna Carta as precedent for their political goals may almost have been equalled by the appeal of holding up a proclamation from Rome, and saying "if you're against our agenda you side with the pope!"

Neither his politics nor his precedents won Cotton much favor from King Charles I, of course. Their broad appeal among Charles' critics only helped get Cotton and his library, both, imprisoned via precisely the kind of means that Magna Carta forswears. In the end Charles paid a price for his heavy-handedness. Despite which, even when England at last renounced unconstrained monarchy once and for all, the charters that now symbolize that struggle fell again on hard times. Only with the creation of the British Museum, and inspectors discovering a much-damaged Charter XIII 31a in a drawer, did it and its sibling copy find some kind of home befitting national treasures. Good intentions still could, and did, go wrong. But Josiah Forshall's botched restoration in the 1820s was the last hurt suffered by either charter, to date.

The status of the great charters since then could hardly be more different. Magna Carta has once more become almost a sacred symbol, not only in Britain but through much of the world. Its prestige is indeed risen so high that many modern historians attempt to nudge it down a bit, and emphasize that far from being a grand declaration of rights, Magna Carta was mostly haggling among the rich and powerful about how pre-eminent their topmost member ought to be. It's true enough. But the real source of astonishment in Magna Carta is that this context produced not only a vague gesture toward rights for some, but a number of genuine and plain declarations of rights for all that still resonate today. That number is small, but prolixity seems beside the point when reading phrases like "No free man shall be seized, imprisoned, dispossessed, outlawed, exiled or ruined in any way... except by the lawful judgement of his peers and the law of the land," or the even more direct "To no one will we sell, to no one will we deny or delay right or justice."

Sir Robert Cotton obviously recognized the importance of these ideas. As, for reasons good and bad, do people today. Richard Godden, an attorney and backer of 2015 anniversary plans, has warned that "The arbitrary authority of the state is just as much a threat today as it was in the day of King John and the principals enshrined in Magna Carta remain essential... we forget them at our peril." More encouragingly, according to the British Library's Claire Breay "Magna Carta is the most popular item in the Library's Treasures gallery." Hopefully, the lessons of its history will remain well attended.

CHAPTER 14

Sir Frederic Madden

O F ALL THE COTTON LIBRARY's many "what-ifs," the most tantalizing may be Humfrey Wanley. Just as the library approached a major crossroads, along came a brilliant young scholar bursting with ideas and eager to launch a great new expedition into its dusty volumes. It's not unreasonable to imagine that, given the chance, Wanley might have transformed the whole history of the collection, and averted its decades-long dark age through sheer personal energy. Instead, of course, the library trustees turned to a succession of absentee librarians, Wanley remained restricted to a minor player in the collection's story, and the Cotton manuscripts eventually joined someone else's grand design considerably the worse for their detour.

Yet time and again, what seems lost to the library has proved merely delayed. A volume may disappear but return decades later; a better catalog may take generations but eventually someone gets around to it; for most of a century damaged manuscripts faced neglect or abuse as their only alternatives, but finally, someone came to their rescue. The arrival of that someone, moreover, represented a kind of second chance for the story of the ambitious prodigy and the Cotton library. Almost one hundred years to the day after Humfrey Wanley's death, Frederic Madden arrived at the British Museum with a background and promise that unavoidably recall his would-be predecessor's.

Frederic Madden was born in Portsmouth six weeks into the new century, on February 16, 1801. Like Wanley, Madden proved an interested and gifted student of history from early life. He excelled at languages including Hebrew, Old English and Norman French. Also like Wanley, he nonetheless had to earn his way into the ranks of scholarship more through patient labor than formal academic routes, and chose much the same methods. Madden studied at Oxford, but the need to support himself diverted him from earning a degree; instead he found employment with the university organizing manuscripts, just as Wanley had done 13 decades earlier. Madden, too, then polished his nascent reputation, as paleographer for a great private library. Madden's catalog of Thomas Coke's collection met with a frustrating end, as had Wanley's Cotton catalog—in Madden's case the work remained unpublished due to expense—but then, crucially, their paths began to diverge. Unlike Sir Robert Harley, whose patronage had not helped Wanley's bid to manage a national collection, Coke's endorsement of Madden won results.

At first those results were limited, and, like much that involved the BM of the day, halting. But Madden, the museum, and the Cotton manuscripts had all arrived at a familiar intersection, and this time they all turned the corner together. Madden's first application to the museum in June 1826 met rejection, but he soon found another way in as a temporary cataloger for the printed books department. From there, his progress was rapid.

By early 1828, Madden was not only a full employee in the department of manuscripts, but very nearly running it single-handedly. Josiah Forshall had only recently been promoted to keeper of manuscripts, but (fortunately for certain items in his charge) he was already busying himself with additional roles at the museum. Madden's timing could hardly have been better. He not only arrived in the department of manuscripts at the right moment to take charge, but at the right time to join a movement for transformation.

Joseph Planta had stirred the pot of the museum's administration, but Madden's generation brought the process of change to a boil. In the spring of 1827, while Madden was still a mere temporary employee in the printed books department, the museum transferred its entire manuscript collection from Montagu House to one of the new buildings gradually supplanting it. In the process, keepers reorganized the lot, including the Cotton library. Sorting onto shelves by size replaced the 200-year-old system of emperor pressmarks, at least physically. The Cotton manuscripts' traditional pressmarks remained in use, but consulting a particular volume thereafter required an additional directory to locate it. The utility of this exercise is debatable, but it clearly demonstrated openness to change. Frederic Madden was ready to respond.

Within a year, he was Forshall's assistant. Like many previous deputy custodians of the Cotton library, he was frequently responsible for the department given its director's other interests; unlike them, Madden was eager and qualified to embrace the role. From 1830 the British Museum embarked on what Edward Edwards describes as "a re-foundation," and Madden made certain that the department of manuscripts played its part. As the de facto, and eventually official, keeper of manuscripts, Madden introduced important reforms and innovations. He brought new focus and professionalism to cataloging, binding and conservation. He embraced the possibilities of change taking place around him; as photographic technology matured he became an early advocate of its use for copying manuscripts, and with a growing if still modest budget, he became the first keeper to expand his department's collection on a significant scale. The *Dictionary of*

National Biography declares "there is no doubt that his energy and industry abruptly ended his department's amiably torpid eighteenth-century ways and advanced it to a standing in the world of scholarship which it has maintained ever since."

Knighted in 1833, Sir Frederic Madden's record as administrator might have been enough, by itself, to secure him a respectable place in history. Yet Madden is genuinely memorable for three things above all else. Only one directly concerns the story of the Cotton library. The origin of Madden's role in that story is, all the same, the perfect opportunity to introduce another of his most notable legacies: his diary.

As a diarist, Madden was prolific, candid, and best of all unhesisitant about naming names (or very obvious initials, at least). His irascible style has provided spice to numerous accounts of both the Cotton collection and the British Museum. The description of Wollaston's failures as "like *biscuit*, and contracted to one third of their original size!" was Madden's, and entirely typical; emphasis, exclamation point and all.

The entry for April 17, 1837, is somewhat more tame. It must count, even so, as one of the most significant in the entire diary. Barely three months away from promotion to keeper of manuscripts, Madden was still officially Forshall's assistant. Whatever patience the keeper-in-waiting had sustained up to that point, though, measurably diminished upon a fateful discovery in the charter garret. Per Madden's diary, he "had always been told there were only a few fragments, not worth the bother of dusting or sorting;" that he trusted this claim is evident from his surprise and dismay at what he found, instead. The garret's "few fragments" amounted to "crusts of vellum enough to fill several bushel baskets," including "a box full of receipts of Sir Robert Cottons" and other items of obvious interest to any genuine manuscript scholar. The contrast with his supervisor's disinterest was distinctly unflattering, and in Madden's view "It is very much to the discredit of Mr F that affairs should have remained thus..."

Alerted to the possibility that the museum's nooks and crannies concealed treasure, Madden soon made a further astonishing find. For years he had sought some trace of Cotton Tiberius D VI, a cartulary of Christ Church Twinham. Like the antiquaries of old, Madden entertained plans for a history of his county, and he longed to consult this early record from Hampshire. To all appearances, though, not even fragments remained. Then, remarkably, Madden "discovered in an old cupboard [the entire volume] very little the worse for the fire, except being wrinkled up!" The same volume, he noted pointedly, that Forshall "had declared to me over and over again could not by any possibility exist!"

Madden's mind was made up. "I saw enough to make me resolve in my own mind," he pledged, "to have the entire [garret] cleared out, whenever it should be my lot to be Keeper of the MSS." That day was approaching sooner than he knew, but Madden did not wait even that long to make a beginning. He began work on restoring some of the fragments immediately. He applied Forshall's methods—soon enough Madden saw room for improvement there, as well, but they provided a starting point— but performed all of the work himself. Likely a little distrustful of everyone in the wake of his discoveries, Madden was skeptical of the in-house binder Charles Tuckett's qualifications in particular.

His own results, by contrast, filled Madden with pride, but they also had an obvious shortcoming. He was only one man, and as of July he was officially keeper of manuscripts. The added authority would be useful to his new cause, but he was still going to need help and he was still determined to recruit it from outside the British Museum. For that, in turn, he was going to need money beyond what his own department could spare. Once again, he was in a position that Humfrey Wanley had known all too well. He, too, was going to need to win over the board of trustees, and could only hope for better results.

Much of the history of the Cotton library told against Madden. In early 1838, he proposed the museum recruit the services of Henry Gough, who had performed delicate restorations for the Bodleian Library and other Oxford collections. The trustees' response was to charge Madden with reporting further on the condition of the manuscripts in question. If they hoped to evade the issue by such a time-honored delaying tactic, though, they had misjudged their petitioner. Rebuffed once, he held nothing back from his second attempt, which verged on a "shock and awe" assault. Prescott describes Madden's report of December 1838 as "a masterly survey of the condition of the Cotton manuscripts... more comprehensive than any previous survey." Madden's impatience with the half-measures represented by the garret's "bushel baskets" of unrestored manuscripts found an equally rich target in the indifference that had concealed them. In the space of months he inventoried the damaged volumes more completely than anyone else had in more than 100 years.

Madden's investigation took nothing for granted. In addition to all the material hidden in the charter garret, he examined every damaged item that predecessors had judged sufficiently restored to place back in service. Nearly all of these needed further conservation, in his view. He forced the trustees to confront the inconvenient fact that many valuable documents had been "constantly receiving fresh injuries" for years, or even decades; then, he followed up with a detailed program of solutions.

Prioritizing those items in immediate danger, Madden divided them into three categories. The first consisted mostly of vellum manuscripts, among them many valuable Old English documents including *Beowulf*, which might have been the prime example of poorly-restored items threatened by renewed handling. Madden advocated setting Gough to work on the 35 items of this category without delay. A second category of mostly paper manuscripts, and a third of loose leaves in cases, Madden regarded as slightly less urgent. He proposed that Charles Tuckett could work on these as time permitted, though Madden did advise at least partial transcription of the most fragile texts beforehand. (For the first category, he concluded the need of conservation was too urgent to delay it for transcription, which would likely be cost-prohibitive anyway.)

According to Prescott, Madden's extensive report "provided the basis on which the work was organized over the next forty years," though that longevity had as much to do with the hesitancy of its audience as with the brilliance of its content. Despite the precision and intensity of his bombardment, Madden was not going to capture the treasury by storm. The trustees' general reluctance was, to an extent, understandable. The British Museum had a firmly limited budget and a nearly unlimited number of worthy projects to pursue. Their skepticism about transcription was certainly reasonable; rebinding volumes with transcriptions inserted after each manuscript page, as Madden suggested at one point, would have involved considerable time and money as well as doubled the size of each volume. Other of the trustees' choices, however, verge on perverse. They not only elected to begin with the second-category paper manuscripts—the opportunity to rely on in-house labor outweighing concern for the first category's fragility—but also rejected any restrictions on access to the brittle vellum manuscripts in the meantime.

Still, they were responding, even if not nearly as swiftly as Madden desired. Over the following years, they approved additional steps in small increments. In 1840 Madden reached agreement with the trustees to entrust some of the first-category manuscripts to Tuckett. Madden continued to lobby for Gough, however, and the following year received approval to fund small, trial experiments. Gough's work produced excellent results, which made Madden all the more impatient. At one point, queried on an issue he believed more than adequately answered already, Madden wrote to the principal librarian "I beg leave to refer to you to my reports of 11 Jany 1838, 13 Dec. 1838, 3 Jan. 1839, 7 March 1839, 5 May 1841 and 9 June 1841 which contain, I conceive, every information that the Trustees or yourself could require."

Such outbursts may not have helped the keeper of manuscripts' case. His frustration with delay was, however, balanced by his capacity for persistence, as well as his youth. History's motto for the Cotton library had proved, in general, "if not today, perhaps in another generation, or another century." Madden's motto was by contrast *carpe diem,* each and every single *diem,* no matter how many times he was rebuffed. So it would remain, even if it eventually took years of this to complete the work of conservation to his satisfaction. Madden was not going to give up.

Fate, unable to dissuade Frederic Madden, seems to have chosen to make sport of him instead. It was certainly easier. Madden did not suffer fools gladly, nor did he have any great tolerance for delay, budgetary constraint, redundant conversation, or indeed bureaucracy in general. This naturally made his career at a large public institution exasperating. Even so the splenetic splendor of Madden's diary might not be half so copious, if not for Anthony Panizzi.

Alongside that diary, and its author's work on behalf of the Cotton manuscripts, Madden's other notable claim to posterity's interest is a bitter feud with his colleague and rival. The Madden-Panizzi conflict has remained near legendary among Britain's national institutions long after both men departed from the scene. In *Treasures of the British Library*, published in 1989, Nicolas Barker wrote of the pair that "Their energy transformed the departments over which they presided; their mutual antipathy pervaded the whole Museum..." The feud receives considerable attention in Madden's *Dictionary of National Biography* entry as well. As the DNB notes, the two were initially friendly enough upon Panizzi's arrival at the museum, a few years after Madden. Yet the timing of their appointments eventually provided spark to the tinder of incompatible personalities.

Like Madden, Panizzi was headstrong and outspoken, and could stir up opponents at least as easily. Panizzi, however, was more effective at balancing these with friends than the comparatively go-it-alone Madden. The British Museum was in a sense simply not big enough for both of them—or at least for both of them to wield all of the influence and resources that their ambition demanded—and Panizzi's political instincts gave him an advantage that Madden endlessly resented.

In fairness, Madden often had reasons to be resentful. The worst involved Panizzi's eventual seniority, acquired as much by unfair happenstance as by gift of personality. In 1837 the museum promoted Panizzi to keeper of printed books at essentially the same time that it promoted Madden—but the principal trustee formalized Madden's appointment three days after Panizzi's. Thus, despite the fact that he had five years' seniority working at the museum, Madden was thereafter stuck a crucial increment lower in its hierarchy than his rival.

The keepers' head-butting affected more than their personal status, although in policy battles, too, Madden usually came in second. A decade after his injury in the seniority system, both keepers had cause to rejoice at the museum's purchase of the Grenville collection. Its 20,000+ volumes "finally put the Museum in the first rank among the libraries of the world" per Barker's history, and should have offered bountiful prizes to the manuscript and printed book departments alike. Unfortunately for Madden, his rival keeper managed to crowd him out, twice over. Panizzi arranged to place the great mass of new material in the recently built West Room, a space that had been promised to Madden. Then he managed to keep the whole collection, including manuscripts, isolated from Madden's department, in which status it remained for decades. Madden had share of neither space, nor contents, and could only rage at the villainy of "Mr. P" and the unfairness of fate.

In spite of sometimes outrageous fortune Madden did enjoy successes, though even these conveyed a hint of mockery, now and then. After several years of besieging the trustees, organizing and reporting on baby-step "test" projects, and trying to keep Gough from losing interest and abandoning the whole idea, Madden finally got his wish. In March 1845 the trustees essentially wrote a blank check approving full-time employment of Gough, as well as his son as an assistant. Over the years that followed, the Goughs busied themselves repairing and protecting some of the Cotton library's most valuable and fragile manuscripts: *Beowulf*, ancient cartularies, an early copy of Bede's history.

As the work proceeded, however, it produced an irony that must have been, at the very least, mildly embarrassing. Even with Gough and his son working full-time, Madden's ambitions to "have the entire room cleared" of damaged fragments left a considerable backlog of documents. The museum's in-house binder Charles Tuckett therefore continued to work alongside Madden's contracted genius, and, in the process, to prove himself entirely competent. Gradually Madden's eagerness overcame his fears, and he entrusted Tuckett with limited work on the damaged vellum manuscripts until then reserved for Gough. Each time Tuckett, whose circumstances suggest a remarkably patient and earnest craftsman, rose to the challenge. After all Madden's fussing and anxiety over pursuing an outside expert, the museum's in-house journeyman was proving equally capable if not more so. In March 1852, Madden acknowledged the faintly awkward reality, at least indirectly; thereafter, he wrote, "I shall put the worst in [Tuckett's] hands. Gough's work could draw to a close in another twelvemonth or so."

Any chagrin on Madden's part was more than compensated for by pride at the restorers' results, which merit credit enough for all. Madden spent years pressing to recruit labor for a grand goal, and in the end the most effective laborer may have been the one available all along. But credit surely belongs also to Gough, for leading the first significant advance in conservation of the Cotton manuscripts since Arthur Onslow's rudimentary beginning ages before. Madden sought to challenge the great failing of every effort since, i.e. that restoration was left incomplete not only in terms of the collection, but also in terms of individual manuscripts left vulnerable to further, irreparable damage. In Gough's work he found the solution.

As restorer, Gough not only reopened and cleaned the damaged leaves so they might once more be accessible to scholars, but provided for their safety afterward. His method combined elegantly simple theory with detailed and sensitive practice: each and every manuscript leaf subject to concern over brittle edges received a custom-prepared, protective frame. Gough, and later Tuckett, traced the contours of each leaf onto two sheets of construction paper. Then he carefully cut a hole in each, a millimeter or two inside of the tracing. Because of the variety of the manuscripts' original formats as well as the damage to most, each frame needed to be specially prepared. But the result was, quietly, brilliant. Sealed between the paired sheets, even the most delicate manuscripts were finally safe to handle for the simple reason that a reader no longer needed to directly handle them, at all.

The practice of "inlaying" manuscripts in this way had shortcomings. Most obviously, the need for the frames to overlap leaves' edges meant concealing letters, where fire or breakage had already eliminated margins around the text. Today's British Library struggles with other limitations that have emerged over time, and these will be examined in due course. But the fact that much of the work of Madden, Gough and Tuckett is still the subject of active evaluation in the 21st century testifies to its quality.

Madden took up one of the Cotton library's perennially unmet challenges, and, to a greater extent than even Planta's bout with cataloging, he won. Even before glimpsing a date when Gough's work could "draw to a close," Madden and his team began collecting just praise for their years of effort. Around 1848, they presented their results to date to a visiting royal commission, and in 1851 many of the restored items appeared in the museum's first public exhibit of manuscripts. Madden generally disapproved of the whole concept of displaying his department's highlights in this way. But even his famous peevishness must have admitted some measure of pride at this exhibit, which included not only restored manuscripts but displays demonstrating their earlier condition. The contrast was a stirring tribute to all he had accomplished.

As a librarian of the Cotton collection Sir Frederic Madden remained part of an ongoing story, even if he had conclusively ended a sub-plot or two. There was always more to do, even before counting the rest of the department of manuscripts' holdings. Madden had sought to enlarge these, moreover, during his years as Forshall's surrogate. In 1829 a bequest from the Earl of Bridgewater provided both manuscripts as well as money, permitting a fruitful period of further acquisitions. In 1831, Madden's department purchased the remaining collection of Thomas Howard, who as Earl of Arundel had been a great patron of the arts and of Sir Robert Cotton. Much of Sir Simonds D'Ewes' library having arrived with the founding Harley collection, the British Museum was gradually reuniting Cotton's collection with those of a number of his friends.

Madden also made efforts, involving more than a little overlap with the preceding, to reunite the Cotton library with its own missing pieces. As in other areas, Madden introduced a thoroughness and organization that had long gone wanting. He compiled a detailed list of "lost and strayed" items, then pursued their recovery to the extent his resources allowed. As he had first discovered in 1837, some "lost" manuscripts were in fact already in the museum. Others turned up in independent collections, from whose owners Madden met varying degrees of sympathy. Sir Thomas Phillips sold Vitellius D IX to the museum on generous terms, according to Prescott; Utrecht University, by contrast, disappointed the keeper of manuscripts' hopes of turning the Utrecht Psalter back into Claudius C VII.

Both bequests and funds for purchases largely dried up, after Madden's early years in the museum. The great exception, as noted, eluded him thanks to Panizzi's diversion of the Grenville collection. Naturally Madden complained of his department's constricted growth. But he was also sufficiently wise—or simply restless—to go on with what constructive work was possible. By dedicating himself to a comprehensive restoration of the Cotton manuscripts, he managed to expand his department anyway, which created still more to do.

By the mid-1850s Tuckett and the Goughs had prepared thousands of inlaid manuscript pages. Between the idiosyncrasy of Cotton's original volumes, disarrangement by the fire and repeated moving, and historic limitations of Cotton manuscript cataloging, making sense of all this represented a genuinely Herculean labor. First, sorters needed to identify fragmentary manuscripts written in any of dozens of languages, many of them archaic. Then they needed to match them up, a task all the more difficult because one might examine every loose leaf and still have only an incomplete text. Once more Madden found masterful assistance close at hand, including his assistant keeper Augustus Bond; in time, Bond went on to succeed Madden as keeper of manuscripts, and eventually to become principal librarian of the entire museum. The aid of Bond and his colleagues was every bit as essential to organizing the manuscripts as Gough and Tuckett had been to restoring them, particularly as the work stretched well into the 1860s even with their help, and Madden's vision deteriorated in later years.

In Andrew Prescott's estimation, "The work performed by Madden and his team on the arrangement of the restored leaves was a bibliographical and paleographical *tour de force*." Human fallibility inevitably meant some degree of error in the massive project, but these were flaws within a system that had not even existed when Madden arrived. Although he had help, chief credit for the transformation was his; over the course of nearly half a lifetime, Madden had practically willed the chaos within the Cotton library back into order through dogged, exhausting effort. Some proportionate reward should have been little enough to hope for.

Again, the past of the Cotton library suggested otherwise. The rejection of Madden's predecessor Humfrey Wanley, as well as the fates of Thomas Smith, and Sir Robert himself, were hardly exemplars of a wise and just cosmos. Nor by any means was the library's own history of suffering. Yet Madden had genuinely changed things. The curse of neglect and abuse that had lingered around the Cotton library, even after its arrival at the British Museum, was broken; the library's story continued, but largely outside the tragicomic genre after Madden's departure.

Unfortunately, Madden himself seemed to remain under a curse that he never managed to dispel, and right up until his departure, Madden's misfortune could also be the Cotton library's.

Both the history of the Cotton library and his own entire life should have prepared Frederic Madden for the events of July 10, 1865. At the same time, though, nothing could have truly prepared a rational mind for the news he received around 9 o'clock that evening: the Cotton manuscripts were burning again.

The main collection itself was safe for the moment—a reassurance he would have grasped quickly after the first shock. But a fire was threatening the bindery where Charles Tuckett worked, and even after 20 years' effort Tuckett was still repairing items from the Cotton library, as well as other collections. All of these were in danger. As Madden hurried toward the bindery—all too near the rest of his department's holdings—his emotions must have been nearly indescribable. The pride of both his department and career was going up in flames. The fire not only imperiled individual manuscripts he had spent decades painstakingly reviving from a similar disaster, it also made a mockery of his entire aspiration to be a better custodian than all those who had allowed such waste.

It would have been little consolation that so many who should have interceded in such a disaster also seemed to fail, all at once. Policemen with relevant keys proved elusive. The museum's fireman was on leave, and no one else had any real training in fire fighting; after locating a hose to bring water from the nearest hydrant, the hose burst. After half an hour, a fire brigade finally arrived—summoned by a new telegraph line just completed the year before—but one of their two engines would not work.

Despite this, the firemen eventually made do. By 10:15, the fire was out. As soon as possible Madden dispatched an assistant named George Gatfield to learn the fate of the manuscripts.

Gatfield returned with some better consolation: most of the manuscripts in the bindery were in an iron safe, and unharmed by the fire. Yet Gatfield also carried, literally, partial confirmation of Madden's worst fears. Emerging from the bindery, he held a bundle of manuscripts that had been sitting out in the work areas. They were burned, and soaked, and a wretched terrible mess.

Madden set other staff to help Gatfield retrieve whatever else had suffered in the fire, then went to inform the trustees of the catastrophe. Much of what followed was all depressingly familiar, multiple times over. In the subsequent weeks, Madden and other staff cleaned and dried the damaged manuscripts, attempted to sort them back into order, and counted up what was lost. Along with hundreds of printed books, the second fire completely destroyed several manuscript volumes, including three Cotton items. One of these consisted of leaves from a volume thought destroyed by the first fire, until Madden sifted out and reunited dozens of pieces that had survived—only for this to happen. More than a dozen other manuscripts suffered significant damage, including much of what remained from Otho A XII after the first fire had incinerated Asser's "Life of King Alfred." The fire also claimed the third part of a map and drawing catalog, to which Madden had devoted considerable time; given that he both resented the project and nonetheless received much criticism in later years for neglecting cataloging work, the sense of demoralization could scarcely have been more complete. As for Tuckett's negligence in fire safety, partly validating the initial distrust which the keeper had since discarded, even Madden may have been at a loss to know how to feel. (The trustees were not, and fired Tuckett despite a far better record of service than Dr. Bentley, whom their predecessors had forgiven after a far worse fire.)

For the British Museum the bindery fire was, realistically, a limited if still terrible loss. Prescott calls it "arguably the greatest single disaster to have struck the collections since the establishment of the Museum in 1753." For Frederic Madden, it was nearly the final, bitter defeat of a career spent suffering them. Nearly final, because Madden remained for another year before one more cruel reverse used up his last ability to endure. A decade earlier the museum had appointed Anthony Panizzi principal librarian, to Madden's fury. In 1866 Panizzi retired—but the trustees passed over his rival once again. Despite all Madden's services, despite his seniority, despite his decades of relatively patient suffering, this was to be his reward. It was too much.

Sir Frederic Madden retired September 29, 1866. In the 40 years since he first applied for employment at the museum he had accomplished an astonishing amount, which neither the work's occasional failings, nor the slights of Panizzi and the board, nor even the humiliation of the bindery fire could efface. In a last memo Madden emphasized this positive view, and laid just claim to the title of "Restorer of the Cottonian Library" as a legacy. As usual, however, his raw and uncensored opinion found vent in his private papers. Here, he also reflected on "my long and arduous labours," but in a much different context. Listing his many services—"*for which I have neither received recompence nor thanks!!*"—he contrasted them with the abuses heaped upon him instead.

The final joke may have been this last tally of ingratitude itself. For, though probably never suspected by its author, both its content and circumstances recall a similar document from nearly 240 years earlier. Madden had thwarted fate's narrative for the Cotton library, but fate had taken its revenge with pointed irony. In his early scholarly promise realized, Frederic Madden had rewritten the story of Humfrey Wanley. In his last miserable inventory of what his services had gained him, however, Madden ended up repeating that of Sir Robert Cotton.

CHAPTER 15

Peace and War

THE WORLD GAINED A NEW Cotton collection in the 1850s, quite literally. Though mostly assembled by Charles Rogers the century before, Rogers's extensive collection of drawings, paintings and sculpture eventually passed to one William Cotton. William, if not any direct relation to the Cottons of Conington, then proved himself at least their spiritual kin. He preserved the collection, expanded it, and ultimately donated it to the city of Plymouth. The city honors his fine gift as the Cottonian Collection, to this day.

Even as Plymouth founded one new Cotton collection, however, the original Cotton collection was witnessing a figurative rebirth of its own. In the last third of the 19th century, the Cotton library began a new era, in some ways the finest era in its whole story to date. The British Museum was at last becoming a world-class institution. Its library still had limitations; in his study of *English Collectors of Books and Manuscripts (1530–1930)*, Seymour de Ricci suggests that even into the early 20th century the museum's collection fell short of the largest private libraries in significant ways. But such private collections came and went. The British Museum library remained, growing and improving slowly and unsteadily, with results that had after 10 decades nonetheless added up to something uniquely magnificent.

The best symbol of this slow-ripening splendor was the museum's iconic Reading Room. By the 1850s the British Museum was expanding on nearly every front, and public use of the library collection had grown to the point where it obviously needed more space, as well. That the museum added not only more space but one of architecture's great spaces is, primarily, a credit to none other than Anthony Panizzi. Though Panizzi infuriated Frederic Madden and more than a few others, the keeper of printed books made contributions to the museum library every bit as important as his rival's, and the Reading Room was the most dazzling. Panizzi envisioned a great, round chamber in the museum courtyard, inspired by no less a model than the Pantheon. The architect Sydney Smirke realized that vision on paper. Then, between 1854 and 1857, through Panizzi's lobbying the museum realized it in iron, glass and concrete.

The first reviews of the Reading Room were mixed. But subsequent generations embraced it as a central depot of knowledge, one both dramatic and practical. Within its round space visitors were surrounded by books in the most fantastic sense. Twenty-five miles of shelves covered the walls; iron frames supported volumes stacked many levels high. The space that they enclosed was almost a physical tribute to bibliophiles. Writing soon after its opening, Edward Edwards recorded with pride how "The new Reading-Room and its appendages can be made to accommodate, in addition to its three-hundred and more of readers, some million, or near it, of volumes, without impediment to their fullest accessibility."

Readers' access remained restricted by tickets, obtained from the principal librarian, but the great and humble alike lined up. Museum archives record tickets issued to Karl Marx, Arthur Conan Doyle, George Orwell and Mahatma Gandhi, among many others. In its eventual fame as a central destination for notables of art, letters and statecraft, the Reading Room was in its way a revival of the Cotton House of the 1620s. Though vastly more grandiose than Sir Robert's narrow storeroom that may once have been a chapel, the Reading Room also became a kind of temple to learning. It even complemented the Cotton library's emperor system with its architectural reference to classical Rome.

Cotton's bronze busts of Julius, Augustus, et al. were probably absent from this picture, however; the British Museum has always maintained that it never received them. The Cotton manuscripts themselves were shelved outside of the new Reading Room, for that matter. By Frederic Madden's last years they shared space with the Harleian and other manuscripts in one of two new "apartments," north of the courtyard, the other hosting the enormous King's Library assembled by George III. Nonetheless, the Cotton library was finally snug and secure—bindery fire excepted—and close at hand to a spectacular new concentration of intellectual activity. After entire lifetimes spent as a political pawn, exile, disputed inheritance, white elephant or burn victim, it could at last be what it had been created to be: a library.

Exploration of the Cotton library never stopped entirely, at least not for long, and certainly not since the British Museum rescued it from the Old Dormitory. But the conditions for scholarship improved markedly during the 19th century. After going almost unnoticed since joining the collection in Sir Robert's time, *Beowulf* finally began to attract notice beginning in the late 1790s— as a result of which, at least several hundred letters crumbled off the brittle manuscript's edges, based on comparisons with the oldest transcripts. Fortunately, Madden's campaign of inlaying the damaged leaves eventually put a stop to this. By the time he bowed out in despair, the Cotton library was, by contrast, in better condition as a resource than it had been in ages. Planta's catalog remained a valuable guide to the collection, as it would into modern times. Madden, Gough and Tuckett restored thousands of damaged leaves to serviceable condition, and made provision for them to remain so.

All of this left work still to do. Manuscript fragments remained even after Madden, and the great volume of material he did restore only exacerbated the shortcomings of Planta's catalog. But nothing was quite so urgent as a few generations earlier. The Cotton library's need for heroes seemed over; by 1870, even a new Madden would have found little to prompt genuine outrage. The balance of the collection's affairs shifted from what it needed back to what it had to offer, which remained considerable. What was more, potential interest in its riches benefitted from both new accessibility and new media. From the mid-19th century the Cotton library begins appearing in news periodicals for things other than great fires.

Around 1883, a number of newspapers noted the discovery of a Cotton manuscript sketch of "The History of Mary Stuart" by her secretary Claude Nau. Apparently an unpublished draft, seized at some point by Mary's Elizabethan jailers, it revealed among other things a miscarriage (the implications of which historians are still debating today) that the Queen of Scots had suffered at Loch Leven. The London *Athenaeum* commented, "strange to say, this remarkable fragment has existed for nearly three centuries in what was almost all along the best-known and the most accessible collection of manuscripts in the whole kingdom." Their first observation was reasonable, but in truth, the recent work of Planta, Madden and others had made the Cotton library considerably more accessible. In the wake of their collective efforts, the fact of renewed discoveries might seem not so much wondrous, as entirely natural.

Strange occurrences remained part of the library's affairs, all the same. In 1861 *The Times* reported another sort of "Curious Literary Discovery" among the Cotton manuscripts. A few years earlier, while examining an ancient volume of the City of London's records, a Mr. H.T. Riley had discovered a gap of more than 100 leaves. The city's library committee proceeded to investigate, but found no explanation. Eventually Riley himself discovered the *Liber Custumarum*'s missing leaves, by chance. They turned out to be precisely where they had been for the past 250 years: bound into Cotton manuscript Claudius D II.

As *The Times* reported, subsequent delving into the city's own archives revealed that this was not the first time it had sought after its manuscript. In 1608, representatives of the city had attempted to relocate a number of missing documents. William Fleetwood, an official of the city and at one time its Member of Parliament, had borrowed some of these, including the *Liber Custumarum*. As Fleetwood had died in 1594, however, his surviving colleagues were somewhat tardy in calling in the loans he had taken out, and tracing them further proved consequently rather more complicated. Eventually they found that most of Fleetwood's books and papers had passed to two antiquarians. As it happened, both gentlemen also had delinquent loans of their own from the city archive. The first borrower, Francis Tate, proved willing enough to return the city's manuscripts. But he faced a difficulty of his own, as he had passed some of them on to the second: his friend and fellow antiquarian, Sir Robert Cotton.

The final details of who acquired what, by what means and from whom, will never be known with certainty. But ultimately the city archivists did conclude that the *Liber Custumarum* had found its way to Cotton, and remained with him. When they sought its return, however, Cotton obviously proved reluctant to cooperate.

Scholars offer varying opinions of the episode. Kevin Sharpe suggests that the refusal to yield back manuscripts that were plainly city property "make it difficult to exonerate Cotton from the charge of theft." Edward Edwards counters with the possibility that "whosoever may have been the original wrongdoer, Sir Robert Cotton had acquired them by a lawful purchase." Meanwhile the broader arguments for and against Cotton's methods have already been examined, and the facts of the *Liber Custumarum* do little to settle them. Cotton certainly had the manuscript, and other city documents, and clearly considered them part of his own collection as he went to the trouble of binding them into new volumes bearing his coat of arms. Regardless of how they reached him, however, the city never formally approved their permanent transfer to anyone, and eventually notified Cotton of this along with its desire to regain them. A desire that Cotton, in the end, appeared to comply with. He returned most of the *Liber Custumarum*. Yet he kept a portion for himself—and made a deliberate attempt to suggest otherwise. As *The Times* reported long afterward, someone—who can only have been Cotton—had not only removed several dozen leaves from the ancient book, but also replaced them with a similar number from some other volume, creating the false appearance of an intact text.

Such methods hardly support a case for Cotton as an entirely honest character. Nonetheless it is impossible to deny some element of humor in their sophomoric cunning, not least because they worked so astonishingly well. Despite having every reason to confirm the return of their missing records in detail, the City of London apparently showed no closer interest in the *Liber Custumarum* than it had for the 14 or more years after William Fleetwood carried it off in the first place. This indifference was likely less than helpful to successors' attempts to claim injustice 250 years later. *The Times*' story concluded by noting that "measures are now being taken by the Court of Common Council to procure their restoration to the book…" Presumably, however, the British Museum was unmoved. As of 2014, the catalog of the

British Library continues to list portions of the *Liber Custumarum*, "Previously owned by: the Guildhall, London," within Claudius D II.

The orderly, comfortable Victorian era that followed in the wake of the bindery fire, with great figures queuing quietly for the Reading Room, and interesting little items in *The Times*, might have gone on and on. The need for interventions of heroic scale, like Madden's, might have ended along with the last guttering flame of an accident that, in turn, might have remained the last such episode in the Cotton library's history. But the larger story that the library had shared in—and in spite of that, preserved—did not end. In the first half of the 20th century, history descended once again on London, and heroic measures proved a long way from being obsolete.

Such measures were primarily a national effort, in the First World War. Though the war was traumatic for Britain and much of Europe, for the British Museum its impacts were mostly temporary, and in the end relatively minor. The most serious disruption involved museum staff pulled away from regular duties by the war effort. In 1917, the same cause in the form of the Air Board attempted to requisition the entire museum, but public protest spared the BM from even this friendly takeover. Meanwhile geography, in combination with the rudimentary technology of long-distance bombing at war's outbreak, spared the museum's collection from enemy action. German zeppelins and, later, heavy aircraft, did drop bombs on London; none fell nearer than 150 yards from the museum.

The nearest misses caused some damage to museum buildings, however. As the war catalyzed the pace of weapons development, museum staff went to greater lengths to keep the collections safe. Initially, they moved material within the museum, to less-exposed areas. By early 1918 they were growing sufficiently concerned to begin a large-scale evacuation. Entire rooms full of valuable objects, including 47 cases of manuscripts, left London for the National Library of Wales.

For the Cotton volumes among them, the evacuation to Aberstwyth represented a strange pairing of milestones. It was the most distant exile of the collection's history, as even the Civil War had not driven the library so far from its London home. On the other hand, compared with so much of the collection's history the museum's exertions in its defense were a stirring demonstration of how far things had come. They were also, essentially, unnecessary. By the end of the same year Allied forces had won the terrible war, a defeated Germany's bombers were grounded, and the British Museum's collection was on its way home.

Unfortunately, all too many activities of the First World War found an indirect use a generation later, as preparation for a second. For the British Museum and its collections the renewed conflict was to prove much more costly.

By the late 1920s a wholly positive interruption to its quiet idyll seemed to await the Cotton library. Though its founder's death might offer a debatable occasion to commemorate, its approaching 300th anniversary prompted fine plans to honor the legacy that had survived Sir Robert. The museum's keeper of manuscripts, Idris Bell, did as noted admit some qualified criticism of Cotton's librarianship. But he more than balanced this with celebration of Cotton's greater accomplishments. In 1931 the museum prepared a special exhibit of Cotton manuscripts—which, as *The Times* pointed out, already constituted the largest portion of the permanent manuscript exhibit by then in place—including rare examples of Cotton's personal papers, illuminated books usually stored behind the scenes, and even the remaining fragments of the Cotton Genesis.

The Genesis fragments had recently been supplemented by

a long-term loan of those pieces that, via Andrew Gifford, had spent more than a century in the collection of Bristol Baptist College. Bell planned another, much more ambitious project, meanwhile, to complement their recovery and the anniversary exhibit. His preface to the exhibit catalog noted plans for a new Cotton library catalog, by that point long desired by library staff and users alike. Since the completion of Planta's catalog not long after Gifford's unintentional division of the Cotton Genesis fragments, much had happened to the Cotton manuscripts, including the absent fragments' return as well as all of Madden's extensive restoration work. Never a flawless catalog even when new, the notes and addenda to Planta had grown to the point where a new start seemed overdue. The museum had recently completed excellent new catalogs for the Old Royal and King's Libraries, and the 1930s should have been the Cotton collection's turn for similar bibliographic pampering.

Instead, the British Museum gradually found its energies once more exhausted in merely keeping that and its other collections intact. In the Second World War, moreover, even their best efforts met with rather less perfect results than in the first.

The difference was not for want of planning. On top of the all-too-recent experience of 1918, the museum's leadership began preparing for renewed hostilities by the mid-1930s. Nor was effort lacking from those plans' execution. By the summer of 1939 all available staff were busy packing manuscripts into more than 3,000 cases held ready for nearly a year; by early 1940, the National Library of Wales sheltered more than 13,000 manuscript refugees. But the bombings of World War II were something new and terrible. Even before the introduction of atomic weaponry at the war's end, adequate preparation for the fire and destruction proved impossible for any of the nations in its path, despite the fact that they were often inflicting the same horrors themselves. Later in the war, Allied bombing of Berlin destroyed dozens of oriental wall paintings, each as ancient as anything in the Cotton library.

The British Museum was not spared by bombing, either. Nor, in contrast to the previous war, were its collections. Though none were literally fixed in place, like the Berlin Ethnological Museum's unfortunate murals, after two centuries the treasures gathered in Bloomsbury were simply too extensive for complete evacuation. On September 23, 1940, an enemy bomb smashed into the King's Library. The explosion destroyed nearly 30′ of bookcases and set many others on fire. Writing nearly 50 years later in *A History of the British Museum Library 1753–1973*, P.R. Harris records that the damage to George III's great collection proved less disastrous than it initially appeared; 428 volumes were destroyed completely and "Not more than 1,500 volumes had been involved" in total. At the time, however, the ruin must have seemed more than bad enough, and worse was to come.

The first months of 1941 proved relatively less harrowing, at least for the British Museum. Despite which its directors continued to worry for the collections, including those already evacuated from London. The National Library of Wales had already moved much valuable material into an underground tunnel, but the BM determined to take no chances. Early the following year they began evacuating more of their treasure, to various remote country houses, and then—some items possibly moving for the third time since war's outbreak—to a disused quarry in Wiltshire. Harris writes that "The rock cover above the area… was about 90′ thick" and eventually sheltered material from more than 30 institutions. The Cotton manuscripts and their fellow exiles would likely be safe, there, from nearly anything that left behind a Britain to remember them.

Their home at the museum still had to take its chances. On May 10, 1941, the British Museum's number came up once more, and this time Harris does not equivocate; in his words, "on that night disaster struck." Multiple incendiary bombs rained onto the southwest portion of the museum. The BM's own firefighters, though grown considerably in numbers and readiness since the bindery fire 76 years before, were overwhelmed, and for the only time in the entire war called for help from London's fire brigade.

Fortunately, the latter were also well prepared for the many demands on them, and the combined forces contained the fire. Better still, though the damage was extensive, it was essentially the last. The museum continued packing material offsite for some time, but after 1941 it suffered no direct hits. What collections remained onsite proved adequately protected from subsequent nearby strikes. Both the Cotton library and its home were going to survive. Years of slaughter and waste remained ahead. Gradually, though, the war's direct impact receded and left the British Museum, and British people, to begin rebuilding once more.

Even in victory, rebuilding from the Second World War was slow for an exhausted Britain. A great many dreams were finished forever. Idris Bell's projected new Cotton library catalog was one of them; as before, the library might survive to other eras and possibilities, but for Bell's generation the chance had passed.

Making do with what they had was not, all the same, a completely grim fate. The fact that the Cotton manuscripts had survived yet another trial, along with the great majority of the museum's library and other artifacts, was indeed worth celebrating. In the years after the war the British Museum celebrated the riches of the Cotton collection twice over, in 1950 and 1953. On the first occasion, "arranged in connexion with the centenary celebrations of the public library movement," the rebuilt King's Library hosted highlights of the Cotton, Harley and Sloane collections along with portraits of their respective founders. Three years later, the British Museum celebrated its own bicentenary, and Cotton manuscripts provided not one but two exhibits. One featured the Lindisfarne and Coronation Gospels, plus other bibles and illuminated works; the second presented other historical manuscripts, from an 11th-century copy of laws of Cnut's England, to a 16th-century letter from the young Elizabeth to her half-brother Edward VI.

The great ambitions of the 1931 exhibit did not reappear with those of the 1950s, however, and researchers went on wishing for a new catalog while muddling through with Planta. The next significant events in the Cotton library's history waited until the following decade. Once more, larger issues directed the library's own fate. In 1962 Parliament took up legislation to reform the British Museum trustees. Their initial membership of 41 had expanded, by 10, but still reserved seats for family of founders dead more than two centuries. *The Times* noted that a Mr. Richard Thompson, distantly descended from Sir Robert Cotton, "gave a rather qualified welcome to a Bill which contained the seeds of his own dissolution as a... trustee." Considerable laughter by Mr. Thompson and his colleagues, however, belied the dour message of his words. Specific pre-war goals like a Cotton catalog weren't yet back on the agenda, but the BM's leadership seemed prepared to meet the larger task of renewal with some measure of bluff enthusiasm, once more.

The prospect of another reform, much larger still, approached throughout the 1960s. To some extent it had been approaching for 200 years, as arguments over dividing the museum's sprawling collections had first begun within years of its founding. By the late 19th century, discussions mostly converged on splitting out the natural history collections, a process that followed by slow stages and was still in progress when Richard Thompson was confronting his "dissolution" with humor. Even as Thompson and other trustees considered reforming their own ranks, however, they were planning further reforms to the British Museum itself. As early as 1960, trustees felt ready to move the museum library to a separate space of its own.

Here, too, the arguments were by no means new. Most of them came down to the same kind of constraints that had prompted the Reading Room's construction in the 1850s. The century since had overwhelmed even its capacious shelving. Even through postwar austerity, the pressure increased, in part because so much of the library's expansion was by then automatic; manuscript purchases might wax and wane, but copies of the nation's new books and periodicals arrived year in and year out. As more optimistic years began, trustees hoped to have the site for a new British Museum Library lined up by 1967.

Building and moving into a new library would obviously involve enormous challenges. But the previous generation had shifted much of the museum's holdings across the country, repeatedly, amid the disruptions of a war. It seemed reasonable to imagine that with some luck, a new library might open to the public by the early 1970s. Reasonable it might even have been. In the event, though, moving the Cotton library and its many siblings back out of the British Museum proved almost as tortuous a process as moving them in.

EX LIBRIS
BEOWULF
Vitellius A XV ff 132r–201v

SINCE ITS DISCOVERY by scholars, *Beowulf* has collected many tributes. In 1876 *The Examiner* called it "the crown of what we possess in Anglo-Saxon literature." More recently, James Grout of the University of Chicago described it as "one of the very first poems in English and its first great literary masterpiece," while longtime literary editor for *The Times* Philip Howard adds that it is "the first major poem in [any] European vernacular language" as well as the most important poem in Old English. Possibly, however, no individual assessment has been more impressive than the total volume of all of them combined. Per University of Kentucky professor Kevin S. Kiernan, "More has been written about *Beowulf*, in fact, than any other literary text in the English language."

This immense bibliography is all the more impressive given how recent most of it is. When George Hickes noted in 1700, amid his examination of Cotton library records, that "I can find nothing yet of Beowulph" it was likely because nothing existed to find, anywhere. In 1884 *The Times* observed that as recently as 70 years earlier, "we may safely assert that the Beowulf had not yet been discovered." Yet once that anonymity lifted, it did so dramatically. Part of the reason is that *Beowulf*'s significance has proved not only deep but broad. At one point in his own extensive commentaries on the poem, Kiernan rattles off a dozen academic disciplines with interest in *Beowulf*. One could easily add to his list, moreover. Though he makes no mention of conservators, out of all the Cotton library's potential case studies for their art *Beowulf* may deserve pride of place, and in part through Kiernan's own work.

Along with all of its other merits, *Beowulf* illustrates the great potential value of original manuscripts—and the great potential challenges to preserving them. The scorch marks on its leaves offer graphic testimony to the manuscript's narrow escape in 1731. That escape was all the more fortunate as no one regarded *Beowulf* as particularly significant at the time, and besides brief quotes in George Hickes's *Thesaurus* no copies of the text existed until several decades later. Yet if Vitellius A XV had perished in the later fire of 1865, it still would have meant the loss of real information, despite multiple transcriptions; even if some calamity had claimed it in 1965 it would have been a loss. Long after scholars had published transcripts and translations of its text, and photography had permitted precise visual records of the manuscript itself, Kevin Kiernan went back to the preserved leaves themselves in the 1970s and found they still had more to reveal.

The full history of *Beowulf*, both poem and manuscript, has remained vague ever since its modern recognition by scholars. Sir Robert Cotton added it to his library some time during his three or four decades as collector. In doing so he presumably combined for the first time two or more codices, including the Nowell Codex that contains *Beowulf*; a name and date on its first folio seems to confirm its previous ownership by Laurence Nowell, the scholarly predecessor who died the year before Cotton's birth. Precisely how the codex then reached Cotton is uncertain, as is nearly all of *Beowulf*'s history before Nowell. Most scholarship has approached the poem itself as an ancient work, composed in the 8th or even 7th century, then transmitted by repeated copying to a sole surviving manuscript produced in the 11th century. With the publication of *Beowulf and the Beowulf Manuscript* in 1981, Kiernan challenged all of this.

Based on detailed study of the manuscript leaves, Kiernan concluded that the Nowell Codex is just as much a composite as Vitellius A XV. In his view the *Beowulf* manuscript began as an entirely separate document that, though based on older stories, was produced firsthand by the author of the combined saga. Thus, Kiernan asserts, the epic known today is not a much-recopied product of the pagan Dark Ages but instead an invention of the 11th century, inspired by legends from a past already distant by its author's time.

Though Kiernan argues his thesis in persuasive detail it remains controversial. Nonetheless, his studies of the *Beowulf* manuscript resulted in some discoveries—or at least rediscoveries—that cannot be disputed. Between the fire of 1731 and Frederic Madden's introduction of protective frames to *Beowulf* and other brittle manuscripts, hundreds of characters vanished as its leaves' edges crumbled away. Madden's campaign successfully halted the decay, but at the cost of concealing more characters beneath the edges of the frames, and a

The first folio of *Beowulf*

century of scholars depended on older transcripts' record of these missing letters. Kiernan, however, proved that those characters not only remained but remained readable beneath the frames. He found that modern lighting technology could reveal what the paper frames had hidden, along with other details of the manuscript such as sections where the scribe had scratched out and rewritten words.

All of this has enhanced scholars' resources for understanding the manuscript and the poem. Kiernan has since worked to make his discoveries accessible to the world. In the 1990s, the Group for Research in Electronically Networked Digital Libraries—GRENDL—helped develop an online replica. Today, replicas of the *Beowulf* manuscript are accessible through the British Library's web site, as well as on a DVD from the University of Chicago that features ultra-high resolution and even ultraviolet images. All of these boons to *Beowulf* studies, for all that they demonstrate the wonders of 21st-century information technology, nonetheless highlight the enduring value of Sir Robert Cotton's 17th-century manuscript collection. If not for the manuscript's acquisition by Cotton—and its preservation by occasional worthy successors—the finest optics and the fastest internet connection in the world would come up blank.

CHAPTER 16

The British Library

THE STORY OF THE COTTON LIBRARY has no ending. More than four centuries after its foundation it continues to provide inspiration, insight and controversy, and there is every reason to hope it may do so for another four, at least. *This* story, however, must end somewhere. It does so at the British Library. For many reasons, it is a very fitting destination for (most of) the Cotton collection. By no means least among those reasons is the fact that, in perfect sympathy with that collection's long history of delays, false starts and recurring events, the life of the modern British Library has at least two beginnings.

This accounting does not include the institution's long prehistory, or various abortive beginnings, either, though at least one of the latter features also. The museum trustees' hopes of 1960 gradually bogged down amid various arguments, particularly over the location for a new library. By the end of 1967, local opposition and parliamentary reversal effectively sank a planned new complex south of the museum. The planners returned to square one. Over the next six years, multiple reports issued, all essentially restating the need for a new national library without committing to any specific plan for housing it. These culminated in 1973 with the British Library Act. On paper, the act converted the British Museum's library into a new, independent organization. In reality, the core of the British Library remained very literally within the BM, and would remain there for another quarter century.

The library stayed within the British Museum so long largely because of the same challenge that had originally driven its independence. Britain's national library collection was large—and growing ever larger, as the Library Act and subsequent mergers appended other national reference institutions to the former museum library—but free space in the capital was limited. The British Library's very first annual report identified a new building as its "most urgent need," and yet, for all that space within the British Museum was crowded, the library at least had some safe claim on it. Laying claim to an even larger space anywhere in central London was far more contentious. For precisely that reason the museum had selected sites at the metropolitan fringe for offsite storage of library collections; a site in Colindale housed newspaper archives, and in the early 1960s further overflow went to rented space in the Royal Arsenal at Woolwich. Like Sir Robert Cotton, however, the new British Library remained committed to operating close to the nexus of government, commerce and cultural activity. In fact the library's board still hoped to find a new home in Bloomsbury.

Instead, they found the same opposition that the museum trustees met with several years earlier. The sparse 18th-century Bloomsbury of Montagu House's day had long ago filled in. Large-scale redevelopment proved no more popular in the 1970s than it had in the 1960s, and the library's second attempt at house-hunting ended almost as soon as it began.

At which point, arguably, the searchers got somewhat more realistic and also got a bit of luck. Having been rebuffed by incumbent residents twice, they began looking for a more or less unoccupied space; remarkably, they found one, large enough for their goals and not so far from the British Museum. As the library itself describes it, the third-try site "was a derelict goods yard immediately to the west of St. Pancras Station." It was not quite the most glamorous site in London, and indeed is not exactly that even today. But this was essentially its great advantage. The library could build there. After centuries of floating around London, first with Robert Cotton and later under the parliamentary trustees, then sharing space in the British Museum, the Cotton manuscripts would finally have a purpose-built home in a formal national library.

The architect Colin St. John, reflecting on his work on the British Library, once described it as a "thirty-year war." He might have been understating things. The long, long awaited fulfillment of the British Library Act, and in some sense of preceding acts stretching back to 1701, took until 1998. That June, the library's new St. Pancras building finally opened its doors. After all of the delays the result was still something of a compromise; former British Library board chairman Sir Anthony Kenny has reflected that "As might be expected of such a large construction project, the British Library building became the victim of delays and rising costs." Eventually patience wore thin, and "In 1988 the Conservative government then in power indicated that it would provide enough funding for a building approximately two thirds the size of the original plan."

The result is nonetheless a far cry from the days of Ashburnham House or the Old Dormitory, and rivals even the grand scale of Victorian construction. The library offers an assortment of numbers: 10 million bricks, 180,000 tons of concrete, 112,000 square meters total area. "The largest public building constructed in the UK in the 20th century" may convey the scale best. The style of the St. Pancras building is not to everyone's taste, and it will probably never be an architectural icon like the old Reading Room. But as the original Cotton library demonstrated, a great library does not depend on a great space. A great library is measured best by its contents, and by the use made of those contents.

The contents of the modern British Library are staggering. Their diversity far exceeds even the varied Cotton library, making any count an approximation. But its collection is well past 150 million items and growing by three million per year. More importantly the library is committed to enabling study and appreciation of that collection, in ways that Robert Cotton never could have imagined. Though the library's reading rooms can accommodate 1,200 people, more than 10 times that number access the collection every day thanks to online services. In 2008, the library's first curator of digital manuscripts took office; today, the library's web site provides access to electronic reproductions of more than a dozen manuscripts just from the Cotton library, alone. Several highlights of the Cotton manuscripts are also on perpetual display in the library's Treasures gallery. But digitized manuscripts offer 24/7 viewing from any corner of the world, and—unlike the original volumes motionless inside a glass case—provide access to every leaf.

Meanwhile, the library sponsors plentiful new research and scholarship, for popular and specialist audiences alike. In addition to the permanent Treasures exhibit, new temporary exhibitions are always opening. Cotton manuscripts inevitably feature in many of these. Understanding of the Cotton library has also benefitted enormously from books, journals, events and electronic publications produced under the British Library banner. Colin Tite's 1993 lectures on the Cotton library, for example, were originally delivered as part of an annual series, then published in book form, in both cases thanks to the British Library. It's fair to say that without this and other studies, published as books or articles for *British Library Journal* or on the library's manuscripts

Entrance to the British Library, St. Pancras, London
Photograph by Mike Peel (www.mikepeel.net)

blog, this history would have been much poorer if it existed at all.

For Tite and other scholarly authors, there is still no substitute for direct study of the Cotton manuscripts themselves of course. There, too, the British Library supports further scholarship through its care and organization of the collection. The task, as history has shown, is unlikely ever to be truly complete. The Cotton library is so large and complex it is in some sense a living system. Even if a catalog could ever meet with universal acclaim, it would eventually require updating as users and their expectations changed around it. A catalog optimized for the political and religious interests of Sir Robert's day would have been ill-suited to Georgian-era users, for example.

By the same token a hypothetical, completed 1930s cataloging project would be woefully out of date today. Modern library users bring not only different interests and new frameworks to the Cotton manuscripts, but significantly different methods compared with just a few decades ago, thanks to computerization. The British Library has responded, in an impressively prompt fashion compared with earlier Cotton custodians. In 1990 Dr. Nigel Ramsay was already laying the groundwork for an electronic Cotton manuscripts catalog. From 1997 to 1998, the University of Sheffield's Humanities Resource Institute assisted the British Library in developing an updated, online catalog; today, helpful entries for Cotton manuscript items are instantly searchable through the British Library's web site.

Areas for improvement always remain. Restrictions on use of digital manuscripts—nearly as draconian as those on the original documents—suggest some confusion about the relevant technology, or else about the purpose of a public institution. But study of the Cotton library almost imposes by force an appreciation of the long term. From that perspective, there is ample reason to hope for further beneficial reforms one day, and to recognize that the modern library, even with faults, offers much to be grateful for.

Despite centuries of change, aspects of the manuscripts' modern organization would be familiar to figures from their past. Though in recent years the library has again promised a new catalog as forthcoming, as of 2014 that particular grail remains elusive, and online catalog entries are still descendants of Planta's 1802 catalog and the even older directories he reused. Much of Cotton's original system remains in place, too, in that the British Library still associates his manuscripts with the compilations and emperor pressmarks that Sir Robert introduced. (Their precise physical arrangements are classified, officially, for security concerns.) Some of these volumes are, at this point, mostly re-creations after disruption by one calamity or another, and for many manuscripts and fragments a shared place within a single volume is now more theoretical than physical. Yet even today, approximately 40 volumes still have at least partial Cotton family bindings; some may be from after Sir Robert's time but at least a few are likely his own handiwork.

Sir Frederic Madden would find much of his contribution to the library still in place as well. The majority of the protective paper frames that Gough and Tuckett assembled are still in use. Their commendable work is at last showing its age; acid content is yellowing some frames, while the different behavior of parchment and paper is causing nearly all of the frames to buckle, and tug at brittle 150-year-old paste. In recent decades, the library has turned to plastic sleeves to protect some of these, as well as various of the seemingly inexhaustible supply of leftover loose fragments. But these, too, have their drawbacks. For the time being no perfect permanent fix exists, and curators simply do their best to slow damage rather than stop or reverse it. Even with their faults, Madden's paper frames have done more good than harm over a long period, and will likely remain part of the library for many years to come.

The library remains optimistic that the manuscripts also have a long life still ahead of them. Extending that life nonetheless depends, in large part, on limiting access to them. For that reason, preparation of replicas is doubly valuable, and the British Library continues this work as well using both new and old technology. For a small but growing number of Cotton manuscripts, the same library web site that notes tight restrictions on the original now hosts high-resolution online facsimiles. One of the most precious of all items in the collection has, by contrast, been reproduced through slower and far more painstaking means.

In the late 1970s, the British Library offered artist Marian Wenzel extensive access to the remaining pieces of the Cotton Genesis, to prepare monochrome and color studies of every fragment. As she noted in *British Library Journal*, smoke and fire left even the most legible of the celebrated miniatures "too badly damaged for simple photographic reconstruction" to be of real use. Yet even without resorting to guesswork, a surprising amount of information remained recognizable to the human eye through patient study of a fragment from both sides. Over the course of hundreds of hours Wenzel teased out and then transcribed this information. Describing her work as "accurate I hope, painstaking I know," she related ultimately "rejoicing where many commentators have despaired, since it is my conviction that it is possible to say quite a lot not only about small details in the pictures… but also about the styles (and there are several) employed by the Cotton Genesis artists." The remarkable Otho B VI, even after sharing the worst misfortunes of the Cotton library, still testifies to great unfinished story awaiting within.

Marian Wenzel's work on the Genesis fragments took place before they, and the new library, moved out of the British Museum. Some of those same fragments had already left the museum once, before being borrowed back from Bristol Baptist College.

In 1962 the museum purchased their permanent return—in light of the BM's stance on the *Liber Custumarum* and other, more famous contested objects, it had the dignity not to expect their return *gratis*—only for the Library Act to herald their departure again just nine years later.

Owing to the long delays that followed, the British Museum and Library nonetheless had ample time to sort out the details of their amicable divorce. Compared with most occasions of items being severed from the Cotton library, the bulk of the collection's removal to another public institution barely a mile away from the British Museum is hardly tragic.

Cotton's larger collection has never been completely unified anyway. His stone inscriptions remain in Cambridge—although in another curious example of synchronicity, they also changed hands around the same time as the manuscripts. Since their arrival in 1750, the Cotton stones had occupied niches in Trinity College's Wren Library. In 1969, however, the university transferred them to its Museum of Archaeology and Anthropology. The move has meant removal of most of the stones out of public view and into storage, but scholars can now examine sides that had been concealed for more than 200 years; Cotton stones also feature in temporary displays such as a 2012 exhibit.

To a great extent the Cotton library has been screened from public view through most of its history, and on balance it is today more public than ever. Most of the cabinet of curiosities material remains at the British Museum, where practical limitations also keep a majority of objects behind the scenes. The BM nonetheless offers a small but generous acknowledgement of the Cottons' gifts in its ongoing displays. Its Enlightenment Gallery includes recognition of antiquaries and alchemists, who laid the groundwork for modern sciences. Though many of Cotton's odder ornaments have vanished over the years, some reminders of them still exist; a selection of Dr. Dee's instruments are on display in this gallery. As are several of Cotton's coins, and, casting a watchful eye over this small piece of his collection, a fine bust of Sir Robert by Louis-François Roubiliac.

The core of the Cotton library, naturally, remains its documents. Nearly all of these are stored in the manuscripts department of the British Library today (with a few exotic items distributed among the Asia, Pacific and Africa collections). As part of its commitment to public engagement, however, the library balances the missions of preservation and accessibility. Sir Robert knew the same balancing act quite well, and he would no doubt greatly appreciate the advantages of sharing digital images via the internet as opposed to packing off original volumes to de Peiresc or some other correspondent. Even so, seeing an original document in person retains a quality of magic. With its well-trafficked public displays in the heart of a great international city, the British Library is ideally positioned to keep the Cotton library accessible in this way as well. Nearly a dozen of its best known highlights appear in the permanent Treasures of the British Library exhibit, including the Lindisfarne Gospels, *Beowulf* and one copy of Magna Carta. This last is, appropriately, further honored with a thoughtful sub-exhibit of its own.

Recent decades have reaffirmed that there are no guaranteed "safe" assets, nor any "end of history" so long as people remain. One cannot say what another two or three centuries may have in store for a collection that is already 400 years old, and contains many items more than twice that age. Nonetheless, in its homes at the British Library and other prestigious institutions, the Cotton library seems about as safe as an unpredictable world will ever permit. An otherwise minor news item from 2003 underscores just how much things have changed. On June 23, the BBC reported a fire the previous day at the British Library. The presumed source in an electrical fault offers a reminder that no

Bust of Sir Robert Cotton by Roubiliac
In the British Museum Enlightenment Gallery

system is ever foolproof. Yet after repeated lessons in this principal, the guardians of the Cotton library seem at least to have these sorts of vulnerabilities in hand. Per the BBC, the basement fire "was brought under control before fire crews arrived."

Happily, safety has not meant that the story of the Cotton library has become dull. Aside from all the perennial interest in its contents, the library continues to produce surprises. In 2009 a Cotton volume provided the answer to a long-unsolved art mystery. Art historians had long wondered why a series of drawings recording Henry VIII's military campaigns left out the aftermath of 1544's Siege of Boulogne, even though its successful outcome seemed an obvious conclusion for the series' three known parts. Peter Barber, head of the British Library's map collections, finally found the answer while preparing another update of the Cotton library catalog; the fourth drawing did exist, and was in fact at the library among the Cotton manuscripts. Identified only as "A view of some French town after a siege," it had gone unnoticed through entire ages. Similar oversight misidentified a noteworthy letter from Robert the Bruce to the king of England, until Dauvit Broun of the University of Glasgow reappraised it in 2013. If and when a thorough new Cotton catalog arrives, one suspects that even more discoveries will follow.

Some small measure of controversy persists, as well. According to the BBC, a group called the Northumbrian Association has for several years lobbied for transferring the Lindisfarne Gospels to "a permanent home in the North East" of England. Nor are they alone in seeking to reverse a long trend of centralization in London by repatriating a piece of the Cotton library to its place of origin. More recently, the Surrey County Council has sought the long-term loan of a copy of Magna Carta for a visitor center at Runnymede. Such debates over proper custodianship are entirely fitting, given the origins of the Cotton library itself.

Likewise the British Library maintains Sir Robert's policy of readiness to share out the most valuable objects in his collection—up to a point. The library has agreed to loan both its copies of Magna Carta during an anniversary event in 2015, reuniting all four surviving copies for the first time. The Lindisfarne Gospels are currently offered to their northeastern admirers on a septennial basis, for loans of up to three months. Beyond this, however, the heirs of Sir Robert Cotton appear even more firm in defending the collection's integrity than its founder. Per the library's statement to the BBC, its board "would be seriously derelict in its obligation to provide access to these manuscripts for people of all faiths and nationalities, if we allowed this collection to be broken up by removing one of its greatest treasures." For the time being, the Northumbrian Association will likely remain disappointed.

The contents of the Cotton library are, for practical purposes, now fixed. Barring future accidental damage or massive political realignment, nothing more will be permanently lost; another Utrecht Psalter is exceedingly unlikely at this point. The collection is even less likely to grow. Aside from a very small number of notes stored with fragmentary items, the most recent Cotton manuscript result returned by the British Library catalog dates from the early 18th century. The odds are very small that anyone will ever begin a 15th press for Emperor Nerva. At most, additional items once included in the collection may occasionally find their way back to the British Library. Even this is certain to be a rare occurrence, owing largely to the quality of Cotton's original collection and the esteem it has since earned as an institution. Many strayed items are now known as part of other collections, but none will be eager to part with them.

The same goes for many items that were never officially part of the Cotton library, yet provide essential evidence to modern understanding of the collection and its history. In one further irony the Cotton library contains remarkably few of the records of its own past. Even those from its first century, while the Cottons themselves maintained it as a private collection, have by one means or another escaped the national owners that succeeded them. Nearly all of the known early catalogs are parts of other collections. Thomas Smith's invaluable papers are found in Oxford's Bodleian Library. Most of these documents will, undoubtedly, be waiting at least as long as the Lindisfarne Gospels or Magna Carta for any permanent "homecoming."

Which only goes to make one particular exception all the more special. In 1985 the British Library acquired what may be the most important Cotton library "appendix" document of all, from both libraries' perspective. Nicolas Barker records—quite appropriately in *Treasures of the British Library*—that one "recently acquired charter is a document whose presence in these incomparable collections is particularly fitting: the will of Sir Robert Cotton, 1631..." Colin Tite has proposed that Cotton "has some right to be regarded as the founder of the British Library." To the extent that he is, Cotton's will is the library's founding charter.

Like the sale of baronetcies and indeed most of Sir Robert's successes, such a credit attracts multiple other claimants. Cotton's claim seems in some ways one of the poorest among them, too; by a literal standard his efforts to found a national library were more failure than success, part of the long line stretching back through Dee and Parker, and forward for decades after.

Yet such a grim accounting requires ignoring the central significance of Sir Robert Cotton, as a librarian: the greatest part of his achievements, by far, are found in the legacy he left to those that followed. Despite an impressive career as collector, scholar and politician, Cotton's own life ended in frustration. Almost certainly he wrote his last will amid more despair than hope. Yet even if, weighed by illness and persecution, he could not see it, Cotton had already created in his library what might almost be the cornerstone of true, lasting progress. He had created something *worth* having hopes for. Ideas can inspire people, but the hope that motivates perseverance in the face of setbacks wants a stronger foundation, and Cotton had built one. He advocated for causes worth fighting to advance, but more significantly—when his petitions met with rejection—he created something, himself, worth fighting to preserve. This is the essence of Sir Robert Cotton's claim to importance as a library founder. He did not found the British Library, or even the Academye for the Studye of Antiquity and History. But he founded *a* library that was great in every way that counts. As a collector he acquired great treasures, while as a librarian he worked to keep them in use by a community, informing useful new works from their mingling.

Cotton preserved pieces of the past, but left to the future something more than the sum of their parts. For centuries after, that was enough for others to keep working to perpetuate that legacy. It proved a difficult charge, and many times its trustees' fallibility threatened the Cotton library's ruin. Yet the modern British Library, though it might well have existed without Cotton's legacy, is in some sense still a lineal descendant of a small collection begun in Huntingdonshire more than 420 years ago. That collection lasted because, ultimately, its founder achieved all that anyone can in a brief life in an uncertain world. He led the way, personally, then trusted that posterity would prove wise enough to take responsibility.

Acknowledgements

First, thanks to everyone who read my first book. Your interest has meant a great deal to me, and helped me persevere through doing it all over again.

Katie Fortney provided invaluable criticism; *Cotton's Library* could not have asked for a better editor than an accredited librarian ready to tell me "cut the crap and clearly say what happened." Thanks also to Joan Husmann for assistance with proofreading.

A number of people aided in my research: Drs. Joel and Sara Uckelman, Ian Leins at the British Museum, Imogen Gunn at the Cambridge Museum of Archaeology and Anthropology, and Alison Whittlestone at the British Library. I also want to thank John Ronayne, for his wonderful illustration of the Cotton library in Cotton House and his tremendous generosity in allowing it to appear herein.

Finally, I am deeply grateful to Colin G.C. Tite, Kevin Sharpe, and all of the other scholars who have so patiently and painstakingly documented the Cotton library's history before me.

Discovering More

THE LIBRARY TODAY

Dozens of institutions today possess one or more items that formed part of the Cotton library at one time or another. The British Library is home to the great majority of the documentary objects, however, with the British Museum and Cambridge's Museum of Archaeology and Anthropology holding important ancillary collections.

The British Library
96 Euston Road
London NW1 2DB
http://www.bl.uk

The Department of Manuscripts is on the second floor. Note that access to Cotton manuscripts is closely restricted, and will likely require an appointment and letter of introduction. The Sir John Ritblat Gallery: Treasures of the British Library exhibit is on the ground floor and open to the public.

The British Library's web site is a sprawling resource which may well merit a catalog of its own some day; the following offer excellent starting points for Cotton library inquiries:

http://www.bl.uk/treasures/treasuresinfull.html
http://www.bl.uk/manuscripts
http://www.bl.uk/eblj
http://britishlibrary.typepad.co.uk/digitisedmanuscripts

The British Museum
Great Russell Street
London C1B 3DG
http://www.britishmuseum.org

Selected Cotton coins and other items of interest are displayed in the Enlightenment Gallery, on the ground floor. The rest of the coins are accessible via the Study Room by appointment; contact CoinsID@britishmuseum.org for details.

Museum of Archaeology and Anthropology
Downing Street
Cambridge CB2 3DZ
http://maa.cam.ac.uk

Most Cotton stones are stored behind the scenes; check the museum web site for special exhibits, or contact the museum to make an appointment for viewing them.

RECOMMENDED READING

For more on Cotton and his library, there are no better places to begin than Colin Tite's collected lectures and Kevin Sharpe's biography. Fascinating, informative and engaging, I give both my highest possible recommendation.

Among other major sources, Edwards provides a 104-page biography focusing on major turning points of Cotton's life, as well as information on the collection's later fate and the British Museum up through the mid-19th century. Through the vagaries of copyright law, this is one of the most accessible of the following, via the world wide web. Many of the essays in *Sir Robert Cotton as Collector* are also freely accessible online, as articles for *British Library Journal* (http://www.bl.uk/eblj). As is Andrew Prescott's exhaustive and invaluable "'Their Present Miserable State of Cremation': The Restoration of the Cotton Library."

Memory's Library is worth note for Summit's deep contextual insights into Cotton's library and daring extrapolations about its significance. Mirrlees's biography is an odd volume, frequently wandering far from its main subject and essentially leaving out the eventful last 16 years of Cotton's life—but its details on his early life and background substantially reward the reader's patience.

Edwards, Edward. *Lives of the Founders of the British Museum*. London: Turner and Co., 1870.
http://books.google.com/books?id=p50E6TN3JrAC

Mirrlees, Hope. *A Fly in Amber: Being an Extravagant Biography of the Romantic Antiquary, Sir Robert Bruce Cotton*. London: Faber and Faber, 1962.

Prescott, Andrew. "'Their Present Miserable State of Cremation': The Restoration of the Cotton Library." (Originally published in *Sir Robert Cotton as Collector*.) http://www.uky.edu/~kiernan/eBeo_archives/articles90s/ajp-pms.htm

Sharpe, Kevin. *Sir Robert Cotton, 1586–1631: History and Politics in Early Modern England*. Oxford: Oxford University Press, 1979.

Summit, Jennifer. *Memory's Library: Medieval Books in Early Modern England*. Chicago: The University of Chicago Press, 2008.

Tite, Colin G.C. *The Panizzi Lectures 1993: The Manuscript Library of Sir Robert Cotton*. London: The British Library, 1994.

Wright, C.J., et al. *Sir Robert Cotton As Collector: Essays on an Early Stuart Courtier and his Legacy*. London: The British Library, 1997.

BIBLIOGRAPHY

To make the following list of sources more useful, I have attempted to sort them by several categories, although a number of items naturally may touch on more than one. For the same reason, I have provided URLs for every item accessible online. As some of these are of wearying length, all of the online entries from this bibliography are published as hyperlinks at:
www.mattkuhns.com/cottons-library

General Cotton Library

Birkwood, Katherine. "'Our Learned Primate' and that 'rare treasurie': James Ussher's Use of Sir Robert Cotton's manuscript library, c. 1603–1655." *Library & Information History* 26.1 (Mar. 2010): 33-42. https://www.repository.cam.ac.uk/handle/1810/241606

Hooper, Samuel. *A catalogue of the manuscripts in the Cottonian library. To which are added, many emendations and additions. With an appendix, containing an account of the damage sustained by the fire in 1731; and also a catalogue of the charters preserved in the same library.* London: Samuel Hooper, 1777. https://archive.org/details/acataloguemanus00astlgoog

Keynes, Simon. "The reconstruction of a burnt Cottonian manuscript: the case of Cotton Ms. Otho A. I." *British Library Journal* (1996): 113-160. http://www.bl.uk/eblj/1996articles/pdf/article6.pdf

Lee, S.D. "Two fragments from Cotton MS. Otho B. X." *British Library Journal* (1991): 83-87.
http://www.bl.uk/eblj/1991articles/pdf/article5.pdf

Levelt, Sjoerd. "The Manuscripts of Jan van Naaldwijk's Chronicles of Holland, Cotton MSS. Vitellius F. XV and Tiberius C. IV." *The Electronic British Library Journal* (2012) Article 4.
http://www.bl.uk/eblj/2012articles/pdf/ebljarticle42012.pdf

"THE COTTONIAN MANUSCRIPTS." *The Morning Chronicle* (London), 5 Sept. 1823: 3.

"THE COTTONIAN MANUSCRIPTS." *The Morning Chronicle* (London), 12 Sept. 1823: 4.

Thornbury, Walter. "The royal palace of Westminster." *Old and New London: Volume 3*, British History Online. http://www.british-history.ac.uk/report.aspx?compid=45170

Tite, Colin G.C. *The Panizzi Lectures 1993: The Manuscript Library of Sir Robert Cotton*. London: The British Library, 1994.

———. "The Printed Books of the Cotton Family and Their Dispersal." *Libraries Within the Library: The Origins of the British Library's Printed Collections*. Ed. Giles Mandelbrote and Barry Taylor. London: The British Library, 2009.

———. "'Lost or stolen or strayed': a survey of manuscripts formerly in the Cotton Library." *British Library Journal* (1992): 107-147. http://www.bl.uk/eblj/1992articles/pdf/article8.pdf

Background/Context

Aubrey, John. *Brief Lives*. Oxford: Clarendon Press, 1898. https://archive.org/details/cu31924088005628

"ARCHÆOLOGY IN ENGLAND." *The Morning Chronicle* (London), 9 Oct. 1850: 7.

Bale, John, and John Leland. *The Laboryouse Journey & Serche of John Leylande for Englandes Antiquitees Geven of Hym as a Newe Years Gyfte to Kynge Henry the VIII in the Xxxvii. Yeare of His Reygne*. Ed. W.A. Coppinger. Manchester, England: The Priory Press, 1895. http://books.google.com/books?id=nDgLAAAAYAAJ

de Ricci, Seymour. *English Collectors of Books and Manuscripts (1530–1930)*. Bloomington, Indiana: Indiana University Press, 1960.

"DEATH OF MR. WILLIAM COTTON, F.S.A." *The Morning Post* (London), 24 Jan. 1863: 6.

Gittleson, Kim. "Trade secrets of oldest family firm in US." *BBC News*. British Broadcasting Corporation, 6 June 2012. http://www.bbc.com/news/business-18261045

Kenyon, J.P. *Stuart England*. New York: St. Martin's Press, 1978.

McKisack, May. *Medieval History in the Tudor Age*. Oxford: Clarendon Press, 1971.

Raymond, Irwin. *The Origins of the English Library*. London: Allen & Unwin, 1958.

Summit, Jennifer. *Memory's Library: Medieval Books in Early Modern England*. Chicago: The University of Chicago Press, 2008.

Trevor-Roper, Hugh. Introduction. *The Decline and Fall of the Roman Empire*. By Edward Gibbon. New York: Alfred A. Knopf, 1993.

Wormald, Francis and C.E. Wright, ed. *The English Library Before 1700*. London: The University of London / Athlone Press, 1958.

Young, Joyce. *The Dissolution of the Monasteries*. London: George Allen & Unwin Ltd, 1971.

Sir Robert Cotton

Backhouse, Janet. "Sir Robert Cotton's record of a royal bookshelf." *British Library Journal* (1992): 44-51.
http://www.bl.uk/eblj/1992articles/pdf/article3.pdf

Brown, Michell P. "Sir Robert Cotton, Collector and Connoisseur." *Illuminating the Book: Makers & Interpreters: Essays in Honour of Janet Backhouse*. Ed. Michelle P. Brown and Scot McKendrick. Toronto: The British Library and University of Toronto Press, 1998.

Carley, James P. "The Royal Library as a source for Sir Robert Cotton's collection: a preliminary list of acquisitions." *British Library Journal* (1992): 52-73. http://www.bl.uk/eblj/1992articles/pdf/article4.pdf

Edwards, Edward. *Lives of the Founders of the British Museum*. London: Turner and Co., 1870.
http:// books.google.com/books?id=p50E6TN3JrAC

Harrison, Julian. "Printed Material and the Cotton Manuscripts." *Libraries Within the Library: The Origins of the British Library's Printed Collections*. Ed. Giles Mandelbrote and Barry Taylor. London: The British Library, 2009.

Howarth, David. "Sir Robert Cotton and the commemoration of famous men." *British Library Journal* (1992): 1-28.
http://www.bl.uk/eblj/1992articles/pdf/article1.pdf

"LIBRARY THIEVES." *The Graphic* (London), 23 May 1891: 15.

Montague, Bruce R. "Robert Bruce Cotton, 1571-1631." *The Montague Millennium*. Larry Montague, 2006. http://www.montaguemillennium.com/familyresearch/h_1631_cotton.htm

Mirrlees, Hope. *A Fly in Amber: Being an Extravagant Biography of the Romantic Antiquary, Sir Robert Bruce Cotton*. London: Faber and Faber, 1962.

Selden, John. *Table Talk: being the discourses of John Selden, Esq*. Ed. Edward Arber. London: A. Murray & Son, 1869. https://archive.org/details/tabletalk00seld

Sharpe, Kevin. *Sir Robert Cotton, 1586–1631: History and Politics in Early Modern England*. Oxford: Oxford University Press, 1979.

"Sir Robert Cotton: A Great English Collector." *The Times* (London), 6 May 1931: 17.

"Sir Robert Cotton." *Kemble: The Anglo-Saxon Charters Website*. The British Academy - Royal Historical Society Joint Committee on Anglo-Saxon Charters. http://www.kemble.asnc.cam.ac.uk/node/34

Society of Antiquaries of London. *Archaeologia: or miscellaneous tracts relating to antiquity*. Vol. 1 The Society of Antiquaries of London, 1770. https://archive.org/details/archaeologiaormi01sociuoft

Parry, Graham. *The Trophies of Time: English Antiquarians of the Seventeenth Century*. Oxford: Oxford University Press, 1995.

Interregnum

Dugdale, William. *The Life of that Learned Antiquary, Sir William Dugdale. Kt. Garter Principal, King of Arms*. London: E. Curli, 1713. https://archive.org/details/lifeofthatlearne00dugd
———. *The Life, Diary and Correspondence of Sir William Dugdale, Knight, Sometimes Garter Principal of Arms*. Ed. William Hamper, Esq. F.S.A. London: Harding, Lepart, & Co., 1827.

Peacey, Jason. "Sir Thomas Cotton's Consumption of News in 1650s England." *The Library: The Transactions of the Bibliographical Society* 7.1 (2006): 3-24. http://muse.jhu.edu/journals/the_library_the_transactions_of_the_bibliographical_society/v007/7.1peacey.html

Heyworth, P.L. "Thomas Smith, Humfrey Wanley and the Cottonian Library." *The Times Literary Supplement*. 31 Aug. 1962: 660.

Joy, Eileen A. "Thomas Smith, Humfrey Wanley, and the 'Little-Known Country' of the Cotton Library." *The Electronic British Library Journal* (2005) Article 1.
http://www.bl.uk/eblj/2005articles/pdf/article1.pdf

Cataloging

Tite, Colin G.C. "The early catalogues of the Cottonian Library." *British Library Journal* (1980): 144-157.
http://www.bl.uk/eblj/1980articles/pdf/article12.pdf
———. *The Early Records of Sir Robert Cotton's Library: Formation, Cataloguing, Use.* London: The British Library, 2003.

Teviotdale, E.C. "Some classified catalogues of the Cottonian Library." *British Library Journal* (1992): 74-87.
http://www.bl.uk/eblj/1992articles/pdf/article5.pdf

Nationalization

"Preface," *Calendar of Treasury Papers, Volume 3: 1702-1707.* Ed. Joseph Redington. British History Online.
http://www.british-history.ac.uk/report.aspx?compid=79578

"Volume 98: April 1-June 29, 1706." *Calendar of Treasury Papers, Volume 3: 1702-1707.* Ed. Joseph Redington. British History Online.
http://www.british-history.ac.uk/report.aspx?compid=79598

"Volume 192: September 2-October 31, 1715." *Calendar of Treasury Papers, Volume 5: 1714-1719.* Ed. Joseph Redington. British History Online. http://www.british-history.ac.uk/report.aspx?compid=85023

"Volume 199: April 3-July 31, 1716." *Calendar of Treasury Papers, Volume 5: 1714-1719.* Ed. Joseph Redington. British History Online.
http://www.british-history.ac.uk/report.aspx?compid=85030

"Warrant Books: December 1707, 1-15." *Calendar of Treasury Books, Volume 21: 1706-1707.* Ed. William A. Shaw. British History Online.
http://www.british-history.ac.uk/report.aspx?compid=90488

"William III, 1700 & 1701: An Act for the better settling and preserving the Library kept in the House at Westminster called Cotton House in the Name and Family of the Cottons for the Benefit of the Publick [Chapter VII. Rot. Parl. 12 § 13 Gul. III. p. 1. n. 7.]." *Statutes of the Realm: volume 7: 1695-1701.* Ed. John Raithby. British History Online. http://www.british-history.ac.uk/report.aspx?compid=46991

The Fire

Parliamentary Committee Appointed to View the Cottonian Library. *A Report from The Committee Appointed to View the Cottonian Library, &c.* London: The House of Commons, 1732. http://books.google.com/books?id=t3o7AAAAMAAJ

Pollard, Justin. *Alfred the Great: The Man Who Made England.* London: John Murray, 2005.

Tomalak, Ann. "Crisp as a Poppadom." *Medieval manuscripts blog.* The British Library, 25 Feb. 2013. http://britishlibrary.typepad.co.uk/digitisedmanuscripts/2013/02/crisp-as-a-poppadom.html

The British Museum

Borrie, Michael. "Panizzi and Madden." *British Library Journal* (1979): 18-36. http://www.bl.uk/eblj/1979articles/pdf/article2.pdf

"British Museum in need of money as well as modern organization." *The Times* (London), 21 Dec. 1962: 4.

"Curious Literary Discovery." *The Times* (London), 19 Apr. 1861: 9.

"FROM OUR MUSEUMS CORRESPONDENT: British Museum Library: History Portrayed in Exhibition." *The Times* (London), 20 Sept. 1950: 5.

Harris, P.R. *A History of the British Museum Library 1753-1973.* London: The British Library, 1998

"History of the British Museum." The British Museum. http://www.britishmuseum.org/about_us/the_museums_story/general_history.aspx

"History of the collection." The British Museum. http://www.britishmuseum.org/about_us/the_museums_story/the_collection.aspx

"Illuminated manuscripts: a guide to the British Library's collections: The foundation collections." The British Library. http://www.bl.uk/catalogues/illuminatedmanuscripts/TourCollFound.asp

"New Facts About Mary Stuart." *St. Louis Globe-Democrat*, 14 May 1883: 7.

"NEW READING ROOMS, BRITISH MUSEUM." *The Morning Chronicle* (London), 13 Sept. 1838: 4.

Prescott, Andrew. "'Their Present Miserable State of Cremation': The Restoration of the Cotton Library." *Sir Robert Cotton as Collector: Essays on an Early Stuart Courtier and His Legacy*. Ed. C. J. Wright. London: British Library Publications, 1997. 391-454. http://www.uky.edu/~kiernan/eBeo_archives/articles90s/ajp-pms.htm

"Reading Room." The British Museum. http://www.britishmuseum.org/about_us/the_museums_story/reading_room.aspx

"Selections From the Cotton Library." *The Times*, 10 Jan. 1953: 8.

"Sir Hans Sloane." The British Museum. http://www.britishmuseum.org/about_us/the_museums_story/sir_hans_sloane.aspx

"The Cottonian Manuscripts: Exhibition in British Museum." *The Times* (London), 26 May 1931: 17.

The British Library

Barker, Nicolas, et al. *Treasures of the British Library*. New York: Harry N. Abrams, Inc., 1989

"Cotton Manuscripts Project." *HRI Digital*. The University of Sheffield, 2013. http://hridigital.shef.ac.uk/cotton-manuscripts

Davies, Caroline. "Lost drawing of Henry VIII's great victory uncovered." *The Guardian* (London), 4 Apr. 2009. http://www.theguardian.com/artanddesign/2009/apr/05/henry-eighth-drawing-uncovered-siege

Howard, Philip. *The British Library: A Treasure House of Knowledge*. London: Scala Publishers Ltd in association with The British Library, 2008.

"Library treasures escape fire." *BBC News*. British Broadcasting Corporation, 23 July 2003. http://news.bbc.co.uk/1/hi/england/london/3089341.stm

Medieval manuscripts blog. The British Library. http://britishlibrary.typepad.co.uk/digitisedmanuscripts/

Coins

Archibald, Marion M. "Cotton's Anglo-Saxon Coins in the Light of the Peiresc Inventory of 1606." *British Numismatic Journal* 76 (2006): 171-203. http://www.britnumsoc.org/publications/Digital BNJ/pdfs/2006_BNJ_76_1_7.pdf

Blunt, C. E., C.S.S. Lyon and B.H.I.H. Stewart. *Coinage in Tenth-Century England: from Edward the Elder to Edgar's Reform*. Oxford: The Oxford University Press, 1989.

Grueber, Herbert A. and Charles Francis Keary. *A Catalogue of English Coins in the British Museum: Anglo-Saxon Series, vol. II*. London: The Trustees of the British Museum, 1893. https://archive.org/details/catalogueofengli02brit

Keary, Charles Francis. *A Catalogue of English Coins in the British Museum: Anglo-Saxon Series, vol. I*. London: The Trustees of the British Museum, 1887. http://books.google.com/books?id=OcMWAAAAYAAJ

North, Jeffrey James. *English Hammered Coinage. Vol. 1* London: Spink, 1960.

Seaby, P.J. *The Story of British Coinage*. London: Seaby, 1985.

Specific Highlights

"Appeal for return of Magna Carta to Runnymede." *BBC News*. British Broadcasting Corporation, 28 Oct. 2012. http://www.bbc.com/news/uk-england-surrey-20116242

"Beowulf." *Online Gallery*. The British Library. http://www.bl.uk/onlinegallery/onlineex/englit/beowulf/index.html

Borrie, Michael. "What became of Magna Carta?" *British Library Journal* (1976): 1-7. http://www.bl.uk/eblj/1976articles/pdf/article1.pdf

Danziger, Danny, and Robert Lacey. *The Year 1000: What Life Was Like at the Turn of the First Millennium: an Englishman's World*. New York: Little, Brown and Co., 1999.

Di Consiglio, Flavia. "Lindisfarne Gospels: Why is this book so special?" *BBC Religion & Ethics*. British Broadcasting Corporation, 20 Mar. 2013. http://www.bbc.co.uk/religion/0/21588667

Edward VI. *Chronicle and Political Papers*. Ed. Wilbur Kitchener Jordan. Ithaca, New York: Cornell University Press, 1966.

"Gospels to return to North East." *BBC News*. British Broadcasting Corporation, 24 Mar. 2009. http://news.bbc.co.uk/2/hi/uk_news/england/7961968.stm

Heney, Seamus. *Beowulf: A New Verse Translation*. New York: Farrar, Straus & Giroux, 2000.

Kiernan, Kevin S. *Beowulf and the Beowulf Manuscript*. Ann Arbor, Michigan: The University of Michigan Press, 1996.
———. "Electronic Beowulf Archives, 1993-1997." The University of Kentucky / The British Library. http://www.uky.edu/~kiernan/eBeo_archives

Kiernan, Kevin S., et al. *Electronic Beowulf - Third Edition*. The University of Kentucky / The British Library. http://ebeowulf.uky.edu

"LITERATURE: BEOWULF." *The Examiner* (London), 30 Dec. 1876: 16-17.

"Magna Carta copies to be united to mark 800th anniversary." *BBC News*. British Broadcasting Corporation, 14 July 2013. http://www.bbc.com/news/uk-23304764

Merwin, W.S. *Sir Gawain and the Green Knight: A new verse translation*. New York: Alfred A. Knopf, 2002.

Paul, Jim. *The Rune Poem: Wisdom's Fulfillment, Prophecy's Reach*. San Francisco: Chronicle Books, 1996.

"Sacred Texts: Lindisfarne Gospels." *Online Gallery*. The British Library. http://www.bl.uk/onlinegallery/sacredtexts/lindisfarne.html

Siebold, Jim. "The Cottoniana or Anglo-Saxon Map." *Ancient Maps 6,200 BC to 600 AD*. http://cartographic-images.net/Cartographic_Images/210_The_Cottoniana_or_Anglo-Saxon_Map.html

"The Beowulf." *The Times* (London), 25 Aug. 1884: 6.

"Treasures in Full: Magna Carta." The British Library. http://www.bl.uk/treasures/magnacarta/index.html

Wenzel, Marian. "Deciphering the Cotton Genesis miniatures: preliminary observations concerning the use of colour." *British Library Journal* (1987): 79-100.
http://www.bl.uk/eblj/1987articles/pdf/article7.pdf

"Viz creator urges gospels return." *BBC News*. British Broadcasting Corporation, 20 Mar. 2008.
http://news.bbc.co.uk/1/hi/england/7306234.stm

Index

Aethelward 181, 182
Agarde, Arthur 26, 28, 50
Alfred the Great 55, 57, 161, 182
Anglo-Saxons 42, 55, 56, 57, 59, 137, 139, 161, 182
antiquarians 9–10, 25, 32, 43, 98, 103, 107, 112, 124, 174. *See also* Society of Antiquaries
Arundel, Earl of. *See* Howard, Thomas (Earl of Arundel)
Ashburnham House 146–152, 156, 160, 163
Asser's Life of Alfred 161, 213
Astle, Thomas 189, 190
Athelstan 182–184

Bacon, Francis 21, 25, 36, 38, 82
Bale, John 3–4, 6
baronetcies 34–35, 170
 Cotton family 35, 125–126, 174
 sale of 88, 246
Becket, Thomas 38, 52
Bedfordshire 97, 99, 100, 105
Bell, Idris 61, 222, 225
Bentley, Dr. Richard 140, 142, 145, 148–152

Beowulf xiii, 26, 54, 55, 60, 64, 117, 156, 161, 203, 207, 217, 228, 229, 230, 231, 232, 242, 260, 261
Bernard's Catalogue 113, 115
Bloomsbury 170, 178, 234
Bodleian Library 68, 88, 106, 108, 113, 135, 203, 245
Bodley, Thomas 29, 106
bombing 221–225
brass busts 64, 217
Bristol Baptist College 187, 223, 240
Britannia (book) 7, 21, 36
British Library xiii, 51, 57, 60, 73, 104, 124, 135, 157, 197, 209, 221, 233–246
 online/digital services 104, 232, 236, 238, 240
 separation from British Museum 227, 233–234, 241
 St. Pancras building 235–236
 Treasures Gallery xiii, 197, 236, 242
British Library Act of 1973 234–246
British Museum xiii, 73, 117, 135, 168–181, 185–194
 exhibits 61, 209, 222, 226
 in 21st century 241–242

INDEX

Reading Room 216–217, 227, 236
tickets 179
trustees 176–177, 186–190, 192, 203–204, 206–207, 213, 226–227, 233
Buckingham, Duke of 75–87
Byzantine Empire 72–73

Cambridge 6, 22, 62, 76, 145, 173–174, 241
Museum of Archaeology and Anthropology 241
Trinity College 145, 148, 241
Camden, William 6–8, 10, 13, 21, 35–36, 40, 52, 129
Carr, Robert 46–51, 75
cartularies 202, 207
Casley, David 145, 150, 157, 175, 187
catalogs xvi, 53, 63, 66, 95, 111–116, 130, 141, 143, 159, 188–191, 223, 225–226, 238–239, 244, 245
Bernard 113, 115
classified 109, 113, 141
Cotton/James 28, 68, 109
Hooper 189
Planta 188–191, 218, 226
Smith 39, 111–115, 114–116, 159, 189, 190
Wanley 113, 115–116, 133–134, 199
Catholicism 10, 16, 37–38, 47, 110–111
Cecil, Robert 23, 26, 31, 34, 45
Cecil, William 4–5
chained libraries 22
Charles I 65, 77–87, 89–90, 93–96, 99, 123, 196
Charles II 47, 101, 105, 110
charter garret 186, 191, 192, 194, 201–202, 203
charters 55, 64, 93, 107, 115, 129, 133, 175, 179, 192, 246
great charter. *See* Magna Carta
Christianity 10, 44, 86, 118

Civil War, English xii, 79, 81, 96–99, 106, 222
Codex Purpureus 72–74
coins 36, 52, 64, 120, 156, 175–176, 181–184, 186, 242
Coke, Sir Edward 49
Conington 5, 52, 131, 173
coronation fiasco, 1626 54, 77–78, 81–82, 83, 101
Coronation Gospel 54, 77–78, 101
Corpus Christi College 68, 122
Cotton Genesis x–xiii, xv, 21, 54, 65, 107, 150, 161, 187–188, 193, 222, 240–241
Cotton House 23, 51, 69–71, 77–78, 81–82, 96, 99–100, 105, 108, 113, 123–124, 131, 140–141, 143, 144–146, 217
sale of 140–141, 143, 144
Cottoniana 55–59
Cottonian Collection (Plymouth) 215
Cottoni Posthuma 35, 100
Cotton library
comparisons with peers 22, 37, 62, 108
compilations 31, 40, 54, 60, 63, 107, 160–161
contents of 51–55, 85, 112, 141, 179, 236, 243, 245
home in Cotton House 51, 69–71, 100, 108, 123, 140. *See also* Cotton House
lending xi, 21, 30, 52, 54, 55, 63, 65, 87, 93, 95, 101, 108, 110, 148, 244
nationalization 122–136, 140–144
online replicas xiii, 104, 232, 236, 238, 240
origins of 2–6, 8, 18–21, 26–29, 39, 90, 92, 142, 147, 244–247
restoration xiii, 159–160, 186, 191–193, 196, 202–205, 207–211, 214, 218, 223
Cotton, Sir John (2nd baronet) x–xii, 93–94, 106–108, 110–115, 120–128, 130–131, 170, 187

Cotton, Sir Robert (1st baronet) xi,
    xiii–xv, 2, 5–14, 17–40, 44–56,
    60–71, 73–90, 93–95, 100–101,
    103, 106, 111, 112, 117,
    123, 124, 139, 147, 155, 170,
    173–174, 176, 193, 195–197,
    210–211, 214, 219–220, 222,
    229–230, 232, 234, 239, 242,
    243, 244, 246–247
  arrests 46, 49–50, 86
  collecting 18–20, 26–30, 35, 36,
    39, 44, 46, 51–52, 54, 56, 60,
    68, 71, 88, 89. *See also* Cotton
    library, origins of
  criticisms as librarian 26, 60–61,
    138, 222
  last will 84, 89, 123, 246
  marriage 9, 46, 50, 94
  scholarship 6, 9, 11, 24, 35–36,
    38–40
  service in Parliament 23, 35, 71, 80,
    87, 94
Cotton, Sir Thomas 93–101, 105,
    107–108, 112, 120–121
Cottons, other 121, 125–128,
    131–132, 145, 173–174
Cotton, William 215

Dark Ages. *See* Middle Ages
Dee, Dr. John 4–5, 13, 18–19, 37, 52,
    62, 92, 241
Dering, Sir Edward 87, 163
D'Ewes, Sir Simonds 61, 78, 93,
    107–108, 134, 143, 210
Dissolution of the Monasteries 2–5,
    12–13, 18, 22, 37, 146
Dudley, Robert 85
Dugdale, Sir William xii, 98, 107–110,
    114, 124, 160

Edwards, Arthur 169
Edward the Elder 182
Edward VI 4, 15–17, 38, 43, 226
Elizabeth I xi, 4–5, 11–14, 17, 23, 28,
    38, 45–47, 47, 79, 86, 226
Ellis, Sir Henry 192
Elphinstone, John 141, 145, 148

emperor system xii, 64–65, 68, 69,
    154, 179, 189–190, 200, 217,
    239
Essex House 146
exhibits. *See* British Museum exhibits

Fire of 1731 xiii, 148–158, 160–162,
    169, 172, 187, 193, 202, 213,
    229–230
  consequences 156–161, 176, 187,
    209, 210
  report 154, 162, 164
  restoration. *See* Cotton library
    restoration
  salvage 155–160, 176
Fire of 1865 212–214, 217, 225
Fleetwood, William 219–220
Forshall, Josiah 192–194, 196, 199,
    201–202

Galba Psalter 138, 190
Sir Gawain and the Green Knight
    See Pearl poems
George II 171, 172, 178
Gifford, Andrew 187, 223
Glorious Revolution of 1688 108,
    111–112, 123
Gough, Henry 203–205, 207–211,
    218, 239

Hanbury, William 128–129, 131–132,
    134–135, 140–141, 144
Harleian Collection 134–135, 170,
    172–173, 177–178, 186, 210,
    217, 225
Harley, Edward 135, 140, 142, 172
Harley, Robert 132, 134–135, 141,
    170, 172, 199
Henry VIII xi, 2–4, 13, 15, 22, 38, 62,
    103, 122, 161, 177, 187, 244
heraldry 11, 26–27, 53
Hickes, George 111, 115–116,
    228–229
Hooper, Samuel 189
Howard, Frances 46–48, 50

INDEX

Howard, Henry (Earl of Northampton) 19, 23–25, 33–34, 45–48, 49–50, 71, 77
Howard, Thomas (Earl of Arundel) xi, 19, 53, 71, 76–78, 80, 82, 94, 209
Howard, Thomas (Earl of Suffolk) 24

inscriptions. *See* stone inscriptions

James I 14, 18, 23–27, 28, 33, 39, 43, 45–48, 75–77, 82, 85, 142
James II 110–112
James, Richard 29, 66–68, 86, 98, 109, 114
Jonson, Ben 36
Julius work calendar 137–139, 190

Kiernan, Kevin S. 228–230, 232
King's Library 217, 224–225

Leland, John 4, 6–7, 13
Liber Custumarum 29, 219–221, 241
Liber Vitae of Durham 102–104
library keeper contest 116, 125–136, 140, 148
Little Dean's Yard 147
London 6, 11, 23, 27, 71, 95, 105–107, 118, 120, 131, 145–147, 149, 170, 221–222, 225, 234–235, 244
   government of 29, 149, 219–221
Louis XIV 122

Madden, Sir Frederic 117, 124, 199–214, 216, 217, 218, 223, 230, 239
   diary 201–202, 205, 208, 214
   feud with Panizzi 205–206, 210, 214, 216
Magna Carta xiii, 21, 26, 87, 161, 163–164, 177, 193–197, 242, 244
Mappa Mundi. *See* Cottoniana
Mary Queen of Scots 88, 218
Mary Tudor 4, 13, 16–17
Maty, Matthew 176, 189

Middle Ages 3, 42–43, 54–55, 56–59, 65, 102–104, 137–139, 161, 181–184, 230
Montagu House 178, 179, 200, 234

National Library of Wales 222–224
naval investigations 33, 45, 82, 88
non-jurors 111, 130–131, 132
Northampton, Earl of. *See* Howard, Henry (Earl of Northampton)
Northumbrian Association 244–245
Nowell, Laurence 4, 6, 229–230

Old Dormitory 156, 163, 175, 189, 217, 235. *See also* Westminster School
Old English 43, 55, 59, 116, 199, 203, 228
Old Royal Library 12, 142–143, 146, 152, 156, 168, 178
Onslow, Arthur 155–159, 161–164, 172, 175, 178, 180, 208
Overbury, Sir Thomas 46–49
Oxford 22, 28–29, 68, 110, 113, 199, 203, 245. *See also* Bodleian Library

Panizzi, Anthony 205–206, 210, 214, 216
parchment 32, 52, 72, 151, 153, 156, 158–159, 186, 203–204, 239
Parker, Matthew 5, 13, 20, 122, 246
Parliament 23, 25, 32, 34–35, 69–71, 76, 79–85, 87, 94, 96–100, 111, 123–124, 144, 154–155, 160, 162, 164, 169, 171–172, 177, 188, 194, 226, 233, 235
Pearl poems 54, 117–119
de Peiresc, Nicolas Claude Fabri xi, 20, 38, 57, 242
pennies *See* coins
Pepys, Samuel 110, 132, 135
petition for Queen Elizabeth Academy 11–14, 18, 24, 81, 84, 90, 177, 246

266 COTTON'S LIBRARY

Planta, Joseph 187–191, 193–194, 200, 209, 218. *See also* catalogs: Planta
precedent 12, 25, 31–32, 34, 53, 71, 81, 108, 155, 196

Queen's Library. *See* Old Royal Library

Raleigh, Sir Walter 36
Reading Room. *See* British Museum: Reading Room
Reformation, English 2, 4, 15–16, 31, 37–39, 111
Registers 53
Report of 1732. *See* Fire of 1731: report
Restoration, 1660 101, 105, 109
restoration of Cotton manuscripts xiii, 159, 160, 175, 186, 191–194, 202–205, 207–209, 210–214, 218
    Forshall 192–194, 196, 202
    Gough method 208, 239
    Madden 202–205, 207–210, 213–214, 217–218, 223, 230, 239
    Planta 191, 194
Rimius, Henry 176, 189
Royal Society 142, 169
Rune Poem 55, 116
Runnymede 244. *See also* Magna Carta

Scotland 12, 24, 40, 177
    Union with England 25, 142
Selden, John 21, 36, 62, 86, 97–98
Shakespeare, William 8
Sloane, Sir Hans 142–143, 168–173, 177–178, 189, 225
Smith, Thomas 110–116, 124–125, 128–136, 141, 159, 189–190, 211, 245
Society of Antiquaries 7, 9–14, 24–25, 27–28, 64, 76, 90, 106–107, 128, 142, 169
Somerset, Earl of. *See* Carr, Robert
Spain 12, 25, 47–48, 76
Speed, John 35, 52, 175

Spelman, Sir Henry 24, 107
state papers 10, 26–28, 37, 51, 53, 54, 71, 95, 134, 147, 155, 190
stone inscriptions 52, 57, 173–174, 175, 241

Thomason, George 98
Thompson, Richard 226
Tower of London 27–28, 47, 82, 86, 162
trustees, British Museum. *See* British Museum: trustees
trustees, parliamentary 123–125, 128–136, 140–147, 164, 169, 174, 177, 185–186, 235
Tuckett, Charles 202, 204, 207–209, 210, 212–213, 218, 239

Union of England and Scotland. *See* Scotland: Union with England
university libraries 4, 22–23, 62, 76, 108, 122, 203
Ussher, Archbishop James 39, 98

vellum. *See* parchment
Vikings 42, 182–184
Villiers, George. *See* Buckingham, Duke of

Wanley, Humfrey 112–113, 115–116, 128–129, 132–135, 141, 143, 198–199, 203, 211, 214
West, James 173, 175
Westminster 23, 70, 146–147, 148
Westminster Abbey 27–28, 77–78
Westminster School 6, 147, 153, 155–156, 164, 189
William of Orange 111, 123–124
Wilson, Thomas 26–28, 29
Wollaston, William 192, 201
World War I 221–222
World War II 222–225

About the Author

Matt Kuhns grew up in small-town Iowa, graduating with honors from Iowa State University. In his always eventful career as a graphic designer, he has worked for a private university, a boutique design studio and a craft products retail chain, as well as various nonprofit institutions and several advertising agencies. He currently operates an independent design practice as Modern Alchemy LLC. As a writer, his previous work includes *Brilliant Deduction: The Story of Real-Life Great Detectives*. He lives in Lakewood, Ohio.

www.ingramcontent.com/pod-product-compliance
Lightning Source LLC
Chambersburg PA
CBHW031946080426
42735CB00007B/279